PETERSON'S®

SAT® PREP GUIDE 1600:
PREP FOR THE PERFECT SCORE

PETERSON'S®

PETERSON'S®

About Peterson's®

Peterson's is everywhere that education happens. For over five decades, Peterson's has provided products and services that keep students and their families engaged throughout the pre-college, college, and post-college experience. From the first day of kindergarten through high school graduation and beyond, Peterson's is a single source of educational content to help families maximize their student's learning and opportunities for success. Whether a fifth-grader needs help with geometry or a high school junior could benefit from essay-writing tips, Peterson's is the ultimate source for the highest quality educational resources.

For more information, contact Peterson's, 3 Columbia Circle, Suite 205, Albany, NY 12203, 800-338-3282 Ext. 54229; or find us online at *www.petersons.com*.

©Copyright 2017 Peterson's, a Nelnet company

Peterson's SAT® Prep Guide 1600

ISBN 978-0-7689-4152-4

Printed in the United States of America

10 9 8 7 6 5 4 3 2 1   19 18 17

First Edition

TABLE OF CONTENTS

CHAPTER 1: ALL ABOUT THE SAT® EXAM

OVERVIEW

- The SAT® Exam: An Overview
- Registering for the SAT® Exam
- Scoring
- Getting Ready for Test Day
- Summing It Up

You're reading this book for one specific—and admirable—reason: You have a goal of achieving a *perfect score* on the SAT® exam, and nothing short of perfection will satisfy you. You likely have a target college in your sights, and you want to stand out from the ultra-competitive and similarly talented group of top-tier students vying for the same admissions spot. You know that a flawless score will impress any college admissions staff and make your goal of getting into your target school within reach.

Getting into a good college is no easy task, and despite your track record of stellar academic achievement and success, the *last thing* you want to have happen is to stumble on this important test and leave your future academic success in the hands of fate. You're just not that type of person—you're an elite student, and you chose this book to take control of your fate and turn your perfect score goal into a reality.

If this description sounds like you, then you've got the right book in your hands. We *completely* get it, and we're here to help make your goal of a perfect score a reality. So keep reading!

Peterson's SAT® Prep Guide 1600: Prep for the Perfect Score is your ultra-elite, top-tier test-prep coach and your indispensable guide for achieving your target scores on test day. It's designed by exam experts to help you master every aspect of the SAT® exam. This helpful test-prep guide includes the following:

- **Comprehensive coverage of the entire SAT® exam format:** After reading this book, you'll know the structure and format of the exam from start to finish and have all the information needed for success on test day.

- **In-depth, rigorous test review:** You'll get a thorough review of every test section of the SAT® exam and effective study and attack plans for reaching your goal scores.

- **Expert tips, advice, and strategies:** We know what it takes to get a top score on the SAT® exam—you'll get the expert tools that have *proven* to be effective for test-day success.

- **Challenging, effective test practice:** Get ready to practice with the most *challenging* practice questions for the SAT® exam around, along with detailed answer explanations to guide you, to get you in top test-taking form!

We know that a perfect score is important to you, and we're here to ensure you of two things. First, you've come to the right place and have purchased the right book. Second, we understand your quest and will be your helpful guide on this journey to SAT® perfection. Everything you need to make your goal of a perfect score attainable is in the sections and chapters that follow. Let's move forward!

What Is a Perfect SAT® Exam Score?

Your SAT® exam score will range from a low of 400 to a perfect 1600 (your target score). This score is comprised of the following:

- A score ranging from 200 to 800 on the Evidence-Based Reading and Writing section.
- A score ranging from 200 to 800 on the Math section.

Your essay score—if you choose to take this optional part of the exam—will be reported separately. You'll receive a score ranging from 2 to 8 for each of the three dimensions measured.

THE SAT® EXAM: AN OVERVIEW

The first step to acing the SAT® exam is to know the structure and format of the exam and the test basics you'll need to know. We know you're eager to get to the test practice and review, but having a thorough understanding of the exam from top to bottom will give you a real advantage—and put you ahead of the test-taking competition.

Consider your scores on the SAT® exam as an important component of your college admissions package. Along with your impressive GPA, resume of extraordinary extra-curricular activities, stellar letters of recommendation, and application and essay, your scores on this high-stakes test will be among the most important factors that college admissions panels will use to decide whether or not to grant you admission.

Your test scores will help college admissions panels determine if you're ready and capable of handling college-level coursework and whether you possess any specific aptitudes or deficits in any tested area. Your SAT® exam scores will also help your future college advisors make decisions regarding class-level placement.

> **NOTE:** Make sure you're *fully* aware of the admissions requirements of each college or university that you're applying to. Nothing ruins a superlative admissions application quite so effectively as a glaring omission.

The SAT® exam is carefully designed by recognized experts in the field of education to test your proficiency in the following core subjects, which you've studied throughout your academic career: **Reading, Writing and Language,** and **Mathematics.** We'll delve into an in-depth analysis of each section of the exam—along with comprehensive review and practice—in subsequent chapters of this book.

SAT® Timing and Pacing

The SAT® is a **3-hour exam** consisting of **141 multiple-choice questions** and (in the Math section) **13 grid-in questions.** Add in an extra 50 minutes if you're taking the optional Essay.

Make sure you're comfortable with the format and timing of the SAT® exam and develop an effective test-taking pace *before* test day through thorough practice and review under timed and simulated test-like conditions!

The SAT® Exam: Changing Focus

The SAT® exam underwent some critical changes in March 2016—everything from test length and scoring to test components and score reporting were altered by the College Board, the official SAT® test makers. But don't worry: The information in this book reflects the *most current* test specs and information available. For a complete overview of how the test has changed, visit the official College Board website at *www.collegboard.org*.

Some important features of the redesigned SAT® are as follows:

- **Greater focus on real-world college and career readiness:** The College Board has made a concerted effort to have the redesigned SAT® focus on the knowledge and skills that are most essential for real-world college and career success.

- **Greater emphasis and focus on context:** The redesigned SAT® has a greater focus on word meaning in context and the impact of word choice on shaping overall meaning and tone.

- **Greater assessment of command of evidence:** The newly designated Evidence-Based Reading and Writing section of the exam and the optional SAT® Essay section measure your ability to analyze and interpret information from a variety of sources, including infographics, charts, graphs, tables, and text.

- **Math questions with a practical focus:** The Math section of the redesigned SAT® now features questions in three key areas that have a practical application in the real world: Problem Solving and Data Analysis, Passport to Advanced Math, and Heart of Algebra.

- **Eye on science and History and social studies:** The redesigned SAT® will gauge your ability to answer math and reading and writing questions that are grounded in science, history, and social studies contexts.

- **Simplified scoring:** The College Board has simplified the redesigned SAT® scoring and instituted rights-only scoring—you now simply earn points for correctly answered questions, ***with no penalty for guessing***. There's no reason to leave any question unanswered.

Let's take a closer look at each section of the SAT® exam. Remember, knowledge is power, and the more you know about this important exam, the better prepared you will be to achieve a perfect score!

The Reading Test

The Reading Test is one of two tests that comprise the Evidence-Based Reading and Writing section of the SAT® exam (the other being the Writing and Language Test). The Reading Test is a 65-minute exam that consists of 52 questions. It's designed to test your ability to synthesize and analyze information in a variety of practical contexts. The test makers want to assess your skills at engaging with thought-provoking, evidence-based discussions on topics with real-world relevance and in answering questions based on the information you'll encounter.

On this section of the SAT® exam, you'll encounter a series of reading passages and will answer a series of multiple-choice questions based on either the reading or supplementary material that accompanies them—this may include informational graphics, such as charts, graphs, tables, or other graphic media.

Passages in the Reading Test are designed to test your real-world reading skills, which will serve you well throughout your academic and professional career. The breakdown of passage topics that you'll encounter on test day will comprise the following:

- One passage from a historically relevant U.S. founding document or a piece of text that represents the great global conversation (e.g., the Declaration of Independence or a speech by Martin Luther King Jr.).

- One passage from a recognized work of literature. This can be either a classic or contemporary piece of work and can be a work from the United States or anywhere in the world.

- One passage from the social sciences—this may include sociology, psychology, economics, or another branch of discipline.

- Two science-based passages that represent and examine core concepts in biology, chemistry, Earth science, or physics.

Passages for these topic areas may appear alone or in pairs.

NOTE: Although the passages you'll encounter on the SAT® Reading Test will span a broad range of topics, one key point to remember is that no prior knowledge of the topics is required to answer any of the questions—all you need is the passage content and your existing abilities.

Although not a completely exhaustive list, questions on the SAT® Reading Test will ask you to do the following:

- Analyze information provided in the passage.
- Interpret supplemental graphical material and how it relates to the passage.
- Draw conclusions based on information provided.
- Locate and assess information directly from the passages. These could include a word, a line, or a series of lines in the passage.
- Understand and identify implications based on the author's words.

The SAT® Reading Test is designed to measure the following reading comprehension skills:

Command of Evidence

The SAT® Reading Test will assess your ability to identify, understand, and draw conclusions from evidence presented in the reading passages or associated information graphics, including how authors use evidence to bolster their claims.

Words in Context

On the Reading Test, you'll need to understand and answer questions based on key words, phrases, and context clues that appear in the reading passages, including how these words help define and shape each author's style, meaning, and tone. Words in context questions are carefully selected for their practical application—both in the classroom and the workplace.

Analytic Skills in History and Science Disciplines

The passages and associated questions in these topic areas will gauge your ability to apply your existing reading skills to practical application in these fields. This includes such concepts as interpreting data, considering larger-scale implications, and examining hypotheses.

The SAT®: *Not* a Cram Exam!

Doing well on today's SAT® is not a race to memorize as many facts, figures, and formulas as possible between now and test day.

It's designed to test your ability to process, analyze, and apply real-world information in various practical applications, on top of the knowledge you've acquired throughout your academic career—simply put, it's testing the everyday tools you'll need to succeed in college!

THE WRITING AND LANGUAGE TEST

The Writing and Language Test is one of two tests that comprise the Evidence-Based Reading and Writing section of the SAT® exam (the other being the Reading Test). The Writing and Language Test is a 35-minute exam that consists of 44 questions. This test is designed to gauge your ability to recognize errors in construction, language, style, organization, and grammar and to make corrections as needed in an effort to improve the passages.

NOTE: Being able to effectively edit and proofread written material is a practical skill that will serve you well—both in college and the world of work.

On this section of the exam, you'll encounter a series of passages that can touch upon a variety of topic areas, including:

- Social sciences
- History
- Careers
- Science
- The humanities
- Nonfiction narratives

You'll be tasked with answering a series of multiple-choice questions based on a passage and/or supplementary material that accompanies it (this may include charts, graphs, tables, or other graphic media, just like on the Reading Test). Also similar to the Reading Test, no prior knowledge of the topics that the passages are based on is required—you just need a sharp editorial eye!

Here's a look at the types of questions you'll encounter on the SAT® Writing and Language Test:

Standard English Conventions

Some questions on the Writing and Language Test will correspond to underlined portions of text in the passage and will ask you to determine if the underlined text is correct as written (for which you'd select the NO CHANGE option), or if it requires revision—and if so, which choices among the answer options is correct. These questions typically focus on the fundamentals of good writing, including grammar, usage, style, and tone.

Expression of Ideas

Other questions will ask you to make decisions regarding the structure and organization of text within a paragraph or passage—again, with an eye on improving the flow and impact of the writing.

Command of Evidence

You'll also encounter questions that will ask you to make decisions about how an author develops his or her ideas. This may entail adding or deleting information from the passage based on available contextual evidence, with the goal of sharpening an author's claims or bolstering a point of view with relevant supporting details.

Words in Context

You'll be tasked with making critical decisions regarding word choice throughout the passages on test day. Your job will be to ensure that the best possible word choices are deployed throughout the passages—based on available contextual evidence—for maximum impact and to improve style, tone, or syntax.

Analysis in History and Social Studies and in Science

As mentioned, the SAT® exam will assess your ability to apply your analytical and writing skills to improve passages based on topics in science, social studies, and history. Why? Because these skills will be essential for long-term success—not only in the classroom, but in your professional life after graduation.

THE MATH TEST

The SAT® Math Test is an 80-minute test that consists of 58 questions. It is designed to test your ability to answer practical math questions with a focus on the following skills:

- Using algebraic structure
- Using tools strategically
- Modeling
- Problem solving

The Math Test focuses on the following core foundational areas: **Problem Solving and Data Analysis, Heart of Algebra, Passport to Advanced Math,** and **Additional Topics in Math.** Let's take a closer look at each of these, so you'll know just what to expect on test day.

Problem Solving and Data Analysis

These questions will test your quantitative literacy and ability to answer questions that require significant quantitative reasoning and analytical thinking. You'll need to be able to:

- Create conceptual representations of problems and consider relevant quantitative relationships.
- Examine various objects, including their properties and appropriate units of measure.
- Effectively deploy a range of mathematical operations to arrive at the correct answers.
- Analyze data sets, including identifying patterns and deviations.

Questions from this domain will include both multiple-choice and student-produced response types, also known as **grid-in questions.** In addition, use of a calculator will be permitted for some questions. However, a calculator will not always be recommended or needed to arrive at the correct answers.

The types of questions you'll likely encounter from this mathematical domain will ask you to do the following:

- Solve single-step and multi-step math questions involving percentages, units, unit conversion, and measurement.
- Answer questions involving rates, ratios, scale, and proportional relationships.
- Answer questions involving linear and exponential growth.
- Interpret scatterplots and describe the relationships between variables using quadratic, linear, and exponential models.
- Analyze key features of graphs and graphical data.
- Make inferences based on sample data provided.
- Use statistics to analyze spread, center, and shape and to investigate measures of center.
- Calculate conditional probability and use two-way tables to summarize relative frequencies and categorical data.
- Evaluate data collection methods and reports to make inferences and draw conclusions.

Since you're an elite student aiming for a perfect score, you'll have undoubtedly used these skills to handle a wide range of math challenges throughout your academic career. You'll simply need to make sure that your well-honed skills are razor-sharp for test day!

Heart of Algebra

Foundational algebraic concepts are clearly the focus here, including mastery of linear equations and systems. You'll need to be able to:

- Analyze and conceptualize linear equations and inequalities using procedural algebraic skills.
- Solve algebraic equations and systems of equations.
- Demonstrate algebraic fluency, strategic thinking, and logical reasoning towards interpreting graphical and algebraic representations.

Just like the Problem Solving and Data Analysis domain, questions from this domain will include both multiple-choice and student-produced response types, also known as grid-in questions. Again, use of a calculator will be permitted for some questions, but it will not always be recommended or needed to arrive at the correct answers.

The types of questions from this mathematical domain that you'll likely encounter will ask you to:

- Interpret, create, simplify, and solve one-variable linear expressions and equations with rational coefficients.
- Interpret, create, simplify, and solve one-variable linear equalities with rational coefficients.
- Develop linear functions or equations to demonstrate linear relationships between two quantities.
- Interpret, create, and solve systems of linear equalities in two variables.
- Interpret, create, and solve systems of two linear equations in two variables.
- Utilize core algebraic principles to solve inequalities or linear equations in one variable.
- Utilize core algebraic principles to solve two linear equations in two variables.
- Analyze and interpret constants and variables in expressions for linear functions.
- Make connections and draw conclusions between algebraic and graphical representations.

Again, these are *not* new skills that you need to quickly master between now and test day. They are skills that you've been using in your math classes all along, likely to great success. Careful practice and review will help bring you closer to your target perfect score!

SAT® Math Test Question Types: Multiple-Choice and Grid-ins

On the SAT® Math Test, you'll encounter two types of questions:

- **Multiple-choice:** You'll select the correct answer choice from a series of choices. The majority of questions on the test are in multiple-choice format.

- **Grid-ins:** You'll solve problems and enter your answers in grids, which are provided on your answer sheet on test day. Here's what such a grid looks like (Note that answers can begin on the left or the right of the grid):

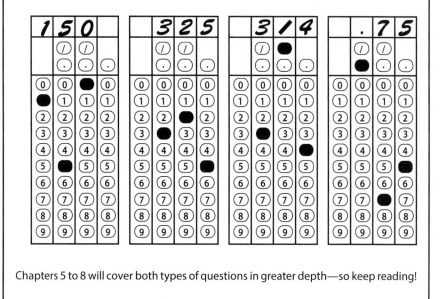

Chapters 5 to 8 will cover both types of questions in greater depth—so keep reading!

Passport to Advanced Math

Some students cringe at the very notion of *advanced mathematics*, but we know that you're a very different type of student. You've got the goal of a perfect SAT® score in your sights, and that means there's no math challenge or concept that you shy away from!

This domain features analysis and manipulation of complex mathematical equations. It tests key skills that should be mastered before moving on to the study of advanced math concepts. You'll need to be able to:

- Understand the structure of complex mathematical expressions.

- Analyze and manipulate complex mathematical expressions and deploy effective logic and reasoning skills to arrive at correct answers.

- Build and interpret functions.

Just like in the other domains, questions from this domain will include both multiple-choice and grid-in questions. Again, use of a calculator will be permitted for some questions, but will not always be recommended or needed to arrive at the correct answers.

NOTE: *Don't* spend your entire study time trying to measure every mathematical formula ever created. Most required formulas will either be provided to you on a handy formula sheet or will appear within the relevant question.

The types of questions you'll likely encounter from this mathematical domain will test your ability to:

- Develop contextually relevant quadratic and exponential functions and equations.
- Create equivalent expressions involving rational exponents.
- Determine the most suitable forms of various mathematical expressions.
- Develop suitable equivalent forms of algebraic expressions.
- Solve quadratic equations and one-variable equations that contain radicals or variables in fraction denominators.
- Solve polynomial expressions using addition, subtraction, and multiplication.
- Solve systems of linear equations and quadratic equations.
- Rewrite simple rational expressions as needed, using core mathematical operations.
- Interpret parts of nonlinear expressions.
- Comprehend mathematical relationships between zeroes and polynomial factors and develop relevant graphs.
- Understand nonlinear relationships between variables when analyzing and interpreting graphs.
- Use function notation to solve questions involving transformation and composition of functions.
- Solve equations involving quantity of interest.

The key to doing well on questions from this domain—and all mathematical domains on the SAT® exam—is thorough practice and review between now and test day, to make sure you're in top test-taking form!

Additional Math Topics

The designers of the SAT® exam have ensured that it covers a wide range of math concepts that relate to successful college and career readiness, including concepts in geometry and trigonometry. This domain features both grid-in and multiple-choice questions. You'll need to be able to:

- Use volume and measurement formulas to solve problems.

- Use the Pythagorean theorem and trigonometric ratios, including sine, cosine, and tangent, to determine lengths of triangle sides and angle measurements.

- Perform mathematical operations involving complex numbers.

- Make conversions between radians and degrees, use radians to determine arc length, and determine radian measure using trigonometric functions.

- Apply circle theorems to determine chord lengths, angle measures, sector areas, and arc lengths.

- Use concepts involving similarity and congruence to solve angle, triangle, and line problems.

- Understand and use knowledge of mathematical relationships between trigonometric ratios, right triangles, and similarity to solve problems.

- Use sine and cosine relationships to solve problems involving complementary angles.

- Develop and use two-variable equations to solve problems involving circles within coordinate planes.

Once again, a calculator is sometimes permitted, but not always recommended or needed.

Use your study time between now and test day—and the helpful practice and review provided in this book—to ensure that you have a firm grasp of these concepts and are ready for test-day success!

A Note About Calculators

Although the makers of the SAT® exam want to test your math skills and problem-solving ability, they recognize the utility of calculators as practical tools in the real world.

Therefore, the SAT® Math Test is divided into two portions:

- **Math Test—Calculator**
- **Math Test—No Calculator**

Remember: Even when a calculator is permitted, that *does not* mean it's always recommended for use. Sometimes, your own problem-solving abilities will help you arrive at the correct answers faster and more effectively than a calculator.

THE OPTIONAL SAT® ESSAY

The optional SAT® Essay is a 50-minute test consisting of a single essay-writing task, similar to a writing task that you'll encounter in a college-level writing course. You'll be tasked with:

- Reading a passage on a specific topic.

- Explaining how effectively the author builds an argument in an effort to persuade readers regarding his or her point of view on the topic.

- Using relevant contextual evidence from the passage to bolster your explanation and analysis.

Your personal opinions on the topic provided will *not* affect your score, and you won't be asked to agree or disagree with a specific topic or position—only the quality of your ideas and writing matter. In addition, you will not be tasked with writing about a specific aspect of your personal experience.

NOTE: Although this is an optional test section, some colleges may require that you take it as part of your admissions application.

For a complete rundown of schools that recommend or require the SAT® Essay, visit the official College Board website:
https://collegereadiness.collegeboard.org/sat/register college-essay-policies.

The Essay Test Prompt

The essay prompt will ask you to read the passage provided and carefully consider how the author develops ideas and uses evidence to support his or her claims on the topic written about. This includes the use of relevant facts and examples, sound reasoning, and effective development of thoughts, as well as such persuasive elements as style, tone, and word choice.

Your essay will be a written response to the things you are being asked to consider within the prompt. All of the information you need to write a high-scoring essay will be provided within the passage and prompt—no additional outside knowledge of the topic is needed to achieve a perfect score.

The Essay Test Topics

The writing passage you'll encounter on test day can be based on a huge array of topic areas, so it's virtually impossible to predict what topic area you should expect to see. That said, there are some common passage elements that will help you know what to expect and give you a leg up on the competition.

The passage you'll encounter will:

- Be written for a wide audience.
- Articulate a specific point of view on a potentially complex subject.
- Analyze ideas, trends, or debates in one or several of the following areas: arts and sciences; civic, cultural, or political life.
- Utilize evidence and logical reasoning to support claims.
- Always include information from published works.

Your essay will be scored by two independent and experienced essay readers, each of whom will grade you on a scale between 1 and 4 points in each of the following three categories:

- **Writing:** Your essay demonstrates a well-crafted, focused, and on-target written response that addresses all aspects of the prompt and utilizes effective and appropriate elements of style, tone, word choice, and grammar.
- **Reading:** Your essay demonstrates a thorough understanding of the passage and the connections between key details and ideas and an effective use of textual evidence.
- **Analysis:** Your essay demonstrates a keen understanding of how the author of the passage constructed and developed his or her argument and uses sound evidence, reasoning, and other persuasive strategies to bolster claims.

> **Your Perfect Score Journey**
>
> The path to a perfect score on the SAT® exam is *not* an easy one. Your skills on each section of the exam have to be razor sharp if you're going to achieve this goal.
>
> This book includes a comprehensive review of the most tested concepts on the exam and practice for the *toughest questions* for each of the sections that comprise the SAT® exam.
>
> Here's the bottom line: Challenging practice under timed conditions will help you get closer to achieving your perfect score goal. But don't worry—we're here to help you through your perfect score journey!

REGISTERING FOR THE SAT® EXAM

Registering online for the SAT® exam is the quickest method—go to ***https://collegereadiness.collegeboard.org/sat/register/online-registration-help***, follow the instructions, and create a free online College Board account to get started and register and to find an appropriate testing center to meet your needs. You can also request makeup testing or get waitlisted online if you missed the registration deadline.

Visit the official SAT® website for additional information if you have special circumstances that need to be addressed or accommodated, including if you have a disability, are home-schooled, need a testing facility closer to home, are over 21 or under 13 years of age, or require Sunday testing.

If you have a special circumstance, you may need to register by mail (paper registration). Check out the College Board website for all the information you need, including deadlines: ***https://collegereadiness.collegeboard.org/sat/register/by-mail***.

REGISTRATION FEES

The fee for taking the SAT® exam is $45, which includes having your score report sent to you, your high school, and as many as four colleges of your choice. If you're taking the SAT® with Essay, the total fee is $57.

NOTE: You may be eligible for a fee waiver to help cover the cost of the SAT® exam. To find out if you're eligible, visit ***https://collegereadiness.collegeboard.org /sat/register/fees/fee-waivers***.

Other options and fees include:

- Additional score reports: $12
- Rush reporting of score reports: $31
- Phone registration: $15
- Changing the location or date of your test: $28
- Late registration (after the regular deadline but before the late registration deadline): $28
- Waitlist fee (if you are admitted on test day): $46

For a complete list of options and fees, visit ***https://collegereadiness.collegeboard.org/sat/register/fees***.

When and How Often Should I Take the SAT® Exam?

In the Unites States, the SAT® exam is given seven times a year—in October, November, December, January, March, May, and June. Select the test date that works best for you and your specific goals, and be sure to check out the registration deadlines on the official SAT® website.

Since you're a perfectionist and nothing short of a top score will satisfy you, review your options for taking and retaking the exam with your academic advisor and visit the official College Board website at ***www.collegboard.org***.

SCORING

Since you're on the hunt for a perfect score, you should carefully familiarize yourself with how the exam is scored. The SAT® exam does *not* penalize you for guessing or selecting a wrong answer. Simply put, you earn points for the questions you answer correctly. Therefore, it is important to answer *every* question on the test, even if you only guess. ***Never* leave a question blank!**

Your total score on the SAT® exam will be the sum of your scores on the two test sections: Evidence-Based Reading and Writing and Math. Your score on each section will range from a low of 200 to a high of 800, with your total score ranging from 400 to a perfect 1600. If you decide to take the SAT® Essay, your score (which will not factor into your total score) will range from a low of 2 to a high of 8.

In addition, your SAT® score reports will include subscores and cross-test scores on a variety of tested domains. These new, additional scores are designed to supply college admissions teams with additional information regarding your skills and capabilities, as well as assess your overall levels of college and career readiness.

Cross-Test Scores

You'll receive two cross-test scores based on selected questions in the Math, Reading, and Writing and Language tests (ranging from 10–40), in the following two areas: **Analysis in History and Social Studies** and **Analysis in Science.** Your scores are designed to indicate your aptitude at analyzing texts and solving problems in these key subject areas.

Subscores

You'll receive seven subscores based on the following seven domains (each ranging from 1 to 15):

- **Math:** Problem Solving and Data Analysis, Heart of Algebra, and Passport to Advanced Math

- **Reading and Writing and Language:** Command of Evidence and Words in Context

- **Writing and Language:** Expression of Ideas and Standard English Conventions

Viewing and Reporting Your Test Scores

You'll be able to view your SAT® scores online by logging into your College Board account. After taking the test, you'll receive an e-mail when your scores are ready, with instructions for how to sign in to your online score report.

Scores are generally available for online viewing approximately 3 weeks after your test. They are sent to the colleges you've indicated while registering (up to four schools) around the same time. If there are additional institutions that you'd like to have your scores sent to, you can request additional reports.

We know you're eager to find out if you achieved your goal of a perfect score, but try to be patient when waiting for your score to be posted. If you'd like additional information on rush score reporting, please visit the official College Board website at ***www.collegboard.org***.

Score Choice™ and SuperScoring

Have you heard about **Score Choice™**? If you've taken the SAT® exam multiple times, this program lets you select which scores you send to colleges (by test date), allowing you to make the best possible impression. Keep in mind that you can't select and combine section scores from one test day with section scores from another test day. In addition, some schools and scholarship programs require that you submit all of your scores.

However, some colleges allow you to take the SAT® exam multiple times and consider your best scores on each of the test sections. This is known as **superscoring,** and it may be a compelling reason to consider taking the exam more than once, especially if you did great on one test section but fell short of your perfect score goal on another.

For additional information on Score Choice™ and superscoring, visit ***https:// collegereadiness.collegeboard.org/sat/scores/sending-scores/score-choice***.

For complete information regarding scoring policies and procedures, visit the official SAT® website at ***https://collegereadiness.collegeboard.org/sat/scores***.

GETTING READY FOR TEST DAY

We know that on test day you'll be ready to attack every test section and question, but knowing the test day fundamentals and preparing for the big day—including selecting a date and location, what to expect when you arrive at your test center, what to bring, and what to leave home—will help you avoid surprises, reduce anxiety, and stay ahead of the competition.

Getting ready for the SAT® exam is essential, but just as important is getting ready for what you'll encounter on test day, so keep reading!

> **ALERT:** For security purposes, you must provide an original, current, valid (unexpired), and legal photo ID in order to be admitted to the test center. A government issued driver's license or non-driver ID, an official ID issued by your school, a passport, or a government-issued military or national identification card are acceptable examples.

CHOOSING YOUR TEST DATE AND LOCATION

When you register online or by mail, you'll be able to choose the test date and test center location that works best for you—so choose wisely! On your quest for a perfect score on the SAT® exam, be sure to choose a test date that:

- Allows you sufficient preparation time.
- Is convenient for you.
- Will not conflict with other activities on your schedule.

The last thing you want on the day of this important exam is to be overbooked or racing around to the point of exhaustion. There are a limited number of test administrations each year, and you're the type of student who knows just how important this test is, so choose carefully and don't put it off until the last minute.

Also be sure that the location you choose for taking the exam is convenient for you, and—this is important—make sure you know *precisely* how long it will take you to get to the testing center. Make a few practice runs, have a route as well as an alternate route to the test location just in case, and don't leave anything to chance. Be sure to take all possible factors into account to ensure you don't arrive late to the test center: traffic, adverse weather conditions, a detour to the gas station, etc. Showing up late for the test is the *quickest* way to derail your quest for a perfect score!

Visit the official SAT® website to find the best test location for you—and register as early as possible to avoid having your preferred test location fill up before you sign up: ***https:// collegereadiness.collegeboard.org/sat/register/find-test-centers***.

WHAT TO EXPECT, WHAT TO BRING, AND WHAT TO LEAVE HOME

Test time starts between 8:30 a.m. and 9:00 a.m. By this time, you should be present and in your assigned seat. Plan to arrive early (doors open at 7:45 a.m.), giving you time to relax, get comfortable, and get settled into test-taking mode; you *definitely* don't want to have to deal with the stress of racing the clock to avoid missing the start of the test, and you will *not* be admitted to take the test if you arrive late.

When you arrive at your test center, the staff will check your photo ID and admissions ticket, admit you into the room, bring you to your assigned seat, and provide you with the required test materials.

Be sure to pay close attention to the test supervisor assigned to your chosen test center. This person will be in charge of reading key test instructions and answering questions, letting you know when to start and stop each test section, when exam breaks start and begin (there will be one 10-minute and one five-minute break during the exam), and collecting your materials when the exam is finished.

Your Test Day Checklist

Use the following helpful checklists to make sure you come to your test center appropriately prepared!

Must Have: Make absolutely certain that you bring the following items with you on test day:

- A printed copy of your admissions ticket
- Acceptable photo ID
- Sharpened No. 2 pencils with erasers
- An approved calculator (keep reading for more information regarding acceptable calculators)

Nice to Have: Consider bringing the following optional items to help maximize your test-taking experience:

- A watch (without an alarm) to help pace yourself through each test section
- A sweater to help you adapt to the test center temperature if the room is cold
- Extra calculator batteries, in case of emergency
- A drink or snack (to have during break time only)

Don't Have: *Do not* bring the following items with you to the test room—you will absolutely not be able to use them:

- The following electronic devices: smartphone, cell phone, iPad or tablet, laptop, digital watch, camera, and any audio device and headphones
- Reading material, textbooks, reference materials (including dictionaries and other study aids), and outside notes
- Protractors, compasses, or rulers
- Extra scratch paper of any kind
- Highlighters, colored pens and pencils, or correction tape/fluid

CALCULATORS AND THE SAT® EXAM

Here's everything you need to know about using a calculator on test day:

- You may use an approved calculator on the Math–Calculator portion of the test only.

- Calculators will not be provided to you; you must bring your own—and no sharing will be permitted.

- You may use only a calculator that uses batteries, not a power cord.

- Any 4-function, scientific, or graphing calculator is acceptable for use on test day, as long as it does not violate any of the rules in this list. Visit the official test website for a list of acceptable calculators: ***https://collegereadiness.collegeboard.org/sat/taking-the-test/calculator-policy***.

- You are responsible for the proper functioning of your calculator, and you are allowed to bring a spare calculator and batteries.

- If you bring or attempt to use a prohibited device on test day, you'll be dismissed from the exam and will not receive a test score.

The following calculators are not permitted for use on the SAT® exam:

- Any calculator with built-in or downloaded computer algebra system functionality

- Handheld, tablet, or laptop computers, or any device that can access the Internet or has audio/recording/camera capabilities

- Calculators built into smartphones, cell phones, or any other electronic communication devices

- Calculators with a typewriter keypad

- Electronic writing pads or pen-input devices

Now you have all the information you need to get started with the targeted, intensive review of all SAT® exam subjects that awaits. Good luck with your studies—we admire your quest for perfection. We know you will leave this preparation with all you need to ace the SAT® exam with the score you desire!

SUMMING IT UP

- The SAT® exam consists of three main sections, each designed to measure practical skills that are essential for college and career success: **Evidence-Based Reading and Writing** (which contains both the Reading and Writing and Language tests), **Math**, and the optional **SAT® Essay,** for a total of 154 questions (155 with the Essay).

- You will have **3 hours** to complete the test (if you choose to take the SAT® Essay, add another 50 minutes).

- **The Reading Test** lasts 65 minutes and consists of 52 questions.

- **The Writing and Language Test** lasts 35 minutes and consists of 44 questions.

- **The Math Test** lasts 80 minutes and consists of 58 questions.

- Your scores on the SAT® exam will be among the most important factors that college admissions panels will use to make admissions decisions. It also gives colleges a good idea of what your skills are in each tested area and will help guide decisions regarding class level placement.

- The maximum total score you can achieve on the SAT® exam is 1600 (800 for each test section).

- The optional **SAT® Essay** is scored on a scale from 1 to 4, and the maximum score you can get is 8, which reflects the sum of your scores from two independent essay readers.

- In addition to your total score, you'll also receive a comprehensive series of subscores and cross-test scores.
  - **Subscores:** You'll receive seven subscores based on the following seven domains (each ranging from 1 to 15):
    - **Math:** Problem Solving and Data Analysis, Heart of Algebra, and Passport to Advanced Math
    - **Reading and Writing and Language:** Command of Evidence and Words in Context
  - **Writing and Language:** Expression of Ideas and Standard English Conventions
  - **Cross-test scores:** You'll receive two cross-test scores based on selected questions in the Math, Reading, and Writing and Language tests (ranging from 10–40), in the following two areas: Analysis in History/Social Studies and Analysis in Science.

- There is no penalty for guessing or choosing an incorrect answer on the SAT® exam, so you should answer every question.

- Registering online for the SAT® exam is the quickest method—go to **https://collegereadiness.collegeboard.org/sat/register**, follow the instructions, and create an online account to get started and register.

- Make sure you're fully aware of all applicable test fees, based on your specific testing and reporting needs.

- Choose the test date and location that works best for you, and make sure you register before the deadline.

- Make sure you have at least one, and preferably an alternate, route to your test location that will get you there with plenty of time to spare.

- Be sure to arrive at the test center well before test time; the test typically begins between 8:30 a.m. and 9:00 a.m.

- Make sure you're fully aware of what you *must bring*, *can bring*, and *cannot bring* with you on test day, as well as calculator guidelines.

- SAT® scores are generally reported to your chosen colleges and available for online viewing approximately 3 weeks after your test date.

- It's your responsibility to make sure that you request to have your score report sent to each college that you're interested in applying to; this includes the colleges you indicate while registering for the test (up to four), as well as any additional schools later on.

- The path to a perfect score on the SAT® exam is *not* an easy one. Your skills on each section of the exam have to be razor sharp if you're going to achieve your goal. Your best approach is to get plenty of practice and review between now and test day and to target your weakest areas for improvement.

- Use this book as your helpful guide throughout your perfect score journey!

CHAPTER 2: SAT® READING: U.S. AND WORLD LITERATURE PASSAGES

OVERVIEW

- About U.S. and World Literature Passages
- Information and Ideas Questions
- Words in Context Questions
- Summing It Up

The SAT® Reading Test will probably be similar to many of the reading comprehension standardized tests you've already taken over your middle and high school careers. You'll have 65 minutes to read four passages ranging between 500 and 750 words, as well as one pair of passages of roughly 350 words each, and answer 52 multiple-choice questions testing your ability to recall information, grasp concepts, make inferences, understand the meaning of words, interpret graphics (maps, charts, diagrams, etc.), and find evidence to support conclusions.

In the next three chapters, you'll learn about all the different passages types on the SAT® Reading Test, as well as the question types you can expect to answer. These different passages will have different purposes. Some will be focused mainly on conveying new information, ideas, and concepts. Others will be more intent on making an argument for or against a particular idea—these are informational passages and deal with history, social studies, or science. Some passages will simply tell a story—these are literary passages, the first kind of passage you're going to learn about here in depth. The section that follows will help you get closer to that perfect 1600 score.

TIP Of the 65 minutes you have to take the SAT® Reading Test, allow yourself about 1 minute and 15 seconds to answer each of the 52 questions. That should leave you enough time to read the passages too.

ABOUT U.S. AND WORLD LITERATURE PASSAGES

There are three different kinds of passages on the SAT® Reading Test. The first type we'll discuss is the U.S. and World Literature passage, which will be the only work of fiction you'll read on the exam. You've probably read fiction for enjoyment, and now you'll be reading it to help you earn a top SAT score.

NOTE: There are a total of 10 questions associated with U.S. and World Literature Passages on the SAT® Reading Test.

U.S. and World Literature passages are excerpted from great works of contemporary and classical fiction. Like most great works of fiction, the main purpose of these passages is to tell a story. The stories may describe an event or an experience, or they may even be more metaphorical, using basic story elements—such as characters, setting, and action—to convey a concept or idea. Your job will be to both understand those basic story elements and interpret what they might say about larger ideas.

It's not easy to tell a complete story in just 500 to 750 words, so U.S. and World Literature passages will often be more about establishing a conflict, introducing characters and relationships, or setting scenes. The passage will still give you all the information and details you'll need to answer the questions.

U.S. and World Literature passages might be excerpts from novels or short stories or, length permitting, complete short stories. Genres include drama, comedy, Gothic fiction, and science fiction, and they might be told from the first- or third-person point of view. Any literary work of appropriate complexity is fair game on the SAT® Reading Test.

TIP: The SAT® Reading Test never requires you to remember what you've learned outside of the test. All questions can be answered using only the information in the passages.

The questions that accompany literature passages may require you to recall basic plot details, but more often you'll have to think a lot deeper about what happens in the stories. You may have to comprehend and identify the main idea of the story or make inferences about characters' behavior and motivations. These kinds of questions fall under the heading of **Information and Ideas** questions, and you'll be learning about those questions and how to master them in this chapter too. Just keep in mind that they can accompany any kind of passage, not literary ones only.

Although they can also accompany any kind of passage, **Words-in-Context** questions are common following U.S. and World Literature passages, too. These are basically vocabulary questions, but instead of demanding you to recall the vocabulary words that are already in your arsenal, they require you to look for clues in the passage to help you decode the meanings of words. This chapter will also give you all the information you'll need to answer this question type.

Like all Reading Test passages, U.S. and World Literature passages can be challenging, but they shouldn't be that different from much of what you've already read in literature classes throughout your high school career. Just remember not to get too bogged down in minor details. The SAT® exam is not a memory test that requires you to store away little useless bits of trivia. Central ideas and key concepts are most important, and your ability to comprehend them will be key to acing the this high-stakes exam.

So now that you have a basic idea of the passages and questions you will encounter, let's examine a couple of those question types in greater detail.

NOTE: There is a range in the complexity of the passages that appear on the SAT® Reading Test. Some will be relatively easy. Others will be more complex, requiring a greater degree of concentration. In the next chapter, you will learn how to read actively and closely to help you digest the most complex passages.

INFORMATION AND IDEAS QUESTIONS

One of the fascinating things about great pieces of literature is that they often work on two levels. On one level, the author is basically telling you a story. On another level, the author is using that story and its characters, events, descriptions, and details to convey a philosophical message. For example, Franz Kafka's famous novella *The Metamorphosis* can be read on one level as a fantastical story about a salesman who discovers he has transformed into a giant insect. On another level, the story can be read as a metaphor for the dehumanizing nature of the work world.

Information and Ideas questions on the SAT® Reading Test will assess your ability to comprehend both the basic details stated in a story and what those details imply about the author's message.

Stated details in a passage are explicit:

> *One morning, when Gregor Samsa woke from troubled dreams, he found himself transformed in his bed into a horrible vermin. . . . "Oh, God," he thought, "what a strenuous career it is that I've chosen!"*

These lines from *The Metamorphosis* explicitly state that the salesman, Gregor Samsa, has transformed into a vermin, or insect.

Implied details are not explicit. Read these lines again and think about what the author is merely suggesting:

> One morning, when Gregor Samsa woke from troubled dreams, he found himself transformed in his bed into a horrible vermin. ... "Oh, God," he thought, "what a strenuous career it is that I've chosen!"

Perhaps the author is using this fantastical transformation to say something about how Gregor feels about himself. Perhaps Gregor's grinding job makes him feel as worthless as an insect. The author does not write, "Gregor's career made him feel as worthless as an insect"; Kafka merely implies this by providing clues:

- *Gregor has transformed into a creature often thought to be worthless.*
- *Instead of worrying about this bizarre transformation, he expresses how bad he feels about his career.*

Your ability to interpret those clues will be very important when answering Information and Ideas questions.

There are six types of Information and Ideas questions: Reading Closely, Citing Textual Evidence, Determining Central Ideas and Themes, Summarizing, Understanding Relationships, and Interpreting Words and Phrases in Context. Before we discuss four of these question types in depth, let's address the other two. Interpreting Words and Phrases in Context questions are similar to Words in Context questions, which we will discuss shortly. In Summarizing questions, you might be asked to recognize the option that offers the best summary of the given passage or where a given summary fails to properly summarize the passage.

Now we will explore the ins and outs of each of the four essential question types.

READING CLOSELY QUESTIONS

Reading Closely questions test your ability to comprehend what is stated and implied in a passage. They require you to find details in the passage and use them to make inferences about the author's point. As the name of this question type implies, Reading Closely questions will demand that you read carefully and pay close attention to details even though they tend to be the most general of the Information and Ideas questions. Sometimes they may even require you to draw conclusions about similar situations described in the question but not in the passage.

These examples of Reading Closely questions will help you recognize them on the exam:

- *It can reasonably be inferred that Gregor mentions his career because ...*
- *The narrator indicates that Gregor thinks his career is ...*
- *Gregor's predicament is most like ...*

ALERT: Some questions will begin with phrases such as "According to the passage," "According to the author," or "According to the narrator." The answers to such questions must be determined from information stated explicitly in the passage and not your own outside assumptions. If there is no evidence in the passage to support an answer choice in one of these questions, then that answer choice is wrong.

Determining Central Ideas and Themes

Just as Reading Closely questions require you to make inferences about details in a passage, Determining Central Ideas and Themes questions require you to make grander inferences about the passage as a whole. For example, a Reading Closely question will require you to determine how the specific character of Gregor feels about his career, but a Determining Central Ideas and Themes question will require you to determine what the author is saying about the grind of working life in general.

Incorrect answer choices to Determining Central Ideas and Themes questions will often try to trick you into thinking you're reading a Reading Closely question. They might imply that an author's point about a single detail is the point of the entire passage. For example, if the theme of "beauty is truth" is mentioned in only one sentence and never dealt with again, then it can't be the main theme of the entire paragraph or passage.

You can avoid being fooled by recognizing how the SAT® Reading Test asks Determining Central Ideas and Themes questions. In the following examples, note how such key terms as "main idea," "main purpose," and "central idea" are part of the question:

- *The main idea of the first paragraph is that Gregor is …*

- *The main purpose of the passage is to …*

- *The central idea of the passage is to …*

- *What is the author's central claim in the passage?*

Understanding Relationships Questions

As well as making inferences about individual details and the passage as a whole, you will also have to make inferences about how different details relate to each other. These are Understanding Relationships questions. As is the case with all questions in the Information and Ideas category, these relationships may be stated explicitly in the passage, but more often than not, they will be implied more subtly. There are three main kinds of relationships you may have to recognize on the SAT® Reading Test:

- **Cause-and-effect,** which is how one detail makes something happen. For example, Gregor feels bad because of his career. Gregor's career is the cause, and his bad feelings are the effect.

- **Comparison-contrast,** which is how two things are similar or different. For example, if Gregor hates his job but other salespeople in his office love their jobs, then Gregor's feelings about his job contrast those of the other salespeople.

- **Sequence,** which is the order of events. For example, first Gregor wakes up from troubled dreams, then he discovers he has transformed into a vermin, and then he frets about the strenuousness of his career.

Here are some examples of Understanding Relationships questions:

- *According to the passage, Gregor feels under strain because …* (Cause-and-Effect)

- *The author of the passage suggests that Gregor's coworkers may be more …* (Comparison-Contrast)

- *After Gregor wakes up, he …* (Sequence)

CITING TEXTUAL EVIDENCE QUESTIONS

There are two kinds of questions that require you to find evidence on the SAT® Reading Test: Command of Evidence questions and Citing Textual Evidence questions. Citing Textual Evidence questions fall under the category of Information and Ideas questions and are constructed differently from Command of Evidence questions, as you'll learn in the next chapter.

Citing Textual Evidence questions require you to know *why* the author decided to include particular details or why pieces of evidence were included in the passage. For example:

> *In line 1 ("One morning … dreams), what is the most likely reason the author notes that Gregor's dreams were troubled?*

This detail could be evidence that Gregor was unhappy with his life and career, since unhappiness during waking life can cause troubled dreams.

NOTE: Unlike Citing Textual Evidence questions, Command of Evidence questions require you to cite the lines in the passage that prove the answer to the previous question.

Now it's finally time to read a full-length U.S. and World Literature Passage. As you read, think about which details in the passage may be used in Information and Ideas questions by considering:

- What do characters' behaviors say about those characters?
- What does the author's language say about characters and ideas?
- How are effects caused?
- What is the theme of the passage?
- How are characters and situations the same or different from each other?
- What is the order in which events happen?

 Try doing a quick read of the questions before doing a close read of the passage, so you know which details are important to find as you make your way through.

This passage is excerpted from "Bernice Bobs Her Hair" by F. Scott Fitzgerald.

Warren was nineteen and rather pitying with those of his friends who hadn't gone East to college. But, like most boys, he bragged tremendously about the girls of his city when he was away from it. There was Genevieve Ormonde, who regularly
Line made the rounds of dances, house-parties, and football games at Princeton, Yale,
5 Williams, and Cornell; there was black-eyed Roberta Dillon, who was quite as famous to her own generation as Hiram Johnson or Ty Cobb; and, of course, there was Marjorie Harvey, who besides having a fairylike face and a dazzling, bewildering tongue was already justly celebrated for having turned five cart-wheels in succession during the last pump-and-slipper dance at New Haven.

10 Warren, who had grown up across the street from Marjorie, had long been "crazy about her." Sometimes she seemed to reciprocate his feeling with a faint gratitude, but she had tried him by her infallible test and informed him gravely that she did not love him. Her test was that when she was away from him she forgot him and had affairs with other boys. Warren found this discouraging, especially as Marjorie had
15 been making little trips all summer, and for the first two or three days after each arrival home he saw great heaps of mail on the Harveys' hall table addressed to her in

various masculine handwritings. To make matters worse, all during the month of August she had been visited by her cousin Bernice from Eau Claire, and it seemed impossible to see her alone. It was always necessary to hunt round and find some one to take care of Bernice. As August waned this was becoming more and more difficult.

Much as Warren worshipped Marjorie he had to admit that Cousin Bernice was sorta dopeless. She was pretty, with dark hair and high color, but she was no fun on a party. Every Saturday night he danced a long arduous duty dance with her to please Marjorie, but he had never been anything but bored in her company.

"Warren"—a soft voice at his elbow broke in upon his thoughts, and he turned to see Marjorie, flushed and radiant as usual. She laid a hand on his shoulder and a glow settled almost imperceptibly over him.

"Warren," she whispered "do something for me—dance with Bernice. She's been stuck with little Otis Ormonde for almost an hour."

Warren's glow faded.

"Why—sure," he answered half-heartedly.

"You don't mind, do you? I'll see that you don't get stuck."

"'Sall right."

Marjorie smiled—that smile that was thanks enough.

"You're an angel, and I'm obliged loads."

With a sigh the angel glanced round the veranda, but Bernice and Otis were not in sight. He wandered back inside, and there in front of the women's dressing-room he found Otis in the centre of a group of young men who were convulsed with laughter. Otis was brandishing a piece of timber he had picked up, and discoursing volubly.

"She's gone in to fix her hair," he announced wildly. "I'm waiting to dance another hour with her."

Their laughter was renewed.

"Why don't some of you cut in?" cried Otis resentfully. "She likes more variety."

"Why, Otis," suggested a friend, "you've just barely got used to her."

When two answer choices seem equally logical, always choose the one for which there is direct evidence in the passage. Remember, there is only one correct answer for every question, and there is always a reason why that answer is correct.

Here are some questions you should be able to answer after a first, quick read of the passage.

What does Warren's behavior say about him? Warren is a bit of a hypocrite, because he thinks ill of his friends from his hometown who didn't go away to college even though he brags about the girls from his hometown when he is at college. (Reading Closely)

What does the author's description of the way Warren dances say about how Warren feels about Bernice? In line 23, the author describes the dance as an "arduous duty," which are negative words used to describe something difficult, not an enjoyable dance. Therefore, Warren probably did not want to dance with Bernice because he probably did not like her much. (Reading Closely)

What causes Warren to dance with Bernice? He does so because he loves Marjorie, who wants him to dance with her cousin, Bernice. (Understanding Relationships)

What is the theme of the story? The story is mostly about how Warren does not like Bernice very much, but he wants to dance with her to please Marjorie, whom he "worshipped" (line 21). So the main theme is that love sometimes makes you do things you do not want to do. (Determining Central Ideas and Themes)

How are Bernice and Marjorie different? By discussing Marjorie's "radiant" looks and her power to persuade Warren to do things he doesn't want to do (dance with Bernice), the author shows that Warren thinks Marjorie was an exciting and enchanting person. Bernice, however, is described as "no fun at a party" and the narrator explains that Warren was always "bored in her company," so she is the opposite of exciting: boring. (Understanding Relationships)

What is the order in which events happen in this story? First Warren falls in love with Marjorie, then Marjorie asks him to dance with her cousin Bernice, then Warren notices that Bernice has left the dance, then Otis says that she has left to fix her hair, and finally, Otis's friends mock him for saying that he is waiting for Bernice to return so he can dance with her. (Understanding Relationships)

Now read this passage again and answer the sample Information and Ideas questions that follow it.

This passage is excerpted from "Bernice Bobs Her Hair" by F. Scott Fitzgerald.

Warren was nineteen and rather pitying with those of his friends who hadn't gone East to college. But, like most boys, he bragged tremendously about the girls of his city when he was away from it. There was Genevieve Ormonde, who regularly

Line made the rounds of dances, house-parties, and football games at Princeton, Yale,

5   Williams, and Cornell; there was black-eyed Roberta Dillon, who was quite as famous to her own generation as Hiram Johnson or Ty Cobb; and, of course, there was Marjorie Harvey, who besides having a fairylike face and a dazzling, bewildering tongue was already justly celebrated for having turned five cart-wheels in succession during the last pump-and-slipper dance at New Haven.

10   Warren, who had grown up across the street from Marjorie, had long been "crazy about her." Sometimes she seemed to reciprocate his feeling with a faint gratitude, but she had tried him by her infallible test and informed him gravely that she did not love him. Her test was that when she was away from him she forgot him and had affairs with other boys. Warren found this discouraging, especially as Marjorie had

15   been making little trips all summer, and for the first two or three days after each arrival home he saw great heaps of mail on the Harveys' hall table addressed to her in various masculine handwritings. To make matters worse, all during the month of August she had been visited by her cousin Bernice from Eau Claire, and it seemed impossible to see her alone. It was always necessary to hunt round and find some one

20   to take care of Bernice. As August waned this was becoming more and more difficult.

Much as Warren worshipped Marjorie he had to admit that Cousin Bernice was sorta dopeless. She was pretty, with dark hair and high color, but she was no fun on a party. Every Saturday night he danced a long arduous duty dance with her to please Marjorie, but he had never been anything but bored in her company.

25   "Warren"—a soft voice at his elbow broke in upon his thoughts, and he turned to see Marjorie, flushed and radiant as usual. She laid a hand on his shoulder and a glow settled almost imperceptibly over him.

"Warren," she whispered "do something for me—dance with Bernice. She's been stuck with little Otis Ormonde for almost an hour."

30 Warren's glow faded.

"Why—sure," he answered half-heartedly.

"You don't mind, do you? I'll see that you don't get stuck."

"'Sall right."

Marjorie smiled—that smile that was thanks enough.

35 "You're an angel, and I'm obliged loads."

With a sigh the angel glanced round the veranda, but Bernice and Otis were not in sight. He wandered back inside, and there in front of the women's dressing-room he found Otis in the centre of a group of young men who were convulsed with laughter. Otis was brandishing a piece of timber he had picked up, and discoursing volubly.

40 "She's gone in to fix her hair," he announced wildly. "I'm waiting to dance another hour with her."

Their laughter was renewed.

"Why don't some of you cut in?" cried Otis resentfully. "She likes more variety."

"Why, Otis," suggested a friend, "you've just barely got used to her."

1 According to the narrator, Warren brags about the girls in his hometown because

  A. he thought the girls were remarkably intelligent.
  B. Marjorie was one of those girls and he loved her.
  C. boys of his age tend to be boastful.
  D. he bragged to cover up how awkward he really felt.

2 In lines 26–28 ("She laid a … with Bernice."), what is the most likely reason the author describes Marjorie's behavior?

  A. To show that she is manipulative
  B. To counter the idea that she is bewildering
  C. To contend that she really loved Warren in spite of her behavior
  D. To argue that love is very complicated

3 It can be reasonably inferred that the young men with Otis are laughing because

  A. Otis just told them a hilarious joke.
  B. they are mocking him for dancing with Bernice.
  C. they know that Marjorie asked Warren to dance with Bernice.
  D. Warren is jealous of Otis because Otis got to dance with Bernice.

4 The main idea of the third paragraph is that

  A. Bernice is a pretty girl with dark hair and high color.
  B. Bernice has her appealing qualities, but Warren does not like her.
  C. Bernice was not fun to be around at a party.
  D. Bernice danced with boys because Marjorie made them dance with her.

Answer Key and Explanations

1. C	2. A	3. B	4. B

1. **The correct answer is C.** Evidence supporting this question is explicitly stated in lines 1–3: "Warren was nineteen and rather pitying with those of his friends who hadn't gone East to college. But, like most boys, he bragged tremendously about the girls of his city when he was away from it." So Warren's bragging is just typical of the kind of boastful behavior of boys of his age. However, there is no evidence to support the conclusion that Warren thought the girls of his town were particularly intelligent, so choice A is not the best answer. It is true that Warren loved Marjorie, but the author explicitly offers the fact that Warren is a typical boy as the cause of his boastfulness, so choice B is not as strong of an answer as choice C. It is possible that Warren's boastfulness was really a cover for his true feelings of awkwardness, but the author never suggests this in the passage, and since the author does suggest that Warren was boastful because he is a typical boy, choice D is not as strong of an answer as choice C.

2. **The correct answer is A.** Earlier in the passage, the author noted that Marjorie does not love Warren even though he loves her, but in these lines, she is flirting with him in order to get him to dance with her cousin, which he does not want to do. Therefore, it is reasonable to conclude that the author describes Marjorie's behavior to suggest that she is a manipulative person. If anything, her conflicting messages— she does not love Warren but still flirts with him—are bewildering, which is the opposite of choice B. There is no evidence that there is anything sincere about Marjorie's flirtations with Warren, which means there is no evidence to support the conclusion in choice C. While choice D may be true, this question is about Marjorie's behavior, not Warren's feelings, and since Marjorie is not in love with him, her behavior says nothing about how complicated love is. Therefore, choice D is not the best answer.

3. **The correct answer is B.** No one in the passage seems to be very fond of Bernice, and Otis seems distressed to be with her, complaining that he has to "dance with her another hour" and begging the other young men to "cut in" and take his place dancing with her. Since the author has already established the young men in the passage as emotionally immature (they tend to brag and say cruel things and "worship" girls who do not love them), it is reasonable to infer that the young men are mockingly laughing at Otis because

they think it is funny he had to dance with Bernice for an hour. Otis seems distressed in lines 40–43; he does not seem as though he is sharing a joke with the other young men, so choice A is not a very reasonable inference. Although Marjorie did ask Warren to dance with Bernice, there is no evidence that anyone knows this but Marjorie and Warren, so choice C is not the most reasonable inference either. The author has also established that Warren only dances with Bernice because Marjorie wants him to; he does not actually want to dance with Bernice, so it is illogical to think he would be jealous because Otis got to dance with her. Therefore, choice D is incorrect.

4. **The correct answer is B.** Choice B captures the main idea of the third paragraph, which states that Bernice had her appealing qualities ("She was pretty, with dark hair and high color") but Warren still did not like her because he thought she was boring and "no fun on a party." Choice A only captures part of the idea of the third paragraph; he describes how Bernice had her appealing qualities but fails to indicate the important fact that Warren did not like her. Choice C has the opposite issue; it shows why Warren does not like her (she's no fun at parties), but does not also acknowledge that she has her appealing qualities, too. Choice D misses the entire main idea of the paragraph while also twisting some details. The passage only shows that Marjorie wanted Warren to dance with Bernice; it does not explain why anyone else danced with her.

WORDS IN CONTEXT QUESTIONS

A crucial part of comprehending what you read in U.S. and World Literature passages—and all passages, in general—is understanding the words the author uses. High-level literature tends to use complex vocabulary, and unless you're a walking dictionary, you won't always be familiar with every one of those words.

 A good trick for answering Words in Context questions is to substitute each answer choice for the word as it is originally used in the passage. Incorrect answer choices will either not make sense or sound weak in comparison to the correct answer.

Acing the SAT® exam does not require you to be a walking dictionary, but you will be required to determine the meanings of unfamiliar words based on how the author uses them in the context of a passage. As was the case with a number of Information and Ideas questions, your ability to detect clues will be integral when answering Words in Context questions. The following question illustrates this point.

Say this is a sample line from an SAT® Reading Test passage:

5   *Patrice felt blizblaz after getting an A on her science test.*

Here is a Words in Context question that might follow:

As used in line 5, "blizblaz" most nearly means:

A. proud.
B. bad.
C. indifferent.
D. concerned.

Before going any further, let's just be clear about something you may have already suspected: *blizblaz* is not a real word. However, that should not affect your ability to select the correct answer to this question. Think about its context: *blizblaz* is being used to describe how someone feels after getting an A on a test. How would you feel if you got an A on a test? You'd probably feel pretty proud, and as fortune has it, *proud* is one of the answer choices. Since *proud* is a positive word, you will want to make sure that there aren't any other positive words among the answer choices that might be even better definitions of *blizblaz* than *proud* is. Well, two have negative connotations—*bad* (choice B) and *concerned* (choice D). So go ahead and eliminate those answer choices. *Indifferent* (choice C) is totally neutral without positive or negative connotations.

Realistically, Patrice more likely felt proud than indifferent after getting an A on her science test. So even though *blizblaz* is not a word you will find in any reliable dictionary, you can still answer this question based on context clues.

Many Words in Context questions will require you to find the right definition of a familiar word with more than one meaning. In some instances, the word may not be unfamiliar at all, but you will still need to examine the clues around it to determine the definition the author intends. Some of these incorrect answer choices will be tricky because they will define the word correctly, but they will not define *how* the author uses it in a particular context. In such cases, *precision* is the key.

NOTE: Words in Context questions are not limited to U.S. and World Literature passages by any means. In fact, two Words in Context questions will accompany every passage or paired passage set you will read on the SAT® Reading Test.

For example, you probably already know that the word *shade* can be used to mean a particular hue of a color. You also probably know that *shade* can mean a shadow cast by an object, or the covering of a lamp, or just a general atmosphere of gloominess. So, you know that there are several very different meanings of the word *shade*. A Words in Context question that expects you to find the most precise explanation for how this familiar word is used may go something like this.

Say this is a sample line from an SAT® Reading Test passage:

15   *Davy stood in the shade of the beautifully flourishing tree.*

Here is a Words in Context question that might follow:

As used in line 15, "shade" most nearly means

- **A.** covering.
- **B.** gloominess.
- **C.** hue.
- **D.** shadow.

As you may have already noticed, each answer choice in this question is a synonym for *shade.* Of course, only one of them correctly defines how *shade* is used in this particular context.

Could it be choice A? Well, a tree does create a sort of covering with its branches, so choice A certainly could stay in the running. Let's set it aside for a moment.

 A good hint that an answer choice in a Words in Context question is incorrect is that it is a different part of speech from the word you are being asked to define. For example, a noun cannot be a synonym of an adjective.

Could it be choice B? Well, it is possible that a tree can be described as projecting gloominess. It would be acceptable to say, "Davy stood in the gloominess of the tree." However, does this definition make sense in this particular context? After all, the author describes the tree as "beautifully flourishing," which does not exactly paint a portrait of gloominess. Based on the cheerful description of the tree, it does not likely project gloominess, and you should feel free to eliminate choice B from the running since it does not fit the tone of the line.

Could it be choice C? As already explained, *hue* means the shade of a color. One might say that a tree has a hue, but one cannot really stand in that hue, which is on the surface of the tree's trunk, branches, and leaves. Based on this context, choice C does not really make sense and can be eliminated.

Could it be choice D? Can a tree cast a shadow? Yes, it can. Even a tree that is "beautifully flourishing?" Sure, why not? Can someone stand in that shadow? Absolutely. Are *shadow* and *shade* synonyms? Yes, we already established that. Therefore, choice D is a definite possible answer.

So, let's compare the two answer choices that are still in the running. Choice A still looks plausible, but wait … take a closer look at the wording of line 15:

15 *Davy stood in the shade of the beautifully flourishing tree.*

The tree's covering is its branches, and it may be awkward for Davy to stand *in* those branches. He may stand *under* the branches. He may even stand *on* the branches, but standing *in* the branches might not be as plausible. Therefore, choice D remains the *best* answer.

 Do you see how one small word, such as *in*, can affect the meaning of a word? Always pay close attention to every detail of the context.

Words in Context questions can be even trickier, requiring you to detect the most precise meanings of words by understanding their nuances, the subtle differences between them. Check out this example:

20 *The villain's treatment of his victims was truly abhorrent.*

The Words in Context question to follow might look like this:

> As used in line 20, "abhorrent" most nearly means
>
> **A.**   bad.
> **B.**   horrible.
> **C.**   unpleasant.
> **D.**   poor.

A villain is probably going to treat his victims in a negative manner, but every answer choice in this question implies a negative manner. They are basically all synonyms of *bad*, and choice A actually is *bad*. However, there is an important distinction between them all: each word implies a different degree of badness. *Unpleasant* (choice C) is probably the mildest word, suggesting something that is not pleasant but not intensely bad. *Poor* (choice D) is slightly worse, or more intense, and *bad* (choice A) is as intense as or more intense than choice D. One thing is certain, though: the most intense negative word among the answer choices is *horrible* (choice B).

So let's think a bit more about context. What is happening in this line? There is a villain, which is someone who is so bad that he is defined by his badness. There are also victims: people who are suffering because of this person defined by his badness. Would those deeds be merely *unpleasant, poor,* or even *bad*? Most likely they would be a lot more intense than that, so the most intense answer choice, *horrible*, is the best definition of *abhorrent*.

 ALERT: Don't waste your valuable study time trying to memorize vocabulary lists, even lists of words that are supposedly common to the SAT® Reading Test. There is no way to know if any of them will actually appear on the test, and memorizing definitions won't necessarily help you to determine how words are used according to their particular contexts in the passages you'll read.

Before you answer some practice Words in Context questions, try reading another Literature passage with the following questions in mind:

- Do you notice any unfamiliar words, and are there context clues that indicate their meanings?

- What is the tone of the passage as a whole? Remember that tone affects word meaning.

- How intense are the things described in the passage? Will the author generally use strong words or milder words to be descriptive?

This passage is excerpted from The Canterville Ghost *by Oscar Wilde.*

When Mr. Hiram B. Otis, the American Minister, bought Canterville Chase, every one told him he was doing a very foolish thing, as there was no doubt at all that the place was haunted. Indeed, Lord Canterville himself, who was a man of the most

Line punctilious honour, had felt it his duty to mention the fact to Mr. Otis when they

5 came to discuss terms.

"We have not cared to live in the place ourselves," said Lord Canterville, "since my grandaunt, the Dowager Duchess of Bolton, was frightened into a fit, from which she never really recovered, by two skeleton hands being placed on her shoulders as she was dressing for dinner, and I feel bound to tell you, Mr. Otis, that the ghost has been

10 seen by several living members of my family, as well as by the rector of the parish, the Rev. Augustus Dampier, who is a Fellow of King's College, Cambridge. After the unfortunate accident to the Duchess, none of our younger servants would stay with us, and Lady Canterville often got very little sleep at night, in consequence of the mysterious noises that came from the corridor and the library."

15 "My Lord," answered the Minister, "I will take the furniture and the ghost at a valuation. I have come from a modern country, where we have everything that money can buy; and with all our spry young fellows painting the Old World red, and carrying off your best actors and prima-donnas, I reckon that if there were such a thing as a ghost in Europe, we'd have it at home in a very short time in one of our public

20 museums, or on the road as a show."

"I fear that the ghost exists," said Lord Canterville, smiling, "though it may have resisted the overtures of your enterprising impresarios. It has been well known for three centuries, since 1584 in fact, and always makes its appearance before the death of any member of our family."

25 "Well, so does the family doctor for that matter, Lord Canterville. But there is no such thing, sir, as a ghost, and I guess the laws of Nature are not going to be suspended for the British aristocracy."

"You are certainly very natural in America," answered Lord Canterville, who did not quite understand Mr. Otis's last observation, "and if you don't mind a ghost in the house, it is all right. Only you must remember I warned you."

A few weeks after this, the purchase was concluded, and at the close of the season the Minister and his family went down to Canterville Chase. Mrs. Otis, who, as Miss Lucretia R. Tappan, of West 53d Street, had been a celebrated New York belle, was now a very handsome, middle-aged woman, with fine eyes, and a superb profile. Many American ladies on leaving their native land adopt an appearance of chronic ill-health, under the impression that it is a form of European refinement, but Mrs. Otis had never fallen into this error. She had a magnificent constitution, and a really wonderful amount of animal spirits. Indeed, in many respects, she was quite English, and was an excellent example of the fact that we have really everything in common with America nowadays, except, of course, language. Her eldest son, christened Washington by his parents in a moment of patriotism, which he never ceased to regret, was a fair-haired, rather good-looking young man, who had qualified himself for American diplomacy by leading the German at the Newport Casino for three successive seasons, and even in London was well known as an excellent dancer. Gardenias and the peerage were his only weaknesses. Otherwise he was extremely sensible. Miss Virginia E. Otis was a little girl of fifteen, lithe and lovely as a fawn, and with a fine freedom in her large blue eyes. She was a wonderful Amazon, and had once raced old Lord Bilton on her pony twice round the park, winning by a length and a half, just in front of the Achilles statue, to the huge delight of the young Duke of Cheshire, who proposed for her on the spot, and was sent back to Eton that very night by his guardians, in floods of tears. After Virginia came the twins, who were usually called "The Star and Stripes," as they were always getting swished. They were delightful boys, and, with the exception of the worthy Minister, the only true republicans of the family.

Now let's answer the questions we posed before you read the excerpt from *The Canterville Ghost*.

Did you notice any unfamiliar words, and are there context clues that indicate their meanings? Maybe one of these words was used very early in the passage: *punctilious*. That is probably not a word you use in every day speech, and realistically, there are not many context clues to help you to define it. Was Mr. Otis very honorable? Slightly honorable? Not honorable at all? There's really no way to know from this particular passage, so before you dash for your dictionary, you can rest assured that you will not be expected to define words for which there are no context clues. Incidentally, though, *punctilious* means "meticulous."

What is the tone of the passage as a whole? Although everyone is discussing the existence of ghosts, which is a pretty strange conversation, they do so in very reserved and formal language, which creates a humorous clash between the strangeness of the topic and the formalness with which it is being discussed. This creates a bit of a tricky situation, since mild words may be used to describe wild things such as the existence of ghosts. Be cautious, because this can result in some misleading answer choices.

How intense are the things described in the passage? Will the author generally use strong words or milder words to be descriptive? Once again, we're dealing with a tricky passage. This is not, for example, an adventurous scene full of high danger in which things are generally described with intense language. There are intensely strange things going on, such as the possible existence of ghosts, but the characters speak of them with mild reserve. Meanwhile, intense words such as "magnificent" and "wonderful" are used to describe mortal people. This means you cannot draw any sweeping conclusions about whether the passage will mostly include mild or intense language. There is a mixture of intense and mild words, and each type is not always used where you might most expect it to be. This means you have to pay extra close attention to the context immediately surrounding each word you will have to define.

TIP Science passages in particular may require you to read unfamiliar pieces of jargon or technical language. The SAT® Reading Test is not designed to determine whether or not you're a scientist; approach Words in Context questions that involve jargon or technical language as you would any other.

Now it's time to read that excerpt from *The Canterville Ghost* again and see if you can answer the sample Words in Context questions that follow it.

This passage is excerpted from The Canterville Ghost *by Oscar Wilde.*

When Mr. Hiram B. Otis, the American Minister, bought Canterville Chase, every one told him he was doing a very foolish thing, as there was no doubt at all that the place was haunted. Indeed, Lord Canterville himself, who was a man of the most
Line punctilious honour, had felt it his duty to mention the fact to Mr. Otis when they
5 came to discuss terms.

"We have not cared to live in the place ourselves," said Lord Canterville, "since my grandaunt, the Dowager Duchess of Bolton, was frightened into a fit, from which she never really recovered, by two skeleton hands being placed on her shoulders as she was dressing for dinner, and I feel bound to tell you, Mr. Otis, that the ghost has been
10 seen by several living members of my family, as well as by the rector of the parish, the Rev. Augustus Dampier, who is a Fellow of King's College, Cambridge. After the unfortunate accident to the Duchess, none of our younger servants would stay with us, and Lady Canterville often got very little sleep at night, in consequence of the mysterious noises that came from the corridor and the library."

15 "My Lord," answered the Minister, "I will take the furniture and the ghost at a valuation. I have come from a modern country, where we have everything that money can buy; and with all our spry young fellows painting the Old World red, and carrying off your best actors and prima-donnas, I reckon that if there were such a thing as a ghost in Europe, we'd have it at home in a very short time in one of our public
20 museums, or on the road as a show."

"I fear that the ghost exists," said Lord Canterville, smiling, "though it may have resisted the overtures of your enterprising impresarios. It has been well known for three centuries, since 1584 in fact, and always makes its appearance before the death of any member of our family."

25 "Well, so does the family doctor for that matter, Lord Canterville. But there is no such thing, sir, as a ghost, and I guess the laws of Nature are not going to be suspended for the British aristocracy."

"You are certainly very natural in America," answered Lord Canterville, who did not quite understand Mr. Otis's last observation, "and if you don't mind a ghost in the

30 house, it is all right. Only you must remember I warned you."

A few weeks after this, the purchase was concluded, and at the close of the season the Minister and his family went down to Canterville Chase. Mrs. Otis, who, as Miss Lucretia R. Tappan, of West 53d Street, had been a celebrated New York belle, was now a very handsome, middle-aged woman, with fine eyes, and a superb profile.

35 Many American ladies on leaving their native land adopt an appearance of chronic ill-health, under the impression that it is a form of European refinement, but Mrs. Otis had never fallen into this error. She had a magnificent constitution, and a really wonderful amount of animal spirits. Indeed, in many respects, she was quite English, and was an excellent example of the fact that we have really everything in common

40 with America nowadays, except, of course, language. Her eldest son, christened Washington by his parents in a moment of patriotism, which he never ceased to regret, was a fair-haired, rather good-looking young man, who had qualified himself for American diplomacy by leading the German at the Newport Casino for three successive seasons, and even in London was well known as an excellent dancer.

45 Gardenias and the peerage were his only weaknesses. Otherwise he was extremely sensible. Miss Virginia E. Otis was a little girl of fifteen, lithe and lovely as a fawn, and with a fine freedom in her large blue eyes. She was a wonderful Amazon, and had once raced old Lord Bilton on her pony twice round the park, winning by a length and a half, just in front of the Achilles statue, to the huge delight of the young Duke of

50 Cheshire, who proposed for her on the spot, and was sent back to Eton that very night by his guardians, in floods of tears. After Virginia came the twins, who were usually called "The Star and Stripes," as they were always getting swished. They were delightful boys, and, with the exception of the worthy Minister, the only true republicans of the family.

1 As used in line 7, "fit" most nearly means

   A. form.
   B. set.
   C. match.
   D. convulsion.

2 As used in line 17, "spry" most nearly means

   A. dangerous.
   B. artistic.
   C. lively.
   D. beautiful.

3 As used in line 28, "natural" most nearly means

   A. unaffected.
   B. ordinary.
   C. biological.
   D. native.

4 As used in line 46, "lithe" most nearly means

   A. sneaky.
   B. agile.
   C. aged.
   D. beastly.

Answer Key and Explanations

1. D	**2.** C	**3.** A	**4.** B

1. **The correct answer is D.** Although each answer choice is a synonym of *fit*, only choice D shows how it is used in the context of line 7, which describes how someone was so frightened that he suffered a fit. One could certainly suffer a convulsion, making choice D the best answer. Even if you do not know the meaning of *convulsion*, you can still determine that choice D is correct by the process of elimination: one would not suffer a *form* (choice A), a *set* (choice B), or a *match* (choice C), so all of those choices can be eliminated.

2. **The correct answer is C.** This is a question in which understanding tone will help you find the correct answer. The Minister is speaking lightheartedly about capturing ghosts. The idiom "painting the town red" means "partying," which suggests *liveliness* (choice C). The Minister says the "young fellows" would have put the ghosts in a road show, not destroyed the ghosts, so *dangerous* (choice A) is not the best answer based on that context clue. As already stated, "painting the town red" is an idiom, not a literal description of how artistic someone might be, so *artistic* (choice B) is incorrect. One would not have to be particularly artistic to paint buildings in a town a single color such as red in any event. The Minister never

suggests how the young fellows look, so there are no context clues to support *beautiful* (choice D).

3. **The correct answer is A.** This is another tricky one since the correct answer depends on recognizing that the narrator says that Lord Canterville "did not quite understand Mr. Otis's last observation." The use of "Nature" in that observation is its biological use, but *biological* (choice C) is still incorrect because Lord Canterville did not understand that. Rather, after he categorizes Americans as "natural," he states that they "do not mind a ghost in the house," which means that Americans would be unaffected by such strange and frightening circumstances. Therefore, the best answer is *unaffected* (choice A). *Ordinary* (choice B) and *native* (choice D) are also synonyms of *natural*, but neither make any sense in this particular context.

4. **The correct answer is choice B.** Only one answer choice is a synonym of *lithe* in any context, so this is the least tricky question in this set. However, it will require you to know a little something about fawns. They are agile, so *agile* (choice B) is correct. A fawn could conceivably be sneaky, but *sneaky* has negative connotations, and Miss Otis is definitely being described in a positive tone in lines 46–47, so *sneaky* (choice

A) violates that tone. Fawns are young deer, which eliminates *aged* (choice C), which means "old." Even if you do not know that much about fawns, the narrator states that Miss Otis is only fifteen, which is very young. A fawn is a beast, but *beastly* is another word with negative connotations, suggesting monstrousness more than a resemblance to a pretty and gentle beast such as a fawn, so *beastly* (choice D) violates the tone, as well.

SUMMING IT UP

- The SAT® Reading Test is a 65-minute test comprised of 52 multiple-choice questions, four passages ranging between 500 and 750 words, and one pair of passages of roughly 350 words each.

- The SAT® Reading Test contains one U.S. and World Literature passage, a work of contemporary or classic fiction that ranges between 500 and 750 words.

- Questions on the SAT® Reading Test assess your ability to recall information, grasp concepts, make inferences, understand the meaning of words, interpret graphics, and find evidence to support conclusions.

- **Information and Ideas questions** test your ability to comprehend the basic details stated in a story and what those details imply about the author's message.
  - All information you need to know to answer SAT® Reading Test questions is contained in the passage—you will not have to bring in any specific outside knowledge.

- **Reading Closely questions** test your ability to comprehend what is stated and implied in a passage; Determining Central Ideas and Themes questions require you to make grander inferences about the passage as a whole; Understanding Relationships questions require you to make inferences about how different details relate to each other in a passage.

- **Cause-and-Effect questions** test your ability to recognize how one detail produces the effect in another; comparison-contrast questions test your ability to recognize how two things are different or similar; sequence questions test your ability to recognize the order of events in a passage.

- **Citing Textual Evidence questions** require you to know why the author decided to include particular details or pieces of evidence in the passage.

- **Words in Context questions** require you to determine the meanings of words by using context clues in the passage.
  - Some incorrect answer choices in Words in Context questions are tricky because they define the word correctly but do not define how the author uses the word in a particular context and also because they require you to detect the most precise meanings of words by understanding the subtle differences between them.
  - Tone can affect the meaning of a word in a particular context—don't just answer a question based on the first definition you recognize; make sure to select the correct definition of the word in the *context* of the passage.

CHAPTER 3: SAT® READING: HISTORY AND SOCIAL STUDIES PASSAGES

OVERVIEW

- About History and Social Studies Passages
- Reading Tactics
- Rhetoric Questions
- Command of Evidence Questions
- Summing It Up

ABOUT HISTORY AND SOCIAL STUDIES PASSAGES

In the previous chapter, we focused on the stories creative authors conjured from their imaginations. In this chapter we will shift our attention to the very real stories that occurred throughout the history of the United States and the rest of the world. History and Social Studies passages are particularly important because there are two of them on the SAT® Reading Test: Founding Documents and Social Science.

NOTE: There are a total of 21 questions associated with History and Social Studies passages on the SAT® Reading Test.

Founding Documents

Founding Documents passages are genuine documents of great historical significance. They might be documents detailing important new developments in government, the economy, or international affairs. For example, some of the most famous founding documents of this nature are the United States Declaration of Independence and the Bill of Rights. They might also be speeches made by world leaders or major figures in important political, social, or cultural movements, such as Abraham Lincoln's Gettysburg Address or Martin Luther King Jr.'s "I Have a Dream" speech. Founding documents form the story of the world as told by the people who changed it.

Social Science

Social Science passages on economics, sociology, and political science deal with how society has changed throughout history and how those changes have affected the United States. Passages explaining the Civil Rights Movement, the women's suffrage movement, and the abolition of slavery would fall under the heading of Social Science. Less politically focused topics about how technological developments such as the Internet have affected U.S. society and culture might also appear in Social Science passages.

NOTE: Technically, there could actually be as many as three History and Social Studies passages on the Reading Test since it includes one set of paired passages in either History and Social Studies or Science. However, the two passages in a passage pair are treated like two halves of a single passage of the usual length (500 to 750 words) and followed by the same number of questions that would follow a single passage (10 to 11). You will learn more about paired passages in the next chapter.

As was the case with the U.S. and World Literature passages you learned about in the previous chapter, the History and Social Studies passages will be pretty similar to the kinds of things you've been reading in school for years. They will require you to think about information explicitly stated in the text and ideas that are only implied. So although the content of U.S. and World Literature passages is a bit different from that of History and Social Studies passages, you will still read and answer questions in the same way that you did in the previous chapter. In this chapter, you will also learn some new tactics for reading as effectively as you can. These will be crucial in helping you attain that perfect 1600 score.

History and Social Studies passages may also include questions that will require you to interpret graphics such as diagrams, charts, and maps. You will learn about graphics in the next chapter.

You already learned about Information and Ideas questions and Words in Context questions, which will also accompany History and Social Studies passages. Now, we will cover two additional question types: Rhetoric and Command of Evidence questions, which can be used with all SAT® Reading Test passage types.

READING TACTICS

Before you read some sample History and Social Studies passages and learn all you need to know about Rhetoric and Command of Evidence questions, let's explore some new tactics for reading all kinds of passages as effectively as possible. These tactics will be key, since time is a factor on the SAT® Reading Test. You may think that 65 minutes sounds like a big chunk of time, but remember that you will be reading five passages (six, if you want to count the paired passages as two separate passages) and answering 52 questions during that time. So it is important not to freeze yourself up by struggling with one particularly difficult passage. Doing so will rob you of the precious time you'll need to read the other passages and answer the questions.

 ALERT: Whatever you do, do not skip a passage, no matter how tough it may seem. Not reading a passage will cost you 10 to 11 questions. However, you do not want to spend so much time reading that it slows you down and costs you precious minutes.

READING ACTIVELY

Reading the passages on the SAT® Reading Test carefully is important, but there are also benefits to reading quickly. In fact, when you first read a passage, you should do it quickly just to get a sense of the main ideas and details, making and taking notations as you read. This is known as reading actively.

Your notations should be very simple. In most cases, simply underlining words will do the trick, though you may need to make a brief note to yourself explaining why you underlined those particular words. Underline details that seem important to the passage's overall meaning and take a few seconds to think about what that meaning is. Try to define it in simple words, such as, "It is every American's duty to fight for the equal rights of all."

Try underlining unfamiliar words—though don't waste too much time trying to define them since they may not actually be used in the Words in Context questions that follow. If and when you find those difficult words in Words in Context questions, then it is time to really work to decode their meanings.

Take a look at the following annotated passage to get an idea of how an active reader might mark up a passage. As you will notice, the notes are brief summarizations of the main idea of each paragraph.

This passage is excerpted from American Leaders and Heroes: A Preliminary Text-Book in United States History *by Wilbur F. Gordy.*

American independence, the beginnings of which we have just been considering, was accomplished after a long struggle. Many brave men fought on the battle-field, and many who never shouldered a musket or drew a sword exerted a powerful influence for the good of the patriot cause. One of these men was Benjamin Franklin.

← Benjamin Franklin fought for American Independence.

He was born in Boston in 1706, the fifteenth child in a family of seventeen children. His father was a candle-maker and soap-boiler. Intending to make a clergyman of Benjamin, he sent him, at eight years of age, to a grammar-school, with the purpose of fitting him for college. The boy made rapid progress, but before the end of his first school-year his father took him out on account of the expense, and put him into a school where he would learn more practical subjects, such as writing and arithmetic. The last study proved very difficult for him.

← Franklin was a good student but his father pulled him out of his expensive school to go to one with a more practical education.

Two years later, at the age of ten, he had to go into his father's shop. Here he spent his time in cutting wicks for the candles, filling the moulds with <u>tallow</u>, selling soap in the shop, and acting the part of errand-boy.

← Franklin went to work in his father's candle shop.

Many times he had watched the vessels sailing in and out of Boston Harbor, and often in imagination had gone with them on their journeys. Now he longed to become a sailor, and, quitting the <u>drudgery</u> of the candle-shop, to roam out over the sea in search of more interesting life. But his father wisely refused to let him go. His fondness for the sea, however, took him frequently to the water, and he learned to swim like a fish and to row and sail boats with great skill. In these sports, as in others, he became a leader among his playmates.

← Franklin wanted to be a sailor, but settled for water sports instead.

Once you take these notes, it will be easier to locate a paragraph containing the information that applies to a particular question. Also, notice that the active reader underlined a couple of unfamiliar words: *tallow* and *drudgery*.

READING CLOSELY

After you get the essential details with a quick, active read, it is time to look at the questions. Once you know exactly what you are being asked, you can go back to the passage for a closer reading to spot the details and ideas that will help you accurately answer the questions. Paying attention to clues in the questions will make reading closely easier. Your notes will be very helpful when it comes to questions that ask you to think about the passage as a whole. For example:

- *According to the passage, Martin Luther King Jr. generally believed that ...*
- *The main purpose of the passage is to ...*

Many SAT® Reading Test questions will direct you to the exact lines or paragraphs that pertain to more specific information. For example:

- *In lines 45–57, the author is arguing that the Civil War was ...*
- *According to Paragraph 8, what was the most significant change caused by the invention of the cell phone?*

In these cases, you can jump right to the paragraphs or lines in question to locate the details you will need to answer the questions.

NOTE: Small details are not going to be important on the SAT® Reading Test; you won't be expected to remember someone's middle name or the name of his or her school. As was true of the literature questions, you will be expected to grasp the bigger ideas in the passage.

As you read the sample passages in the following sections on Rhetoric and Command of Evidence questions, try reading actively and closely. This will be especially helpful when answering Command of Evidence questions, but first you'll learn about how writers use words to make a point, which is also known as the art of rhetoric.

RHETORIC QUESTIONS

The most seasoned writers choose their words very carefully, an especially important skill if the writer wants the reader to agree with a point she or he is making. Crafty word choice is known as rhetoric. Most often, you'll hear about rhetoric as it applies to debates or speeches. Since you may be reading a speech among the History and Social Studies passages on the test, you will want to pay close attention to the rhetoric the writer uses in that speech.

Speeches are generally composed to make a convincing argument. The writer wants to convince the audience that his or her point is the correct one. In his famous "I Have a

Dream" speech, Martin Luther King Jr. was trying to convince his fellow Americans that civil rights were an important and just issue. King's speech is celebrated as a masterful piece of rhetoric. You don't have to be as skilled or as convincing as King to employ rhetoric to get your points across. Sometimes, people may use rhetoric in an attempt to hide the fact that their central arguments are weak.

On the SAT® Reading Test, you will need to think about the words authors choose, as well as the ways passages are structured, in order to answer Rhetoric questions. While rhetoric is especially important as it pertains to arguments and speeches, Rhetoric questions can accompany any kind of passage. Remember when we discussed how authors of fiction often use their stories to imply messages in the previous chapter? Well, the way authors use words to imply those messages is rhetoric.

There are five kinds of Rhetoric questions that will appear on the SAT® Reading Test: Analyzing Arguments, Analyzing Point of View, Analyzing Purpose, Analyzing Text Structure, and Analyzing Word Choice. Let's discuss them in depth.

ANALYZING ARGUMENTS

These questions ask you to identify when an argument is strong or weak. You will do so by analyzing important rhetorical elements, including:

- **Claims**—the author's essential stance on a topic. Occasionally, an author will announce her or his claims with phrases such as *I believe* or *my point is*, but usually they will be tucked into the passage with greater subtlety.

- **Counterclaims**—the author's claims that contradict the claims. Counterclaims might begin with words and phrases such as *on the other hand*, *but*, *however*, or *despite*.

- **Reasoning**—the thought process that led the author to take her or his stance.

- **Evidence**—the facts, data, statistics, surveys, case studies, etc. that support the author's stance. The author might use words and phrases such as *for example*, *because*, and *statistics show* to signal the introduction of evidence. Some of these questions may ask you to identify the kind of evidence the author uses *most*, such as personal anecdotes or statistics.

Sometimes, an author includes a quotation from an outside source as evidence to support an idea. This rhetorical device shows that the author is not alone in his or her opinions. The more authoritative the source, the better the quote suits the author's rhetorical purposes.

You may also have to identify kinds of evidence, such as:

- **Statistical evidence:** numerical evidence based on surveys
- **Testimonial evidence:** spoken evidence from experts, authorities, or anyone else
- **Anecdotal evidence:** evidence based on observations
- **Analogical evidence:** evidence that makes a comparison

Here are a few examples of how Analyzing Arguments questions might appear on the Reading Test:

- *What is King's central claim?*
- *The question that begins paragraph 13 primarily serves to …*
- *Which of the following claims is supported by paragraph 7?*
- *As presented in the passage, King's argument primarily relies on which type of evidence?*

NOTE: Analyzing Arguments questions tend to announce themselves. They often contain such key words as *claim*, *reason*, and *evidence*. If they contain the word *evidence*, don't confuse them with Command of Evidence questions.

ANALYZING POINT OF VIEW

These questions require you to understand how the author conveys information (for example, is she discussing her own experiences or those of others) and how that influences meaning and tone. Analyzing Point of View questions may also require you to determine the author's attitude. Is the author taking a negative or positive stance on the topic? Is the argument fueled by anger or love?

Analyzing Point of View questions might appear on the Reading Test like so:

- *The passage is written from the point of view of a …*
- *The passage most strongly suggests that the central message of the Declaration of Independence has been …*

Analyzing Purpose

Analyzing Purpose questions are like main idea questions, except they focus specifically on the author's central argument. However, others require more abstract thought. You might have to figure out why the author includes a particular image or references a particular incident in the passage. What is the message the author is trying to convey in his passage?

Notice how Analyzing Purpose questions might appear on the Reading Test:

- *In lines 14–15, King makes which point about the Declaration of Independence?*

- *King uses the image of the dream (lines 80–100) most likely to …*

When reading a passage, try anticipating Analyzing Purpose questions by briefly defining the point of the passage after you are done reading. Even if there aren't any Analyzing Purpose questions, doing this may help you answer other kinds of questions, such as ones about point of view or main idea.

Analyzing Text Structure

These questions require you to take a broader view of the passage, testing your ability to understand how the organization of a passage affects meaning. They may ask you to analyze the structure of the passage as a whole (for example, does the author follow a cause-and-effect structure, a chronological structure, or a question-and-answer structure), how the focus of arguments change over the course of the passage, or how individual elements of the passage (a particular paragraph or even a single quote, for example) affect the entire passage.

Here are a few examples of how Analyzing Text Structure questions may appear:

- *The primary function of the first paragraph (lines 1–2) is to …*

- *Over the course of the passage, the main focus shifts from a discussion of historic U.S. documents to …*

Analyzing Text Structure questions can be similar to questions about main idea in that incorrect answer choices may place too much importance on a particular detail instead of the wider structure of the passage. Do not confuse a passage's individual details with the grander functions of its structure.

ANALYZING WORD CHOICE

These questions are very different from Words in Context questions. They test your understanding of the essence of rhetoric. They ask you *how* authors choose words to convey their messages, not the basic definitions of those words. You will be expected to understand how those words affect meaning and tone.

Analyzing Word Choice questions might appear in this way on the Reading Test:

- *King uses the words "withering justice" (line 6) mainly to emphasize that …*
- *The primary impression created by King's description of the Emancipation Proclamation as "a great beacon of light and hope" (lines 4–5) is that it is …*

Now we will put your newfound knowledge of Rhetoric questions to the test. Read the following passage and answer the three practice questions that follow it. Beware: This passage is pretty dense and difficult. Now would be a good time to use those reading tactics you learned about at the beginning of this passage: reading actively and closely.

This passage is excerpted from The Frontier in American History *by Frederick Jackson Turner.*

Nothing in our educational history is more striking than the steady pressure of democracy upon its universities to adapt them to the requirements of all the people. From the State Universities of the Middle West, shaped under pioneer ideals, have

Line
come the fuller recognition of scientific studies, and especially those of applied

5   science devoted to the conquest of nature; the breaking down of the traditional required curriculum; the union of vocational and college work in the same institution; the development of agricultural and engineering colleges and business courses; the training of lawyers, administrators, public men, and journalists—all under the ideal of service to democracy rather than of individual advancement alone. Other universities

10   do the same thing; but the head springs and the main current of this great stream of tendency come from the land of the pioneers, the democratic states of the Middle West. And the people themselves, through their boards of trustees and the legislature, are in the last resort the court of appeal as to the directions and conditions of growth, as well as have the fountain of income from which these

15   universities derive their existence.

The State University has thus both a peculiar power in the directness of its influence upon the whole people and a peculiar limitation in its dependence upon

---

the people. The ideals of the people constitute the atmosphere in which it moves, though it can itself affect this atmosphere. Herein is the source of its strength and the direction of its difficulties. For to fulfill its mission of uplifting the state to continuously higher levels the University must, in the words of Mr. Bryce, "serve the time without yielding to it"; it must recognize new needs without becoming subordinate to the immediately practical, to the short-sightedly expedient. It must not sacrifice the higher efficiency for the more obvious but lower efficiency. It must have the wisdom to make expenditures for results which pay manifold in the enrichment of civilization, but which are not immediate and palpable.

In the transitional condition of American democracy which I have tried to indicate, the mission of the university is most important. The times call for educated leaders. General experience and rule-of-thumb information are inadequate for the solution of the problems of a democracy which no longer owns the safety fund of an unlimited quantity of untouched resources. Scientific farming must increase the yield of the field, scientific forestry must economize the woodlands, scientific experiment and construction by chemist, physicist, biologist and engineer must be applied to all of nature's forces in our complex modern society. The test tube and the microscope are needed rather than ax and rifle in this new ideal of conquest. The very discoveries of science in such fields as public health and manufacturing processes have made it necessary to depend upon the expert, and if the ranks of experts are to be recruited broadly from the democratic masses as well as from those of larger means, the State Universities must furnish at least as liberal opportunities for research and training as the universities based on private endowments furnish. It needs no argument to show that it is not to the advantage of democracy to give over the training of the expert exclusively to privately endowed institutions.

But quite as much in the field of legislation and of public life in general as in the industrial world is the expert needed. The industrial conditions which shape society are too complex, problems of labor, finance, social reform too difficult to be dealt with intelligently and wisely without the leadership of highly educated men familiar with the legislation and literature on social questions in other States and nations.

1 The primary function of the first paragraph (lines 1–15) is to

   A. show how all U.S. universities serve democracy in the same way that Middle West universities do.

   B. contrast Middle West universities with those of the rest of the United States.

   C. argue that democracy's pressure on state universities is more striking than anything in educational history.

   D. describe the breaking down of the traditional state university curriculum.

---

2 The author uses the word *peculiar* (line 16) mainly to emphasize that

   A. the state university's power is complex and contradictory.

   B. state universities are strange institutions.

   C. there are severe limitations on state universities' power.

   D. state universities are too influential on people.

3 The author uses the quote from Mr. Bryce (lines 21–22) most likely to

   A. show that everyone agrees with the author's position.

   B. prove that state universities must recognize new needs.

   C. admit that the author's ideas are not original.

   D. indicate that another authority agrees with his position.

ANSWER KEY AND EXPLANATIONS

1. B	2. A	3. D

1. **The correct answer is B.** This is an Analyzing Text Structure question that requires you to interpret the overall purpose of the entire first paragraph of the passage. The paragraph is basically split between an extended description of the contrasting natures of state universities of the Middle West (lines 3–9, "From the State … advancement alone.") and one of other U.S. universities (lines 9–15, "Other universities … their existence."). Therefore, the best answer is choice B. Choice A makes a crucial error: The beginning of the discussion of other universities begins with the misleading phrase "Other universities do the same thing" (lines 9–10), before indicating a counterclaim with the word *but*. Therefore, the author is showing that he is going to explain how other universities are different from Middle West ones, not similar. Choice C is tricky because it paraphrases the first sentence of the paragraph, and the first paragraph will often announce its purpose, but that is not the case here. The paragraph is more concerned with contrasting two different kinds of universities than emphasizing that the pressure of democracy on state universities is more striking than anything else in educational history. Choice D does a common thing in questions of this sort; it picks out a single detail in the paragraph.

   Answer choices such as these fail to take all of the details in the paragraph into account, which is what this question requires you to do.

2. **The correct answer is A.** The author follows his statement that the state university has a "peculiar power" with a more detailed description of that power. On the one hand, it influences people directly; on the other hand, it is limited because it relies on those people. This relationship is both complex and contradictory, so choice A is the best answer to this Analyzing Word Choice question. Choice B makes the mistake of treating this question as if it is a Words in Context question. It defines *peculiar* as "strange," but the author's use of *peculiar* is much more complex than this, and this answer choice simply is not as thorough and accurate as choice A is. Remember that this question asks you to figure out what the author is "mainly" trying to emphasize, and he is more concerned with the complexity and contradictory nature of the state university than the much simpler idea that such institutions are "strange." Choice C is true in itself, but it only addresses half of the issue. By not dealing with the fact that state universities not only have power limitations but also have a direct influence on people, choice C fails to address the complete reason the author uses the word

peculiar in this context. Choice D makes the same mistake, only addressing the influence state universities have on people, while making the additional error of interpreting a judgment on the part of the author by suggesting such institutions are "*too* influential."

3. **The correct answer is D.** Here's another tricky one, because we do not really know who Mr. Bryce is from this excerpt. However, the fact that the author is quoting him suggests that Mr. Bryce is some sort of authority. The fact that the author immediately rewords Mr. Bryce's quotation to clarify it indicates that he didn't really need to include Mr. Bryce's quotation in the passage. So the author is not including the quotation for what is being stated in itself; he is using it because he wants to show that someone else shares his opinion about how universities need to "recognize new needs without becoming subordinate to the immediately practical." Choice A is much too extreme; the quote shows only that "Mr. Bryce" agrees with his position, not that *everyone* does. Choice B is a tricky incorrect answer: It cites the passage directly, but mistakenly suggests that the mere quoting of a source proves a point. We don't really know who Mr. Bryce is, so simply quoting this source is not enough to indicate that what he says is adequate proof. Choice C misinterprets the quotation, too. One generally does not include a quote to confess a lack of originality; it is done to support the argument. If there were some confessional purpose to the quote, the author would probably be more explicit about that.

COMMAND OF EVIDENCE QUESTIONS

As you might have gathered from the previous section, rhetoric is most effective when there is strong evidence to support it. Is a writer merely making up assertions—"talking out of his hat," as the saying goes? Or are there concrete facts, data, and details that support those assertions? And if there are such pieces of evidence in the passage, where are they?

Command of Evidence questions test your ability to locate evidence to support conclusions. That evidence may be a detail that shows something is stated explicitly in the passage, but it might also be more abstract, supporting the idea that the author feels a particular way about the topic being discussed. This is a very unique question type because it is the only kind that is always used in conjunction with the question that precedes it. Basically, you'll answer an Information and Ideas, Rhetoric, or Synthesis (more on that in the next chapter) question before answering a Command of Evidence question that asks you to find the evidence that supports your answer to the previous question.

NOTE: There are 10 Command of Evidence questions on the SAT® Reading Test; two of them accompany each of the test's five passages.

Command of Evidence questions are easy to spot because they always have the same stem (that's the question part itself), and their answer choices always follow the same format. Here is an example of how a Command of Evidence question looks:

Which choice provides the best evidence for the answer to the previous question?

    A.   Line 1 ("Women were once … to vote.")
    B.   Lines 1–2 ("This unjust situation … suffrage movement.")
    C.   Line 2 ("It all began … Seneca Falls.")
    D.   Line 3 ("That is where … Rights Convention.")

Although Command of Evidence questions always follow the exact same format, they require you to understand that authors use evidence to support their claims in different ways. They might use that evidence to prove a conclusion, support an argument, or show that a graphic supports an idea (you'll learn more about graphics in the next chapter).

Command of Evidence questions can pose a challenge because you have to answer the preceding question correctly in order to answer the Command of Evidence question correctly. Let's look at a super-simple History and Social Studies paragraph, and then see how a Command of Evidence question might follow a Rhetoric question.

---

1 Women were once denied the right to vote. This unjust situation led to the

2 women's suffrage movement. It all began in 1948 in New York's scenic Seneca Falls.

3 That is where the first women's rights convention took place.

---

1 Which of the following claims is supported by the paragraph?

A. The denial of women's suffrage was unjust.

B. The suffrage movement was very scenic.

C. Women worked hard to earn their suffrage.

D. The U.S. voting system is deeply flawed.

2 Which choice provides the best evidence for the answer to the previous question?

A. Line 1 ("Women were once … to vote.")

B. Lines 1–2 ("This unjust situation … suffrage movement.")

C. Line 2 ("It all began … Seneca Falls.")

D. Line 3 ("That is where … Rights Convention.")

As you may have deduced, the correct answer to Question 1 is choice A. However, if you failed to answer that question correctly, it could make answering Question 2 tough. We'll make it easy on you this time by revealing that the correct answer to Question 2 is choice B. As you can probably tell, both answer choices reference the fact that the denial of women's suffrage was unjust. However, if you thought that the answer to Question 1 was choice B, then you might have selected choice C as the answer to Question 2.

Understanding Command of Evidence questions is integral to the SAT® Reading Test, but it can also help you when you take the SAT® Essay. In that section of the exam, you will also have to display a strong ability to present your own evidence.

The good news? If you did select the correct answer to Question 1, then Question 2 should be relatively easy to answer. After all, Question 2 is only requiring you to locate that key descriptive word *unjust* in the passage. Of course, the Command of Evidence questions on the SAT® Reading Test won't be as easy as this example. If this were a real test question, Question 1 probably would have used a synonym of *unjust*.

Another potentially good thing about Command of Evidence questions is that they may make you think twice about your answers to the questions that precede them. By looking for the evidence in the passage, you may realize that there is no evidence to support your answer to the previous question and that you need to select a different answer.

So, there's another way Command of Evidence questions are unique: They are the only kind of Reading Test questions that could actually help you choose the right answers to other questions!

> To prepare for Command of Evidence questions, consider the author's opinions while reading the passage and how you know those are her or his opinions. The "how" is the evidence.

Now it's time to answer some more complex Command of Evidence questions. Since they need to be asked in conjunction with other questions, you will also be answering three more that test rhetoric. Read the History and Social Studies passage that follows, and then answer all six Rhetoric and Command of Evidence questions.

This passage is excerpted from President Franklin Delano Roosevelt's first inaugural address.

I am certain that my fellow Americans expect that on my induction into the

Presidency I will address them with a candor and a decision which the present

situation of our Nation impels. This is preeminently the time to speak the truth, the

Line whole truth, frankly and boldly. Nor need we shrink from honestly facing conditions

5   in our country today. This great Nation will endure as it has endured, will revive and

will prosper. So, first of all, let me assert my firm belief that the only thing we have to

fear is fear itself—nameless, unreasoning, unjustified terror which paralyzes needed

efforts to convert retreat into advance. In every dark hour of our national life a

leadership of frankness and vigor has met with that understanding and support of

10   the people themselves which is essential to victory. I am convinced that you will again

give that support to leadership in these critical days.

In such a spirit on my part and on yours we face our common difficulties. They

concern, thank God, only material things. Values have shrunken to fantastic levels;

taxes have risen; our ability to pay has fallen; government of all kinds is faced by

15   serious curtailment of income; the means of exchange are frozen in the currents of

trade; the withered leaves of industrial enterprise lie on every side; farmers find no

markets for their produce; the savings of many years in thousands of families are

gone.

More important, a host of unemployed citizens face the grim problem of

20 existence, and an equally great number toil with little return. Only a foolish optimist

can deny the dark realities of the moment.

Yet our distress comes from no failure of substance. We are stricken by no plague

of locusts. Compared with the perils which our forefathers conquered because they

believed and were not afraid, we have still much to be thankful for. Nature still offers

25 her bounty and human efforts have multiplied it. Plenty is at our doorstep, but a

generous use of it languishes in the very sight of the supply. Primarily this is because

rulers of the exchange of mankind's goods have failed through their own

stubbornness and their own incompetence, have admitted their failure, and have

abdicated. Practices of the unscrupulous money changers stand indicted in the court

30 of public opinion, rejected by the hearts and minds of men.

True they have tried, but their efforts have been cast in the pattern of an

outworn tradition. Faced by failure of credit they have proposed only the lending of

more money. Stripped of the lure of profit by which to induce our people to follow

their false leadership, they have resorted to exhortations, pleading tearfully for

35 restored confidence. They know only the rules of a generation of self-seekers. They

have no vision, and when there is no vision the people perish.

The money changers have fled from their high seats in the temple of our

civilization. We may now restore that temple to the ancient truths. The measure of the

restoration lies in the extent to which we apply social values more noble than mere

40 monetary profit.

Happiness lies not in the mere possession of money; it lies in the joy of

achievement, in the thrill of creative effort. The joy and moral stimulation of work no

longer must be forgotten in the mad chase of evanescent profits. These dark days will

be worth all they cost us if they teach us that our true destiny is not to be ministered

45 unto but to minister to ourselves and to our fellow men.

Recognition of the falsity of material wealth as the standard of success goes

hand in hand with the abandonment of the false belief that public office and high political position are to be valued only by the standards of pride of place and personal profit; and there must be an end to a conduct in banking and in business

50 which too often has given to a sacred trust the likeness of callous and selfish wrongdoing. Small wonder that confidence languishes, for it thrives only on honesty, on honor, on the sacredness of obligations, on faithful protection, on unselfish performance; without them it cannot live. Restoration calls, however, not for changes in ethics alone. This Nation asks for action, and action now.

1 The passage is written from the point of view of

A. a person who values money above all else.

B. an unscrupulous money changer.

C. a teller of difficult truths.

D. an extremely religious man.

2 Which choice provides the best evidence for the answer to the previous question?

A. Lines 2–3 ("I will address … Nation impels.")

B. Lines 12–13 ("They concern … levels;")

C. Lines 16–18 ("… the withered … are gone.")

D. Lines 29–30 ("Practices of … of men.")

3 What is Roosevelt's central claim in paragraph 4 (lines 22–30)?

A. America is suffering from a failure of substance.

B. Money changers, not its natural resources, have failed America.

C. America's natural resources are extremely strong.

D. America's forefathers suffered worse than the people of Roosevelt's time.

4 Which choice provides the best evidence for the answer to the previous question?

A. Lines 22–23 ("Yet our … locusts.")

B. Lines 23–24 ("Compared with … thankful for.")

C. Lines 24–25 ("Nature still … multiplied it.")

D. Lines 25–28 ("Plenty is at … stubbornness …")

5 In lines 46–51 , Roosevelt makes which point about attaining political office?

- **A.** It should be motivated by the desire to do public good, not personal gain.
- **B.** It is as false a measure of success as the accumulation of material wealth.
- **C.** It should be accomplished as one runs a successful business.
- **D.** It can only be accomplished after abandoning false beliefs.

6 Which choice provides the best evidence for the answer to the previous question?

- **A.** Line 46 ("Recognition of … of success …")
- **B.** Lines 47–49 ("… the false … personal profit;")
- **C.** Lines 49–51 ("… there must … wrongdoing.")
- **D.** Lines 51–53 ("Small wonder … performance; …")

Answer Key and Explanations

1. C	**3.** B	**5.** A
2. A	**4.** D	**6.** B

1. **The correct answer is C.** The answer to this Analyzing Point of View question is summed up by President Roosevelt's numerous invocations of "the truth," and he is speaking the truth about the difficult matter of America's plunge into an economic depression. However, as important and dire as the economic crisis is, President Roosevelt also drops hints that money is not everything, so choice A is incorrect. Choice B is incorrect as well; Roosevelt refers to the "unscrupulous money changers" who caused the economic crisis. He is not claiming to be such a person himself. Choice D makes too much of Roosevelt's one mention of God in this passage. Savvy readers might also notice the allusion to a Biblical story in Paragraph 6, but whether or not Roosevelt is religious is not nearly as important to his address as the fact that he is a fearless teller of difficult truths.

2. **The correct answer is A.** Although lines 2–3 are not the ones in which Roosevelt explicitly uses the word "truth" multiple times, he is still casting himself as a teller of difficult truths by saying he will address Americans with "candor" (truth) in the face of the nation's "present situation," which is difficult, indeed. So

choice A is the best answer. Choice B seems to make the mistake that choice D was the correct answer to the previous question since this is the one that references "God" explicitly. Choice C also makes a mistake, though a less careless one. Roosevelt's focus on the economic situation throughout the passage may have led you to conclude that he "values money above all else" in the previous question. However, that was not the correct answer, so choice C, which details all the ways the depression is causing Americans to suffer, is incorrect. Choice D makes another careless error, seemingly assuming that choice B was the correct answer to the previous question since both choices reference "unscrupulous money changers."

3. **The correct answer is B.** The paragraph as a whole explains Roosevelt's claim that a failure of natural resources has not caused the depression; only a failure of money changers have caused the crisis. Therefore, choice B is the best answer. Choice A misinterprets Roosevelt completely; he is saying the opposite of this in paragraph 4; America is *not* suffering from a failure of substance. Choice C only

takes into account half of the central claim; it also needs to acknowledge that people who deal with money caused the crisis, which is the focus of the last two sentences of the paragraph. Choice D is just one fairly incidental detail in a paragraph more focused on rooting out the cause of the depression than comparing current day America to that of America's forefathers.

4. **The correct answer is D.** Choice D includes the only lines in the paragraph that cover both the enduring strength of America's natural resources ("Plenty is at our doorstep") and the failure of money changers ("rulers of the exchange of mankind's good have failed"). It is the best evidence to prove that choice B was the correct answer to the previous question. The other answer choices only take part of that claim into account; choices A, B, and C all show how America's natural resources are not failing, but they fail to also deal with the paragraph's other key claim: that the people who deal with money have caused the crisis.

5. **The correct answer is A.** In this paragraph, Roosevelt rejects the idea that personal gain is a valid reason for attaining political office. Choice A is the best answer. Choice B assumes a comparison where there is not one; Roosevelt does call out the pursuit of material wealth as a false measure of success, but he neither compares nor contrasts that with the attainment of political office. A business does not have to have admirable motivations in order to be successful, so it would not make sense for the president to compare the admirable ideals of one who deserves to attain political office with the qualities that make someone a successful business person. Therefore, choice C is wrong. Roosevelt is saying that people who strive to attain political office *should* abandon false beliefs about it; he is not saying that only those who abandon those beliefs are capable of attaining political office, so choice D is incorrect, too.

6. **The correct answer is B.** In these lines, President Roosevelt is stating that the belief that attaining political office should be motivated by personal gain is false. In doing so, he expresses the idea that the public good, which is the opposite of personal gain, *should* be the main motivation of anyone who wishes to attain political office. Choice A is incorrect because these lines do not reference political office. Similarly, the lines in choice C have moved on from political office to how business people conduct their business, so it cannot be correct. Choice D makes a more general statement about why people are losing faith in business, which again fails to deal with the matter of political office at the center of the previous question.

SUMMING IT UP

- The SAT® Reading Test includes two History and Social Studies passages. One is a Social Science passage and the other is a Founding Document.

  ○ The **Social Science passages** are focused on economics, sociology, and/or political science and deal with how society has changed throughout history and how those changes have affected the United States. It might also include less politically focused topics about how technological developments have affected U.S. society and culture.

  ○ **Founding Documents passages** are documents of great historical significance that might detail important developments in government, the economy, or international affairs. They might also be speeches made by world leaders or major figures in important political, social, or cultural movements.

- The tactics of reading actively and closely will help you manage the limited amount of time you have to take the SAT® Reading Test.

  ○ **Reading actively** involves taking notes, underlining unfamiliar words, and underlining important details to comprehend a difficult passage to the best of your ability.

  ○ **Reading closely** involves paying attention to clues in questions to help you comprehend the passage they accompany better. Some questions may even direct you to the precise lines in which information is located in the passage.

- **Rhetoric questions** test your ability to understand and analyze the various ways writers use words. Rhetoric questions involve analyzing word choice, text structure, point of view, arguments, and purpose.

- **Analyzing Word Choice questions** test your understanding of how authors choose words to convey their messages. You will be expected to understand how those words affect meaning and tone.

- **Analyzing Text Structure questions** test your ability to understand how the organization of a passage affects meaning. They may ask you to analyze the structure of the passage as a whole, how the focus of arguments change over the course of the passage, or how individual elements of the passage affect the entire passage.

- **Analyzing Point of View questions** require you to understand how the author conveys information and how that influences meaning and tone. Analyzing Point of View questions may also require you to determine the author's attitude.

- **Analyzing Arguments questions** require you to analyze the author's claims (the author's essential stance on a topic), counterclaims (the author's claims that contradict the claims), reasoning (the thought process that led the author to take her or his stance), and evidence (the facts, data, statistics, surveys, case studies, etc. that support the author's stance).

- **Analyzing Purpose questions** require you to figure out why the author includes a particular image or references a particular incident in the passage.

- **Command of Evidence questions** test your ability to locate evidence to support conclusions. That evidence may be a detail that shows something is stated explicitly in the passage, or it may be more abstract, supporting the idea that the author feels a particular way about the topic being discussed.

  - ◦ Command of Evidence questions always have the same stem (that's the question itself) and their answer choices always follow the same format.

  - ◦ Every Command of Evidence question refers to the question that preceded it directly. Answering the preceding question correctly is key to answer the Command of Evidence question that follows correctly.

CHAPTER 4: SAT® READING: SCIENCE PASSAGES

ABOUT SCIENCE PASSAGES

The final passage type you'll encounter is the science passage, and there are two of them on the SAT® Reading Test. Science covers a wide variety of topics, so a Science passage may come from any of the following fields:

- **Biology:** The study of life and living things. Specific biology topics might include anatomy, eating habits and diet, and disease.

- **Chemistry:** The study of the properties, structure, composition, and changes of matter. Specific topics might include energy (nuclear, atomic, solar, etc.), developments in medicine, and application of chemical laws.

- **Earth Science:** The study of our planet and its features. Specific earth science topics might include climate and climate change, plate tectonics (the study of the earth's plates), and geology (the study of rocks and minerals).

- **Physics:** The study of movement, space, and time. Specific physics topics might include astronomy, how machines work, the earth's movement, and gravity.

You don't need to study the sciences to answer the questions for Science passages; they test your reading comprehension. Still, you might want to read a few science texts before taking the test to get used to the language used in this type of writing.

These passages should be pretty similar to the kinds of materials you've read in your science classes, but you do not need to be a scientist to answer them correctly. You are not being tested on your knowledge of science. As is the case with the rest of the Reading Test, you are being tested on your ability to comprehend a text. For example, you will not be expected to perform equations as you might in a physics or chemistry class. You will answer the same types of questions you will have to answer with U.S. and World Literature or History and Social Studies passages.

However, Science passages may differ from U.S. and World Literature passages in a couple of significant structural ways: Some could appear as paired passages and/or include informational graphics you will need to comprehend to answer what are known as Synthesis questions. In this chapter, you will learn more about the kinds of Synthesis questions, paired passages, and graphics that will appear on the SAT® Reading Test and how to navigate them to that perfect 1600 score.

NOTE: There are a total of 21 questions associated with the two Science passages on the SAT® exam.

SYNTHESIS QUESTIONS

Synthesis questions are all about drawing ideas together. They involve making comparisons between two similar ideas or contrasting different ones. They may also require you to use one piece of information to better understand another. Since there must be at least two pieces of information to ask a Synthesis question, Science and certain History and Social Studies texts will appear as paired passages or include informational graphics.

Synthesis questions that refer to a paired passage are known as Analyzing Multiple Texts questions. Questions that require you to find data in informational graphics such as diagrams, tables, charts, and maps and relate it to the accompanying passage are known as Analyzing Quantitative Information questions. You will learn more about these question types as we discuss paired passages and informational graphics in greater depth.

ALERT: Beware of extremes. Some answer choices may try to trick you by suggesting that a situation that is true under certain circumstances will be true under *all* circumstances. If the passage does not suggest that the situation in a question is true under all circumstances, then that answer choice is wrong. So watch out for extreme words, such as *always*, *never*, *every*, *none*, and *impossible*.

PAIRED PASSAGES

One of the five question sets that will appear on the SAT® Reading Test will be accompanied by a paired passage. Don't worry, these won't be two full-length 500- to 750-word passages; they will be two shorter passages equaling the length of one single passage. So, each passage in a passage pair will be roughly 250 to 375 words long.

Passages are never paired randomly on the SAT® Reading Test. There will always be a key connection between the two texts. Maybe each passage will present a different stance on the same topic. Maybe they will both deal with the same topic but with a different focus (for example, a passage on the biology of a human paired with a passage on the biology of gorillas). Some passages won't even have different stances or focuses; they will be about the exact same topic but contain different details or be written from different points of view. Some will discuss the same topic but with different levels of specificity.

Every question that follows paired passages won't ask you about how the two passages relate to each other. Information and Ideas, Words in Context, Rhetoric, and Command of Evidence questions may still follow a paired passage, but will only ask about one of the passages in the pair. Only Synthesis questions will require you to draw together the two passages in the pair.

When you face a paired passage set, the first passage will be labeled "Passage 1." The second one will be labeled "Passage 2." This little detail is important because every Analyzing Multiple Texts question will refer you to either Passage 1 or Passage 2. In the case of Synthesis questions, you will be referred to both passages.

Take a look at the following passage pair to get an idea of how they will look on the SAT®
Reading Test.

Passage 1

This passage is excerpted from On the Origin of Species *by Charles Darwin.*

In considering the Origin of Species, it is quite conceivable that a naturalist,
reflecting on the mutual affinities of organic beings, on their embryological relations,
their geographical distribution, geological succession, and other such facts, might
come to the conclusion that each species had not been independently created, but
had descended, like varieties, from other species. Nevertheless, such a conclusion,
even if well founded, would be unsatisfactory, until it could be shown how the
innumerable species inhabiting this world have been modified, so as to acquire that
perfection of structure and coadaptation which most justly excites our admiration.
Naturalists continually refer to external conditions, such as climate, food, etc., as the
only possible cause of variation. In one very limited sense, as we shall hereafter see,
this may be true; but it is preposterous to attribute to mere external conditions, the
structure, for instance, of the woodpecker, with its feet, tail, beak, and tongue, so
admirably adapted to catch insects under the bark of trees. In the case of the
misseltoe, which draws its nourishment from certain trees, which has seeds that must
be transported by certain birds, and which has flowers with separate sexes absolutely
requiring the agency of certain insects to bring pollen from one flower to the other, it
is equally preposterous to account for the structure of this parasite, with its relations
to several distinct organic beings, by the effects of external conditions, or of habit, or
of the volition of the plant itself.

The author of the 'Vestiges of Creation' would, I presume, say that, after a certain
unknown number of generations, some bird had given birth to a woodpecker, and
some plant to the misseltoe, and that these had been produced perfect as we now
see them; but this assumption seems to me to be no explanation, for it leaves the
case of the coadaptations of organic beings to each other and to their physical
conditions of life, untouched and unexplained.

Passage 2

This passage is excerpted from Darwinism *by Alfred Russel Wallace.*

The title of Mr. Darwin's great work is *On the Origin of Species by means of Natural Selection and the Preservation of Favoured Races in the Struggle for Life*. In order to appreciate fully the aim and object of this work, and the change which it has effected
Line not only in natural history but in many other sciences, it is necessary to form a clear
5 conception of the meaning of the term "species," to know what was the general belief regarding them at the time when Mr. Darwin's book first appeared, and to understand what he meant, and what was generally meant, by discovering their "origin." It is for want of this preliminary knowledge that the majority of educated persons who are not naturalists are so ready to accept the innumerable objections, criticisms, and
10 difficulties of its opponents as proofs that the Darwinian theory is unsound, while it also renders them unable to appreciate, or even to comprehend, the vast change which that theory has effected in the whole mass of thought and opinion on the great question of evolution.

The term "species" was thus defined by the celebrated botanist De Candolle: "A
15 species is a collection of all the individuals which resemble each other more than they resemble anything else, which can by mutual fecundation produce fertile individuals, and which reproduce themselves by generation, in such a manner that we may from analogy suppose them all to have sprung from one single individual." And the zoologist Swainson gives a somewhat similar definition: "A species, in the usual
20 acceptation of the term, is an animal which, in a state of nature, is distinguished by certain peculiarities of form, size, colour, or other circumstances, from another animal. It propagates, 'after its kind,' individuals perfectly resembling the parent; its peculiarities, therefore, are permanent."

These passages are a bit dense, but you still probably noticed that they are related to each other quite directly—they both deal with Charles Darwin's book *On the Origin of Species*. Did you also notice some significant differences between the two passages?

Recognizing the essential similarities and differences between the passages in a passage pair will help you answer the Synthesis questions that follow.

Take a look at this basic breakdown of those similarities and differences:

Similarities	Differences
• Both passages are about Charles Darwin's work. • Both passages accept Darwin's theory of evolution. • Both passages refer to people who do not understand or accept the theory of evolution.	• Passage 1 is a firsthand study; Passage 2 is a comment on another work. • Passage 1 was written at an earlier point in history than Passage 2. • Passage 2 quotes other sources; Passage 1 does not. • Passage 1 explains a theory (the theory of evolution); Passage 2 defines a term ("species"). • Passage 1 uses particular plant and animal species as examples; Passage 2 does not.

Some Synthesis questions will use wording similar to that of the Information and Ideas or Rhetoric questions that apply only to a single passage. However, Synthesis questions are about both passages, so do not select an answer choice that applies to only one of the passages.

Any one of these similarities or differences could be used in the Synthesis questions that follow this passage pair. Here are some examples of what a Synthesis question might look like:

- *Based on both passages, both authors would agree with which of the following claims?*

- *Which choice best states the relationship between the two passages?*

- *The primary purpose of each passage is to …*

Some Synthesis questions might be more abstract, dealing with the author's attitudes or assumptions about each other instead of the information stated explicitly in the passages. Such questions might look more like these:

- *Darwin would most likely have reacted to lines 1–3 of Passage 2 with …*

- *Based on the passages, Wallace would most likely describe the attitudes of the naturalists Darwin discusses in lines 9–10 ("Naturalists … variation.") as …*

TIP After reading a paired passage set, it might be helpful to briefly jot down what each passage is trying to accomplish and how they are similar or different. This will give you a clear idea of why the passages were paired in the first place and assist you in answering Analyzing Multiple Texts questions.

Now let's take one of those sample Synthesis questions and figure out the best way to answer it.

Which choice best states the relationship between the two passages?

A. Passage 2 clarifies an important detail in Passage 1.

B. Passage 2 provides additional evidence to prove the main idea of Passage 1.

C. Passage 2 contradicts the main conclusion of Passage 1.

D. Passage 2 presents a refined explanation of the central claim of Passage 1.

The correct answer is A. Consider what exactly the question is asking. It's seeing if you know how the passages are connected—the relationship between them. This does not necessarily signify a similarity. Passages can be connected because one contradicts the other or argues against the other's main point. Is that what is happening between *On the Origin of Species* and *Darwinism*, though? Not really. As we already saw in our chart of similarities and differences between the two passages, they agree that Darwin's theory of evolution is a valid theory. Therefore, you can go ahead and eliminate any answer choices that suggest a fundamental clash between the passages. Words such as *disagrees*, *disproves*, and *contradicts* signal such a clash, and one of our answer choices does include a clashing word: choice C suggests that Passage 2 *contradicts* the main conclusion of Passage 1. Go ahead and eliminate choice C from the running of potential correct answers.

Defining each passage with a simple summary is a good way to get started with answering Synthesis questions, and it would be particularly helpful in answering this one. Maybe something like this:

- *Passage 1 is about how it is absurd to suggest that environmental factors are solely responsible for changes in species.*

- *Passage 2 is about defining the term* species.

These two summarizing statements are very short, but both are packed with valuable information. First of all, they both include a key word: *species*. So that will probably be important in explaining the relationship between the two passages. Also, the summarizing statement for Passage 2 refers to the defining of that word, *species*. To define is to clarify the meaning of a word, and lo and behold, one of our answer choices includes the word *clarifies*.

So what is that detail being clarified? Let's go back to our two summarizing statements. Remember that they each shared a common key word: *species*. Does this align with the idea that Passage 2 clarifies an important detail in Passage 1? Well, it does, if that detail is *species*. Passage 2 clarifies that detail by defining the term *species*, which is something Passage 1 does not do. Everything looks good, so go ahead and feel confident in selecting choice A for the answer to our sample question.

Now that you have an idea of how paired passages appear, the kinds of ideas and information Synthesis questions test, and a strategy for answering such questions, it's time to read another passage pair and answer the Synthesis questions that follow it.

Passage 1

This passage is excerpted from American Pomology: Apples *by Dr. John A. Warder.*

In opening a discussion upon the nosology of vegetation, it may be expected that one who had spent many years of his life in the investigation of the diseases of the human family, and at the same time was something of a student of comparative
Line anatomy and physiology, tracing analogies between the animal and vegetable
5 kingdoms, should be familiar also with the diseases of plants. Such an anticipation, it is feared, will not, in the present instance, be realized. Indeed, the writer feels very much at a loss how to proceed in discussing this branch of the subject, and hardly knows what departures from undoubted health and vigor should be considered worthy of the title of disease. Nor is it easy to trace the causes of the conditions that
10 are generally viewed in the light of maladies. We find the manifestations both in the tree or plant, and in its several parts, and also in the products which chiefly interest us; the fruits themselves, are often deteriorated by what is called diseased action of different kinds. The analogy to diseases of animals is certainly not very distinct. We do not find anything like fevers, or gout, or rheumatism, in plants, but we may consider
15 some of their conditions somewhat in the light of dropsies, and plethora or hypertrophy on the one hand, and of anæmia or atrophy upon the other; we may consider canker and the death of some parts of a plant analogous to gangrene, and mortification in the animal subject. Then again we find congenital defects in individuals among plants, just as we do among animals. Some are always less
20 vigorous than others, and thus certain varieties seem possessed of a degree of

inherent disease that perpetually prevents them from displaying the requisite
strength and vigor which we so much desire in our plantations.

Passage 2

This passage is excerpted from Disease in Plants *by H. Marshall Ward.*

When we come to enquire into the causes of disease, it appears at first an
obvious and easy plan to subdivide them into groups of factors which interfere with
the normal physiology of the plant. Scientific experience shows, however, that the
Line easy and the obvious are here, as elsewhere in nature, only apparent, for disease, like
5 health, is an extremely complex phenomenon, involving many reactions and
interactions between the plant and its environment. If we agree that a living plant in a
state of health is not a fixed and unaltering thing, but is ever varying and undergoing
adaptive changes as its life works out its labyrinthine course through the vicissitudes
of the also ever-varying environment, then we cannot escape the conviction that a
10 diseased plant, so long as it lives, is also varying in response to the environment. The
principal difference between the two cases is, that whereas the normal healthy plant
varies more or less regularly and rhythmically about a mean, the diseased one is
tending to vary too suddenly or too far in some particular directions from the mean;
the healthy plant may, for our present purposes, be roughly likened to a properly
15 balanced top spinning regularly and well, whereas the diseased one is lurching here,
or wobbling there, to the great danger of its stability. For we must recognise at the
outset that disease is but variation in directions dangerous to the life of the plant.
Health consists in variation also, but not in such dangerous grooves. That the passage
from health to disease is gradual and ill-defined in many cases will readily be seen. In
20 fact we cannot completely define disease. Mere abnormality of form, colour, size, etc.,
is not necessarily a sign of disease, in the usual sense of the word, otherwise the
striking variations of our cultivated plants would suggest gloomy thoughts indeed,
whereas we have reason to believe that many cultivated varieties are more healthy—in
the sense of resisting dangerous exigencies of the environment—than the stocks they
25 came from. Strictly speaking, no two buds on a fruit-tree are alike, and the shoots they
produce vary in position, exposure, number, and vigour of leaves, and so forth.

1 The primary purpose of each passage is to

A. describe how common it is to misdiagnosis plant diseases.

B. explain the challenge of recognizing disease in plants.

C. show that it is impossible to diagnose plant diseases accurately.

D. contrast diagnosing human disease with diagnosing plant disease.

2 Based on both passages, both authors would agree with which of the following claims?

A. Plants may display symptoms similar to those of anaemia or atrophy.

B. Cosmetic anomalies in plants do not necessarily signify disease.

C. The causes of plant disease can be inconsistent.

D. Comparative anatomy is important in diagnosing plant diseases.

3 Which choice best states the relationship between the two passages?

A. Passage 2 illustrates the difficulties of an idea presented in Passage 1.

B. Passage 2 takes issue with the primary argument of Passage 1.

C. Passage 2 elaborates upon several ideas introduced in Passage 1.

D. Passage 2 provides an alternate explanation for the position of Passage 1.

4 Based on the passages, the author of Passage 2 would most likely describe the inherent disease of certain plants discussed in lines 18–22 ("Then again … plantations.") of Passage 1 as a

A. hypothesis that requires much more research to prove.

B. glib conclusion not based in scientific research.

C. valid explanation for why diagnosing plant disease is difficult.

D. succinct explanation for the main reason diagnosing plants is difficult.

Answer Key and Explanations

1. B	2. C	3. D	4. C

1. **The correct answer is B.** Although the two passages have some significant differences, they do share a primary purpose: to explain that diagnosing plant diseases can be challenging. Passage 1 shows this by describing how recognizing plant diseases is not as clear as recognizing human diseases. Passage 2 shows this by discussing the complex relationship between plants and their environments and that a plant may seem ill because of natural environmental factors and not disease. While both passages discuss the difficulties of disease diagnosis, and it is conceivable that such difficulties could lead to misdiagnosis, neither passage actually discusses misdiagnosis, so choice A is incorrect. Choice C is too extreme; while the passages show that diagnosing plant disease can be challenging, neither suggests that it is impossible to diagnose them accurately. Choice D only applies to Passage 1, since Passage 2 does not compare diagnosing human disease to diagnosing plant disease.

2. **The correct answer is C.** Both passages indicate that one of the challenges of diagnosing plant disease is the variations among the causes of plant disease. Passage 1 shows this in lines 9–10 ("Nor is ... maladies."). Passage 2 shows it in lines 1–6 ("When we ... its environment."). Choices A and D are incorrect because only Passage 1 compares plant disease to human disease, and only that passage references anaemia, atrophy, and comparative anatomy. Choice B, however, only refers to Passage 2, which explains that "abnormality of form, colour, size, etc., is not necessarily a sign of disease."

3. **The correct answer is D.** Both Passage 1 and Passage 2 share the same essential topic: the difficulty of diagnosing plant disease. However, Passage 2 offers a very different explanation for why it is difficult than Passage 1 does. Passage 1 suggests it is difficult because plant disease cannot be compared to human diseases, while Passage 2 explains that it is difficult by discussing the complex relationship between plants and their environments and explaining that a plant may seem ill because of the difficulties of recognizing how a plant reacts to its environment. Since Passage 2 presents very different examples from those in Passage 1, it cannot really illustrate the difficulties of the ideas in Passage 1, so choice A is incorrect. Choice B suggests that Passage 1 and Passage 2 present opposite sides of an issue when they actually

present the same side, but do so for different reasons. Choice C is trickier, because it recognizes that the passages do share a singular purpose, but Passage 2 does not actually elaborate on the ideas introduced in Passage 2; it just presents an alternate explanation for the main idea of Passage 1.

4. **The correct answer is C.** Although the two passages present very different reasons and examples for their main ideas, they do present one similar idea, which is that some plants are simply more inclined toward disease than others are. Passage 1 shows this in lines 18–22 ("Then again … plantations.") and Passage 2 shows it in lines 23–25 ("cultivated varieties … came from"). Because the authors seem to share an opinion on this matter, choices A and B, which both imply that they differ, are incorrect. Choice D is incorrect, because the main argument of neither passage is the idea that some plants are simply more susceptible to disease than others are. This is just a single detail in each passage. Since choice D indicates that the idea that some plants are more susceptible to disease than others are is the main idea of Passage 2, it is incorrect.

INFORMATIONAL GRAPHICS

Synthesis questions don't only require you to draw connections between two passages. They also require you to draw connections between passages and informational graphics. These might appear as tables, charts, maps, graphs, or diagrams, and there will be two on the SAT® Reading Test. One informational graphic will accompany a History and Social Studies passage, and the other will accompany a Science passage.

Although these Synthesis questions are known as Analyzing Quantitative Information questions, they will not actually require you to perform complex math work. Remember, this is the Reading, not the Math, test (we'll get to that one later). Tallying numbers will not be as important as interpreting information, and you will basically do this in the same ways that you will interpret information for all other question types on the SAT® Reading Test.

 Don't neglect any part of the graphic when studying it. Be sure to not read just the data, but also the title, labels, and any accompanying captions. All of these details are fair game for Synthesis questions.

Informational graphics serve different purposes. Sometimes, they will clarify information in the preceding passage; other times, they will contradict it. The questions that follow them basically require you to either find information relevant to the passage in the graphic or consider the information in both the passage and the graphic and draw reasonable conclusions based on them. Once again, we're dealing with explicitly stated information and implied information: locating details is about finding the explicit, and drawing conclusions is about understanding the implicit.

Let's look at a passage and its accompanying graphic to get a clearer idea of how these questions might appear on the SAT® Reading Test.

This passage is excerpted from "Life Growth—Frogs" by Margaret Warner Morley.

Somewhat higher than the fish in the scale of life is the frog. Although he begins life as a fish, and in the tadpole state breathes by gills, he soon discards the water-diluted air of the pond, and with perfect lungs boldly inhales the pure air of the upper

Line

world. His life as a tadpole, although so fish-like, is much inferior to true fish life: for

5   though the fish has not the perfect lung, he has a modification of it which he fills with air, not for breathing purposes, but as an air-sac to make him float like a bubble in the water. Will he rise to the surface? he inflates the air-bladder. Will he sink to the

bottom? he compresses the air-bladder. But in the frog the air-bladder changes into the lungs, and is never the delicate balloon which floats the fish in aqueous space.

10 When the frog's lungs are perfected, his gills close, and he forever abandons fish-life, though being a cold-blooded creature he needs comparatively little air, and delights to return to his childhood's home in the bottom of the pond. But although he can stay under water for a long time, he is obliged to hold his breath while there, and when he would breathe must come to the surface to do so. It is possible to drown him by

15 holding him under water.

As a feeder the frog relies upon animal life, which he expertly seizes with a tongue fastened by the wrong end, as compared with our tongues. He is a certain marksman, and when he aims at an insect the chances are that the insect will enter his stomach and be there speedily changed into a new form of animal life.

20 Although from the moment the gills disappear the frog is a true land animal, he is obliged, on account of the fish-like character of his young, to lay his eggs in the water. For this purpose the frogs enter the pools in early spring. The surface of every country pond swarms with the bright-eyed little creatures. They have awakened from a long, cold, winter sleep, to find the spring about them and within them. Life has

25 suddenly become abundant and joyous. Their sluggish blood flows faster, their hearts beat quicker; they leap, they swim, they swell out their throats and call to each other in various keys. The toads are with them, and the pretty tree-frogs that change their color to suit their emotions. And all are rapturously screaming. Their voices are not musical, according to man's standard, but seem to afford great satisfaction to the

30 performers in the shrill orchestra of the swamps, who thus give vent to the flood of life that sweeps through them after the still, icy winter.

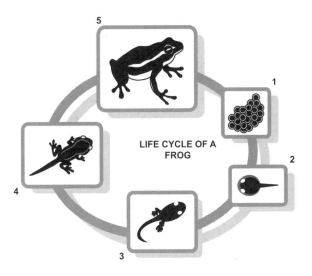

LIFE CYCLE OF A FROG

1   Which off the following claims is supported by the diagram?

A. The frog breathes air in the first stage of its life.

B. The frog no longer breathes with gills in the fifth stage of its life.

C. The frog has not yet risen from the water in the fourth stage of its life.

D. The frog breathes with an air bladder in the fifth stage of its life.

2   Data presented in the diagram most directly support which idea from the passage?

A. Frogs are higher than fish on the scale of life.

B. The first stage of the frog's life is not the most joyous.

C. Frogs have perfect lungs, but fish do not.

D. The sound of the frog is not musical.

Before getting to the questions, let's just take a moment to think about the graphic itself. What is it depicting? Based on the images, and the fact that the passage deals with the life cycle of the frog from egg to the fish-like tadpole stage to the fully formed frog stage, it is safe to conclude that the graphic illustrates that life cycle. Some graphics will be more explicit by including a descriptive title, and since most graphics will be more complex than this one, those titles will be both necessary and important details to consider when answering Synthesis questions.

Question 1 is one of those questions that tests your ability to locate information in both the graphic and the passage. To determine that choice B is the correct answer, you must find the information in the passage explaining that the frog "begins life as a fish, and in the tadpole state breathes by gills, he soon discards the water-diluted air of the pond, and with perfect lungs boldly inhales the pure air of the upper world." Since the graphic shows that the fifth stage is the final one of the frog's life, it is logical that it has stopped breathing through gills at this point.

Question 2 is more concerned with implied information. The author never states that the first stage of the frog's life is not the most joyous, but she does imply that the fifth stage is the most joyous in lines 20–25 ("Although from … joyous."). Therefore, it is logical to conclude that the first stage of the frog's life is not the most joyous one.

Now our example is going to get more complex both in terms of passage and graphic. Read the following passage and answer the sample questions that follow.

This passage is excerpted from The Chemistry of Food and Nutrition *by A.W. Duncan.*

We may define a food to be any substance which will repair the functional waste of the body, increase its growth, or maintain the heat, muscular, and nervous energy. In its most comprehensive sense, the oxygen of the air is a food; as although it is
Line admitted by the lungs, it passes into the blood, and there re-acts upon the other food
5 which has passed through the stomach. It is usual, however, to restrict the term food to such nutriment as enters the body by the intestinal canal. Water is often spoken of as being distinct from food, but for this there is no sufficient reason.

Many popular writers have divided foods into flesh-formers, heat-givers, and bone-formers. Although attractive from its simplicity, this classification will not bear
10 criticism. Flesh-formers are also heat-givers. Only a portion of the mineral matter goes to form bone …

Water forms an essential part of all the tissues of the body. It is the solvent and carrier of other substances.

Mineral Matter or Salts, is left as an ash when food is thoroughly burnt. The most
15 important salts are calcium phosphate, carbonate and fluoride, sodium chloride, potassium phosphate and chloride, and compounds of magnesium, iron and silicon.

Mineral matter is quite as necessary for plant as for animal life, and is therefore present in all food, except in the case of some highly-prepared ones, such as sugar, starch and oil. Children require a good proportion of calcium phosphate for the
20 growth of their bones, whilst adults require less. The outer part of the grain of cereals

is the richest in mineral constituents, white flour and rice are deficient. Wheatmeal and oatmeal are especially recommended for the quantity of phosphates and other salts contained in them. Mineral matter is necessary not only for the bones but for every tissue of the body.

25   When haricots are cooked, the liquid is often thrown away, and the beans served nearly dry, or with parsley or other sauce. Not only is the food less tasty but important saline constituents are lost. The author has made the following experiments: German whole lentils, Egyptian split red lentils and medium haricot beans were soaked all night (16 hours) in just sufficient cold water to keep them covered. The water was

30 poured off and evaporated, the residue heated in the steam-oven to perfect dryness and weighed. After pouring off the water, the haricots were boiled in more water until thoroughly cooked, the liquid being kept as low as possible. The liquid was poured off as clear as possible, from the haricots, evaporated and dried. The ash was taken in each case, and the alkalinity of the water-soluble ash was calculated as potash (K_2O).

35 The quantity of water which could be poured off was with the German lentils, half as much more than the original weight of the pulse; not quite as much could be poured off the others.

      The loss on soaking in cold water, unless the water is preserved, is seen to be considerable. The split lentils, having had the protecting skin removed, lose most. In

40 every case the ash contained a good deal of phosphate and lime. Potatoes are rich in important potash salts; by boiling a large quantity is lost, by steaming less and by baking in the skins, scarcely any. The flavour is also much better after baking.

      The usual addition of common salt (sodium-chloride) to boiled potatoes is no proper substitute for the loss of their natural saline constituents. Natural and properly

45 cooked foods are so rich in sodium chloride and other salts that the addition of common salt is unnecessary. An excess of the latter excites thirst and spoils the natural flavour of the food. It is the custom, especially in restaurants, to add a large quantity of salt to pulse, savoury food, potatoes and soups. Bakers' brown bread is usually very salt, and sometimes white is also. In some persons much salt causes

50 irritation of the skin, and the writer has knowledge of the salt food of vegetarian

restaurants causing or increasing dandruff. As a rule, fondness for salt is an acquired taste, and after its discontinuance for a time, food thus flavoured becomes unpalatable.

	German Lentils	Egyptian Lentils	Haricots	Cooked Haricots
Proportion of liquid	1.5	1.25	1.20	—
Soluble dry matter	0.97	3.38	1.43	7.66
Ash	0.16	0.40	0.28	1.26
Alkalinity as K$_2$O	0.02	0.082	0.084	0.21

1 Based on the table, how much potash do cooked Haricots produce?

A. 1.26%
B. 0.28%
C. 0.084%
D. 0.21%

2 Data presented in the table most directly supports which idea from the passage?

A. German lentils have the highest proportion of water that can be poured off.
B. Important saline constituents are lost when water is poured off haricots.
C. Water needs to evaporate in order to measure its ash content.
D. Egyptian lentils produce less ash than raw haricots do.

3 Based on the table, with which of the following claims would the author of the passage most likely agree?

A. A high proportion of soluble dry matter makes food taste better.
B. Haricots retain more saline than German lentils do.
C. German lentils taste better than Egyptian lentils do.
D. Egyptian lentils take longer to cook than haricots do.

4 Based on the table, which food is most valuable in encouraging bone growth?

A. Cooked haricots
B. Raw haricots
C. Egyptian lentils
D. German lentils

Answer Key and Explanations

| 1. D | 2. A | 3. C | 4. A |

1. **The correct answer is D.** Line 34 of the passage explains that potash is K_2O, and the table reveals that cooked haricots produce 0.21% of K_2O, or potash. Choice A seems to make the error of mistaking ash for potash. However, the passage makes it clear that these are two different materials. Choice B is the amount of ash produced by uncooked haricots. Choice C is the amount of potash produced by uncooked haricots.

2. **The correct answer is A.** The passage explicitly states that German lentils have the highest proportion of water that can be poured off; you can find this information in line 35 ("The quantity … German lentils"). The table supports this information, since at 1.5%, German lentils have the highest proportion of liquid. Choices B and C describe information in the passage that does not also appear in the chart. The passage never makes a comparison between the amount of ash Egyptian lentils produce and the amount of ash raw haricots do, so choice D presents information featured in the table but not in the passage as it pertains to the contents of the table.

3. **The correct answer is C.** In lines 26–27, the author implies that the drier food is, the less tasty it is. According to the table, cooked German lentils retain a higher proportion of liquid than Egyptian lentils do. Therefore, it is reasonable to conclude that the author would find German lentils to be tastier than Egyptian lentils. This also contradicts the conclusion in choice A, which suggests that the author thinks food tastes better when it is drier. In lines 26–27, the author also states that saline is lost with poured-off water. Since the table shows that German lentils retain more water than haricots do, it is unlikely that the author would agree that haricots retain more saline than German lentils do, so choice B is incorrect. The conclusion in choice D is not only incorrect, but there are no details in the table that indicate how long it would take to cook any of the foods in the table. However, according to the passage, all of the foods need to soak for 16 hours, and the haricots were boiled twice, so it took longer to cook them in any event.

4. **The correct answer is A.** This is a very complex question, requiring close reading of different sections of the passage and the table. It would be smart to begin with a search for any mention of bone growth in the passage. You will find this mentioned in lines 19–20 ("Children require … their bones"). Since these lines explain that phosphate is important in stimulating that bone growth, you will then want to check for additional mentions of phosphate in the passage. Line 40 explains that ash is high in phosphate, and since ash appears on the table, finding the food that produces the most ash will give you the answer to this question: it is cooked haricots (choice A). Based on that firm conclusion, you can confidently eliminate choices B, C, and D.

SUMMING IT UP

- The SAT® Reading Test includes one science passage, which might deal with earth science, biology, chemistry, or physics.

- **Synthesis questions** require you to understand how to draw ideas together. They may make comparisons between two similar ideas or contrast different ones. They also involve using one piece of information to better understand another.

- **Paired passages** are two passages equaling the length of one single passage (roughly 250 to 375 words each). There will always be a key connection between the two texts.

- **Analyzing Multiple Texts questions** are Synthesis questions that refer to a paired passage.

- **Informational graphics** will be included with one History and Social Studies passage and one Science passage on the SAT® Reading Test. Synthesis questions require you to draw connections between two passages and may also reference tables, charts, maps, graphs, or diagrams.

- **Analyzing Quantitative Information questions** are Synthesis questions that require you to find data in informational graphics such as diagrams, tables, charts, and maps and relate it to the accompanying passage. They will either require you to find information stated directly in the passage and informational graphic or draw conclusions from ideas only implied in them.

- Not all of the items that follow paired passages will require you to answer questions about how the two passages relate to each other. Information and Ideas, Words in Context, Rhetoric, and Command of Evidence questions may still follow a paired passage, but they will ask about only one of the passages in the pair.

- Taking note of the similarities and differences between the passages in a passage pair may help you to answer the Synthesis questions that follow.

- Reading informational graphics carefully and completely is a key to answering Analyzing Quantitative Information and Synthesis questions correctly.

CHAPTER 5:
HEART OF ALGEBRA

OVERVIEW

- Heart of Algebra: An Overview
- Manipulating Numbers and Expressions
- Solving Heart of Algebra Questions
- Creating and Solving Linear Equations and Inequalities
- Working with Inequalities and Absolute Values
- Heart of Algebra Practice
- Summing It Up

As we discussed in Chapter 1, there are four main content areas the SAT® Math Test will cover. About 90 percent of the questions you will see on test day will fall into three main content areas:

1. **The Heart of Algebra:** These questions concentrate on creating, solving, and interpreting linear equations and systems of linear equations.

2. **Problem Solving and Data Analysis:** These questions focus on applying percentages, ratios, proportions, and unit of measurement conversions to real-world situations.

3. **Passport to Advanced Math:** These questions test your mastery with more advanced functions and equations that are the foundation for college-level courses in math, science, engineering, and technology.

About 10 percent of the questions will fall into the Additional Topics in Math category, which spans geometry, trigonometry, and complex numbers.

The majority of math questions (about 80 percent) will be multiple-choice questions, where you select your answer from four given choices. Approximately 20 percent of the questions will be grid-in questions for which you must come up with your own answer—no answer choices are provided.

In the math review chapters that follow, we'll walk you through both multiple-choice and grid-in questions that test the hardest, most involved concepts you'll see on the SAT® exam. We'll drive this point home through the math review, but let's lay it out there before we even begin: Yes, there are tough math questions, but often, the toughest questions are just a combination of several simpler concepts all bunched together in one problem. You simply need to know what the question asks and what path to take, and—most important—you must work carefully so as not to let careless errors derail you from getting that 1600 you deserve. You know the math; you just need to speak the language of the SAT.

The questions we'll work through will expose you to the careful, considered steps you must take when you tackle difficult SAT® Math Test questions. Trust us when we say that taking your time and understanding the question asked and the information given is often more than half the battle.

Let's get started!

HEART OF ALGEBRA QUESTIONS: AN OVERVIEW

Approximately 33 percent (19 of 58) of the questions on the SAT® Math Test will contain questions that fall into a category called The Heart of Algebra, which covers linear equations and systems. Heart of Algebra questions will be in both the Calculator and the No Calculator sections. Because algebra is a building block for so much of math, having a firm grasp on the topics in this category will help you tackle questions from *every* SAT® Math Test category.

You must have a solid understanding of the following topics to conquer Heart of Algebra questions:

- Manipulating numbers and expressions
- Translating word problems
- Creating and solving linear equations and inequalities
- Solving and graphing systems of linear equations and inequalities
- Working with absolute values

The essence of Heart of Algebra questions is mainly contextual. Remember those word problem sections in your algebra courses? You know, questions that involved finding the speed of a stream's current, determining amounts to invest in two different bank accounts to reach a certain profit, determining how long a project will take if two friends work together, etc.? Well, they play a prominent role in this question category. You will need to set up equations and systems of equations used to solve such problems, interpret parts of equations and inequalities that arise in solving them, and yes, solve some of them algebraically or graphically.

MANIPULATING NUMBERS AND EXPRESSIONS

To successfully solve Heart of Algebra questions, you need to be able to manipulate numbers and all types of expressions involving numbers and variables. The hardest questions you will face typically include multiple steps—that's really what makes them so difficult. Often, the individual steps it takes to solve a problem are pretty basic; you'll just have to perform three to four steps correctly in order to arrive at the correct answer.

These mini-steps within a solution might involve manipulation of fractions, order of operations with several grouping symbols, finding percentages, combining or evaluating rational expressions (that is, fractions involving variables), rearranging terms in a quadratic equation by factoring or completing the square, and sometimes (though not often) simplification involving complex numbers. Let's review some of the trickiest of these concepts.

SIMPLIFYING RATIONAL EXPRESSIONS

When faced with a rational expression, your first step should be to look for a way to simplify. To do this, you will need to pull a **greatest common factor** (GCF) out of the two or more terms presented to you. Always look for a way to do this—simplification is your friend. If you don't see an obvious way to simplify, chances are you can factor a quadratic into the product of two binomials, and then simplify. The SAT® exam is tricky, but usually the tricks lie in making you use your math knowledge to turn a complex problem into a series of simpler problems.

Once your numerator and denominator have been fully factored, see which factors can be canceled out in the expression.

For example, let's say you are asked the following question:

> For all values where the expression is defined, find an expression
>
> equivalent to $\dfrac{2x^3 + 6x^2}{x^2 - 2x - 15}$.

For this example, and those that follow, let's focus on the algebraic process of solving the problem instead of choosing from the answer choices you may see.

In this expression, both the numerator and denominator can be factored. Once you factor each of them, you can cancel out the common factor or factors to find an equivalent, but simplified, expression:

$$\frac{2x^3 + 6x^2}{x^2 - 2x - 15} = \frac{2x^2 \,(x+3)}{(x+3)(x-5)} = \frac{2x^2}{x-5}$$

One way to check your answer is to use a test value. Since the expressions are equivalent, for any value of x you pick (where the first expression is defined), the two expressions will have the same value. For example, pick $x = 1$ and replace each x in both expressions with this value:

$$\frac{2(1)^3 + 6(1)^2}{(1)^2 - 2(1) - 15} = \frac{8}{-16} = -\frac{1}{2}$$

$$\frac{2(1)^2}{(1) - 5} = \frac{2}{-4} = -\frac{1}{2}$$

This isn't perfect. It is possible that two expressions just happen to have the same value as the value of x you pick, but it would be very unlucky to manage to pick such an x! While it is best to know and apply the algebra, you can also use this trick if you get stuck on a problem by checking a value of x in the question expression and all the answer choices. This should only be a last resort, however!

Beware of Careless Simplification Errors!

When simplifying rational expressions, remember that you can only cancel out *factors*, but you may not cancel out individual *terms*. For example, in $\frac{5x - 3}{10x - 3}$, you may not reduce the 5 and 10, nor may you cancel out the 3 on the top and the bottom. $\frac{5x - 3}{10x - 3}$ is fully simplified.

When asked to add or subtract rational expressions, remember you *must* first find a common denominator and, if subtracting, don't forget to distribute the subtraction to *both* terms in the numerator of the second expression.

For $x \neq 1, -1$, find an expression equivalent to $\dfrac{5}{2x^2 - 2} - \dfrac{4}{x + 1}$.

One way to find a common denominator is to simply multiply the two given denominators, and then rewrite each fraction with this denominator. Here, that common denominator would be $(2x^2 - 2)(x + 1)$. This is pretty complicated and would likely result in a huge waste of your precious time.

In this particular example, like with many SAT® Math Test questions, a closer look will save you some work and make things simpler. Take a look at the first denominator. It can be rewritten as follows:

$$2x^2 - 2 = 2(x^2 - 1) = 2(x + 1)(x - 1)$$

 104

Since $x + 1$ (the denominator of the second fraction) is a factor of this larger denominator, you can use this as the common denominator. You just need to multiply the denominator $x + 1$ by the missing piece, $2(x - 1)$. However, since the fraction you get must be equivalent to the original, you will also have to multiply the numerator by this same value.

$$\frac{5}{2x^2 - 2} - \frac{4}{x+1} = \frac{5}{2x^2 - 2} - \left(\frac{4}{x+1}\right)\left(\frac{2(x-1)}{2(x-1)}\right)$$

$$= \frac{5}{2x^2 - 2} - \frac{8(x-1)}{2(x+1)(x-1)}$$

$$= \frac{5}{2x^2 - 2} - \frac{8x - 8}{2x^2 - 2}$$

Now that you have the same denominator for each fraction, you can subtract numerators. Make sure to distribute the negative to each term.

$$\frac{5}{2x^2 - 2} - \frac{8x - 8}{2x^2 - 2} = \frac{5 - 8x + 8}{2x^2 - 2}$$

$$= \frac{-8x + 13}{2x^2 - 2}$$

This is the final answer. Note that this rational expression is completely simplified, but if it weren't, you would likely have to also simplify it to match a given answer choice on the SAT® exam.

A tricky type of question you might face involving rational expressions will ask how a rational expression changes when one of the variables increases or decreases by a certain factor. Here's what this question might look like:

The gravitational force F between two objects with masses m_1 and m_2, in kilograms, is found using the formula $F = g\frac{m_1 m_2}{r^2}$, where g is the gravitational constant and r is the distance between the two objects, in meters. What happens to the gravitational force between two objects if the distance between them is increased by a factor of a, for $a > 1$?

There is a lot going on in this example, but you can use the question itself to guide your first steps. It asks you to figure out what happens to the force, F, when the distance, r, is increased by a factor of a. In other words, if the original distance were r meters, you want to figure out what happens if it were instead ar meters.

To do this, substitute *ar* into the equation in place of *r*.

$$F = g\frac{m_1m_2}{(ar)^2}$$

$$= g\frac{m_1m_2}{a^2r^2}$$

$$= \left(\frac{g}{a^2}\right)\frac{m_1m_2}{r^2}$$

$$= \left(\frac{1}{a^2}\right)g\frac{m_1m_2}{r^2}$$

In the last two steps, we used algebra to manipulate the new expression on the right-hand side of the equation to relate to the expression on the right-hand side of the original formula. These steps show that increasing the distance by a factor of *a* is the same as multiplying the equation for the force by $\frac{1}{a^2}$. This means that the force decreases (since this is a fraction and $a > 1$) by a factor of a^2.

When asked how a change in the value of one variable will impact an entire expression, use substitution to replace the altered variable with its new value. Then, use algebraic manipulations to rewrite the new expression as a product of the original expression and a new factor. This new factor illustrates how the value of the original expression has changed.

RATIO, PROPORTION, AND PERCENT

The SAT® Math Test is big on ratio and percent questions. A ratio is a comparison of one quantity *x* to another quantity *y*, expressed as a fraction $\frac{x}{y}$. This is interpreted as, "for every *x* of one type, there are *y* of the second type." A proportion is an equation relating two ratios. In symbols, a proportion is expressed by setting two fractions equal to each other, say $\frac{a}{b} = \frac{c}{d}$. Proportions come up when solving many different types of problems in all SAT® Math Test sections, including changing units of measure and similar triangles. Proportions are often formulated when one ratio is known and one of the two quantities in an equivalent ratio is unknown.

The word *percent* means "per hundred." To convert from decimal form to percent form, you simply move the decimal point two units to the right and affix the percent sign (%);

to convert in the opposite manner, move the decimal point two units to the left, and drop the percent (%) sign.

Problems involving percentages will most likely be presented to you in one of three varieties:

Problem Type	Method Used to Solve the Problem	Example
"Compute x% of y."	Convert x% to a decimal and multiply by y.	**Q:** Compute 45% of 12. **A:** $0.45(12) = 5.4$
"What percent of x is y?"	Divide y by x, then convert into a percent.	**Q:** What percent of 360 is 280? **A:** $\dfrac{280}{360} = 0.\overline{7} \approx 78\%$
"x is y% of what number z?"	Convert y% to a decimal, multiply it by z, and set equal to x. Solve for z.	**Q:** 33 is 40% of what number z? **A:** Solve $0.40z = 33$ for z to get $z = 82.5$.

 TIP Keep in mind—these computations will usually arise within contextual settings like word problems rather than being presented as plain computational questions.

COMPLEX NUMBERS

A **complex number** is a number of the form $a + bi$, where a and b are both real numbers and $i^2 = -1$.

For example, let's simplify the following expression using i:

$$\sqrt{121} - \sqrt{-144} =$$
$$11 - \sqrt{-1} \cdot \sqrt{144} =$$
$$11 - i \cdot 12 =$$
$$11 - 12i$$

The first four powers of i are the most critical to know, since the values for i^n follow this pattern for all values of $n > 4$. You should memorize this cycle before test day:

- $i = \sqrt{-1}$
- $i^2 = -1$
- $i^3 = i^2 \times i = -i$
- $i^4 = i^2 \times i^2 = -1 \times -1 = 1$

So, when faced with any high power of i, first find the closest multiple of 4 that is no bigger than the exponent. Subtract that multiple from the exponent, and find the value of i to that power for your answer.

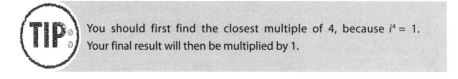

TIP You should first find the closest multiple of 4, because $i^4 = 1$. Your final result will then be multiplied by 1.

Take i^{83}. The closest multiple of 4 to 83 that is lower than 83 is 80:

$$i^{83} = i^{80+3} = 1 \times i^3$$

So, your final answer is i^3, which you know from memorizing the cycle is $-i$.

The following are the basic rules of arithmetic involving complex numbers. This is a super-tricky concept, so make sure you have these rules down. Then you won't second-guess yourself on test day.

Definition (in Symbols)	Definition (in Words)
Sum/Difference $(a + bi) + (c + di) = (a + c) + (b + d)i$ $(a + bi) - (c + di) = (a - c) + (b - d)i$	When adding or subtracting complex numbers, add or subtract the real parts and the imaginary parts separately, and form the complex number using those sums or differences.
Product $(a + bi) \times (c + di) = (ac - bd) + (bc + ad)i$	To multiply two complex numbers, apply the FOIL technique and use the fact that $i^2 = -1$.

Division with complex numbers is another area that you may see on the SAT® Math Test, presented as a fraction that will need to be written in an equivalent form. The main thing to keep in mind is that the denominator of a fraction must always be a rational number— your goal is to make it rational before you calculate.

When a complex number is multiplied by its conjugate, the product will always be a real number. (The conjugate of a complex number $a + bi$ is $a - bi$.) In order to divide with complex numbers, multiply the numerator and denominator by the conjugate of the denominator.

What is an equivalent expression to the quotient $\dfrac{4+3i}{2-4i}$?

In order to rationalize the denominator of $\dfrac{4+3i}{2-4i}$, multiply both numerator and denominator by $2 + 4i$:

$$\frac{4 + 3i}{2 - 4i} = \frac{(4 + 3i)}{(2 - 4i)} \cdot \frac{(2 + 4i)}{(2 + 4i)}$$

$$= \frac{8 + 16i + 6i + 12i^2}{4 + 8i - 8i - 16i^2}$$

$$= \frac{8 + 22i - 12}{4 + 16}$$

$$= \frac{-4 + 22i}{20}$$

$$= \frac{-2 + 11i}{10}$$

SOLVING HEART OF ALGEBRA QUESTIONS

When approaching Heart of Algebra questions, you can usually choose from the following techniques when solving problems:

1. Plugging in and simplifying using arithmetic
2. Reverse engineering (working backwards)
3. Performing algebraic manipulation to alter the form of expressions or solve equations

Let's focus on technique number 3 in this advanced book, since you're likely familiar with the math you'll need to use, and a quick solve via algebra is often the fastest and most efficient method. As we've discussed, the trickiest algebra problems on the SAT® Math Test usually *seem* complicated. Often, simplicity lurks within.

When you approach a tough question, keep in mind that the test makers are sometimes just testing your ability to recognize patterns or ways to turn something hard into something manageable. Take a second to look at a problem that might seem insurmountable, and see how you can make it easier.

Example:

A sinking fund is an account where funds are periodically added until a set future value is reached. The yearly payment required to reach a future value of A dollars after t years is given by the formula $R = \dfrac{Ar}{(1+r)^t - 1}$, where r is the fixed annual interest rate. Use this to find a formula for the value of an account after t years, where R dollars was invested each year at an annual rate of r.

Solution:

To answer this question, we need to find a formula for A. By inspecting the given formula, you can see that the right-hand side of the equation can be rewritten as:

$$\frac{Ar}{(1+r)^t - 1} = A\frac{r}{(1+r)^t - 1}$$

This shows that the right-hand side of the equation really is just a rational expression multiplying A. Remember how you solve a simple equation like $\dfrac{3}{4}x = 5$? As you probably recall, you multiply by the reciprocal $\dfrac{4}{3}$ to get $x = \dfrac{4}{3}(5) = \dfrac{20}{3}$. You can apply that same rule here:

$$R = \frac{Ar}{(1+r)^t - 1}$$

$$R = A\frac{r}{(1+r)^t - 1}$$

$$R\left(\frac{(1+r)^t - 1}{r}\right) = A$$

Often, you will need to use your knowledge of factoring to write a quadratic expression in an equivalent manner. Let's look at an example.

Example:

For nonzero integers a and c, the polynomial $ax^2 - x + c$ can be written as the product of the binomials $3x + m$ and $x + n$, where m and n are also nonzero integers. If $a + c = 1$, then what is the value of $m + n$?

Solution:

The language used in this question is very conceptual, but when you analyze it, it is really just a question that is testing your understanding of factoring. With a question like this, where that might not be obvious, it is best to approach it one sentence at a time. Keep in mind the overall question though: You need to figure out the sum of m and n.

Let's consider the first sentence. It states that $ax^2 - x + c$ can be written as the product of the two given binomials. Mathematically, this means that you can write out the following:

$$ax^2 - x + c = (3x + m)(x + n)$$

It seems natural to FOIL here, so FOIL the right-hand side and see what it shows:

$$ax^2 - x + c = (3x + m)(x + n)$$
$$ax^2 - x + c = 3x^2 + 3nx + mx + mn$$
$$ax^2 - x + c = 3x^2 + (3n + m)x + mn$$

Immediately you can see that $a = 3$, $3n + m = -1$, and $c = mn$. If you are going to figure out the sum of m and n, it looks like you will need to know the value of c.

In the next line of the question, you are told that $a + c = 1$. Since you know that $a = 3$, you can substitute and find that $c = -2$. From the previous equations, you know that $-2 = mn$.

If you wanted to, you could now solve the system of equations $3n + m = -1$ and $-2 = mn$ algebraically. But this is overly complicated. You know the product of m and n is -2. The only possibilities for the value of m and n are: -1 and 2; 1 and -2; 2 and -1; or -2 and 1.

Trying these in the first equation, the only values that work are $m = 2$ and $n = -1$:

$$3n + m = 1$$
$$3(-1) + 2 = -1$$

Therefore, $m + n = 2 + (-1) = 1$.

Notice that if you were stuck at the last step, the sum of each pair of numbers was either 1 or -1. You could therefore have eliminated all but these answer choices and guessed from there!

Translating Words Into Math

First and foremost, make certain to read the questions carefully to be sure you understand what is being asked. Many times, advanced students read the first part of a question and then assume what is being asked, because they've seen something similar in their studies. You're too smart to do that—every test is similar, but every test is also different! As you're reading for understanding, also keep the following in mind: Many SAT® Math Test problems are purposely written in a tricky manner and often include superfluous information.

 For word problems, break up the question, interpret a simple version of each sentence, and then translate this into algebra.

It is very likely that more than one question in this section of the SAT® Math Test will ask you to create an algebraic expression or equation that models an applied scenario.

For instance, consider the following typical question. Pay particular attention to the nature of the distracter choices.

> A cell phone plan including 4 gigabytes of data, unlimited texts, and unlimited minutes has a monthly cost of m, before taxes. For any data over 4 gigabytes, there is an extra, before-tax charge of n per gigabyte. If taxes are 2.1%, which expression represents the monthly bill, in dollars, for someone who uses g gigabytes of data, where $g > 4$?
>
> **A.** $0.021(m + ng)$
> **B.** $0.021m + ng$
> **C.** $1.021(m + ng)$
> **D.** $1.021m + ng$

The key here is to recognize that taxes are charged on the overall total, and not just on the flat monthly charge of m. This eliminates choices B and D, which have a constant multiplying only m.

Someone who uses more than 4 gigabytes of data will pay a total of ng for that extra data. This is in addition to the fee of m. So, before taxes, the user will pay $m + ng$ dollars. The tax of 2.1% is added on to this amount. Therefore, the total charge will be:

$$(m + ng) + 0.021(m + ng) = 1.021(m + ng)$$

The correct answer is C.

CREATING AND SOLVING LINEAR EQUATIONS AND INEQUALITIES

Another skill you must master is manipulating linear equations to solve them. This continues with the theme we've already been hammering home in this chapter—don't take what you've been given and think you must work with it exactly. If you're going to score your best on the SAT® exam, you're going to have to manipulate math so it's easier to work with.

For example, if an equation involves fractions, the first thing you should do is multiply both sides of the equation by the LCD of all fractions appearing in the equation to clear the fractions. Make things as easy as possible for you to work with!

If $\dfrac{x+7}{3} + \dfrac{4}{5} = \dfrac{14}{5}$, then what is the value of $\dfrac{5}{2}(x+7)$?

A. 5

B. $\dfrac{9}{2}$

C. $\dfrac{23}{5}$

D. 15

To clear fractions in the given equation, multiply both sides by 15:

$$15\left(\dfrac{x+7}{3} + \dfrac{4}{5}\right) = 15\left(\dfrac{14}{5}\right)$$
$$5(x + 7) + 3(4) = 3(14)$$
$$5(x + 7) + 12 = 42$$

While this is a relatively simple equation to solve now, this question doesn't just ask you to solve the equation. Instead, like many SAT® questions, it asks for a related value. But also, like a lot of SAT® questions, there is a way to find what you are asked for without too much computation.

Compare the equation that resulted from clearing fractions to the value you need to find: $\dfrac{5}{2}(x + 7)$. With just a little algebraic manipulation, you have:

$$5(x + 7) = 12 + 42$$
$$5(x + 7) = 30$$

Then, multiplying both sides by one-half:

$$\dfrac{5}{2}(x + 7) = 15$$

The correct answer is D.

 Keep in mind that many questions will ask for the answer in a different format than what is given in the question. So be prepared to go the step further when you find your answer. For instance, instead of solving for x and y, you'll be asked to give 5x – y. Another common example is unit conversions (a question might be presented in inches, but ask for its answer in feet).

WORKING WITH INEQUALITIES AND ABSOLUTE VALUES

An inequality is a mathematical relationship that has an inequality symbol, like > or <, instead of an equal sign. You should be completely comfortable solving absolute value inequalities and graphing their solution sets on number lines before test day.

One step that students often forget with inequalities (even if they know it!) is to change the direction of the inequality symbol when the inequality is *divided* or *multiplied* by a negative number. For example, $-3x > 6$ will have the solution set $x < -2$ after both sides are divided by -3.

ALERT: It's easy to forget to switch the direction of the inequality symbol when dividing or multiplying by negatives. Check your answer by testing a value from your solution set in the original inequality.

For any real number a, the *absolute value of a*, denoted $|a|$, is the distance between a and 0. The definition is given in two parts:

$$|a| = \begin{cases} a, \text{ if } a \geq 0 \\ -a, \text{ if } a < 0 \end{cases}$$

For instance, $|9| = 9$ and $|-9| = 9$. This definition works for any type of real number.

The following are some useful properties of absolute values to study and know inside and out:

Property (in Symbols)	Property (in Words)
$\lvert a \rvert = b$, whenever $a = b$ or $a = -b$	Both b and $-b$ are $\lvert b \rvert$ units from the origin.
$\lvert a \cdot b \rvert = \lvert a \rvert \cdot \lvert b \rvert$ $\left\lvert \dfrac{a}{b} \right\rvert = \dfrac{\lvert a \rvert}{\lvert b \rvert}$, whenever $b \neq 0$	The absolute value of a product or quotient is the product or quotient of the absolute values.
In general, $\lvert a + b \rvert \neq \lvert a \rvert + \lvert b \rvert$.	First, compute the expression enclosed by absolute-value bars. Then, take the absolute value of that single number.

A tricky aspect of the solutions to absolute value inequalities is that they will either be bound on two sides ($4 < x < 10$) or they will go on for infinity in two opposite directions: ($x < -2$ and $x > 6$). Let's look at one example of each type.

Find the solution set for the inequality $\left\lvert \dfrac{1}{2}x + 7 \right\rvert < 2$.

Think about the number-line definition of an absolute value. If the absolute value of a number is less than 2, then the distance on the number line between that number and 0 is less than 2. Therefore, all values between −2 and 2 have an absolute value of less than 2.

Applying that to this inequality, if $\left\lvert \dfrac{1}{2}x + 7 \right\rvert < 2$, then it must be that $-2 < \dfrac{1}{2}x + 7 < 2$.

You can now solve this inequality just as you would any other linear inequality. Just make sure that any step is performed to all three parts:

Take the original inequality, $-2 < \dfrac{1}{2}x + 7 < 2$, and subtract 7 from each part:

$$-2 - 7 < \dfrac{1}{2}x + 7 - 7 < 2 - 7$$

$$-9 < \dfrac{1}{2}x < -5$$

Next, multiply each part by 2:

$$(2)(-9) < (2)\left(\dfrac{1}{2}x\right) < (2)(-5)$$

$$-18 < x < -10$$

The solution set is all values between −18 and −10.

Let's look at another example that's a bit more complicated.

Example:

Determine the solution set for the inequality $\left(\left|\dfrac{2}{3}x\right|-11\right)^2 \geq 49$.

Solution:

$\left(\left|\dfrac{2}{3}x\right|-11\right)^2 \geq 49$ looks a lot more complicated than the previous example, but just

approach it step by step, and you will see that it is not as scary as it might appear.

First, take the square root of both sides:

$$\sqrt{\left(\left|\dfrac{2}{3}x\right|-11\right)^2} \geq \sqrt{49}$$

$$\left|\dfrac{2}{3}x\right|-11 \geq 7$$

Next, add 11 to both sides to isolate the absolute-value term: $\left|\dfrac{2}{3}x\right| \geq 18$.

Now recognize that the second part of our solution comes from realizing that $\left|\dfrac{2}{3}x\right|$ will be greater than 18 when $\dfrac{2}{3}x$ is less than -18. (The absolute value of any number less than -18 is greater than 18.) Rewrite $\left|\dfrac{2}{3}x\right| \geq 18$ as two separate inequalities since there will be no overlap between these two solutions (a number cannot be simultaneously greater than 18 and less than -18.) Solve both inequalities by dividing by $\dfrac{2}{3}$:

$$\dfrac{2}{3}x \geq 18 \quad \text{and} \quad \dfrac{2}{3}x \leq -18$$

$$x \geq 18\left(\dfrac{3}{2}\right) \qquad x \leq -18\left(\dfrac{3}{2}\right)$$

$$x \geq 27 \qquad\qquad x \leq -27$$

27 and -27 are the starting points of each part of the solution set, which will expand outwards toward positive and negative infinity.

Solving Systems of Linear Equations and Inequalities

A **system of linear equations** is a pair of linear equations involving x and y that must be satisfied *at the same time*. To solve a system means to identify ordered pairs (x, y) that satisfy *both* equations—not just one, but both! There are only three possibilities that can occur:

Number of Solutions	Geometric Interpretation
0	The graphs of the lines in the system are parallel. Hence, there is no point that is on both lines simultaneously.
1	The graphs of the lines in the system intersect in a single point. The intersection point *is* the solution of the system.
Infinitely many	The graphs of the lines in the system are the same. Every point on the line is a solution of the system.

There are two algebraic methods that you can use to solve a system: the elimination method and the substitution method. Be certain to review these from your algebra coursework in school.

TIP
If you are given a system and asked which of a list of choices is a solution, remember the ordered pair must satisfy *both* equations, not just one of them. Among the choices will be points that satisfy one of the equations, but not the other.

As with most questions in this section, you will likely not be asked to simply solve a system of equations—you'll have to think one step beyond this. The closest you might get to a purely "mechanical" question involving systems of linear equations is finding the value of some expression involving x and y, where (x, y) is the solution of a given system. Even then, there is often an approach that will save you some time in finding the final answer. Consider the following example.

Given the system of equations, what is the value of $\dfrac{x}{y}$?

$$x - 5y = 1$$
$$2x - y = 9$$

A. $\dfrac{7}{9}$

B. $\dfrac{11}{7}$

C. $\dfrac{44}{9}$

D. $\dfrac{44}{7}$

Often, when there is a coefficient of 1 for one of the variables, textbooks will suggest using the substitution method. However, in practice, you will often find that the elimination method is quicker.

When using elimination, which variable to eliminate first is up to you. In this problem, you can eliminate x first by multiplying the first equation by -2. This sets it up so that when you add the equations, you will only be left with an equation involving y:

$$
\begin{aligned}
-2(x-5y) &= -2(1) \\
2x-y &= 9
\end{aligned}
\quad\Rightarrow\quad
\begin{aligned}
-2x+10y &= -2 \\
2x-y &= 9 \\
\hline
9y &= 7 \\
y &= \frac{7}{9}
\end{aligned}
$$

Notice that the first answer choice is this value! Be careful not to be tempted into selecting the first number you calculate that matches an answer choice.

Now, you can use either equation to find x. Let's use the first equation:

$$x - 5y = 1$$
$$x - 5\left(\frac{7}{9}\right) = 1$$
$$x - \frac{35}{9} = 1$$
$$x = 1 + \frac{35}{9} = \frac{9}{9} + \frac{35}{9} = \frac{44}{9}$$

Again, this is also one of the answer choices! But, your job is not to just find x and y, but to find the value of $\frac{x}{y}$. You now have enough information to find this:

$$\frac{x}{y} = \frac{\frac{44}{9}}{\frac{7}{9}} = \frac{44}{7}$$

The correct answer is D.

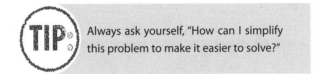 Always ask yourself, "How can I simplify this problem to make it easier to solve?"

Algebraic questions about linear systems more typically involve identifying the value of some constant that ensures that a system has 0, 1, or infinitely many solutions.

If you are asked to identify the value of a coefficient in a linear equation so the solutions of a given system satisfy some condition, use the following facts about lines to find your answer:

- A system has a **unique solution** if the slopes of the two lines are different.

- A system has **no solution** if the slopes of the two lines are equal.

- A system has **infinitely many solutions** if the two lines are constant multiples of each other.

Consider the following problem.

> In the system of equations below, k is a real number.
>
> $$kx - 2y = 10$$
> $$-\frac{9}{2}x + 3y = -15$$
>
> For what value of k does this system have infinitely many solutions?
>
> **A.** 5
>
> **B.** 3
>
> **C.** $-\frac{7}{2}$
>
> **D.** $-\frac{9}{2}$

In order for there to be infinitely many solutions, the two lines must be constant multiples of each other. Use the coefficients for y and the constants to see if you can tell what the first equation is multiplied by to get the second. Considering the $-y$ coefficients first, you can write:

$$-2 \times \text{constant} = 3$$

Solving, this means that the constant multiple would be $-\frac{3}{2}$.

Checking the constants:

$$-\frac{3}{2}(10) = -15$$

This verifies that you have the correct multiple. Now, using the coefficients on x:

$$-\frac{3}{2}k = -\frac{9}{2}$$
$$k = -\frac{9}{2} \times -\frac{2}{3}$$
$$= 3$$

The correct answer is B.

Contextual Problems Featuring Linear Equations and Inequalities

Most of the problems we've worked through so far have been straightforward math, so now let's focus more on your skills relating real-life scenarios to the math methods that can solve them. As we've mentioned, contextual questions involving systems are tested heavily on the SAT® exam. You will likely be asked to either solve a word problem that requires the use of a system of linear equations outright, or you might be asked to set up the system of equations that *would be used* to solve a real-world problem.

Quite often a system of equations will be dressed up in a long word problem with lots of fascinating information. Look for the following key information:

- **The starting point:** the number that doesn't get influenced when other factors change (such as the one-time sign-up fee to join a fitness club—this won't be doubled if you keep your membership for 2 months)

- **The rate of change:** a factor what will cause an increase or decrease in the final value of a relationship as one of the conditions changes (such as the fee per month of a fitness club—you will pay this fee 3 times after 3 months of membership)

In general, you will pull information out from the problem and organize it as such:

$$y = \text{starting point} + (\text{rate of change})x$$

In this equation, x is the **independent variable** that fluctuates (*number of months of gym membership*) and influences the value of the **dependent variable**, y (*total money spent on gym membership*).

The standard linear equation, $y = mx + b$, can be reconstructed to easily model the information you'll be given in word problems: $y = $ starting point + (rate of change) x. Instead of using y and x, choose variables that clearly represent the real-world content of the problem, like m for months and d for dollars spent.

Once you have pulled the information out of a word problem and correctly put it into two linear equations, you can solve the system of linear equations by whichever method you prefer.

Let's take a look at one of the challenging types of questions you might see.

Kayla leaves to drive from Dillon, Colorado, to Moab, Utah, at an average speed of 60 miles per hour. When she is 50 miles into her trip, her friend Ryland calls to say that he is going to also drive from Dillon to Moab. He has just left and will average 70 miles per hour. Which equation would determine the number of hours it will take Ryland to catch up to Kayla if she continues toward Moab at 60 mph?

A. $(70 - 50)h = 60h$
B. $70h = (50 + 60)h$
C. $60h = 50 + 70h$
D. $70h = 50 + 60h$

The correct answer is D. Use distance $=$ rate $\times$ time to model Kayla's distance from Dillon: $d = 60h$. Since Ryland is traveling at 70 miles per hour, his distance from Dillon can be represented as $d = 70h$. Next, incorporate the fact that Kayla was already 50 miles from Dillon when Ryland left Dillon by adding 50 to her original distance: $d = 50 + 60h$. (This shows that when Ryland has traveled h hours, Kayla will have traveled $60h$ miles in addition to her initial 50 miles.) Ryland will catch up to Kayla when their distances are equal, so set the two equations equal: $70h = 50 + 60h$. Choice A is incorrect because it models Ryland going 20 miles per hour. Choice B is incorrect because it models Kayla going 110 miles per hour. Choice C is incorrect because it adds Kayla's initial 50 miles traveled to Ryland's distance.

GRAPHING AND INTERPRETING LINEAR INEQUALITIES IN TWO VARIABLES AND SYSTEMS OF SUCH INEQUALITIES

We talked about absolute value inequalities with one variable earlier in this chapter. Now we'll review graphic solutions of inequalities with two variables. Inequalities are graphed in the standard (x, y) coordinate plane and then shaded *above* or *below* the function. Remember that the inequality sign will determine whether a dotted or solid line is appropriate:

- **> or <**: Use a *dotted line* to show that the solution set does *not* include the values on the line or curve.

- **≥ or ≤**: Use a *solid line* to show that the solution set includes the values on the line or curve.

The most common mistake students make is shading to the *right* or *left* of the line instead of *above* or *below* it. Let's look at an example.

What is the inequality represented by the following graph?

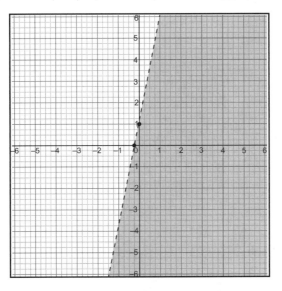

The line graphed has a *y*-intercept at 1 and a slope of 5, so we know the line representing this inequality is $y = 5x + 1$. The line is dotted, so we know that it will be < or >, and not ≤ or ≥. The untrained eye would read this shading as *to the right* of the line and would therefore see this incorrectly as $y > 5x + 1$. However, the shading is *below* the line, indicating that all the shaded values are *less than* the *y*-coordinates on the line. Therefore, the inequality that represents this is $y < 5x + 1$.

 Inequalities are shaded *above* or *below* the line or curve, and not to the right or left of it! (This is for all cases other than inequalities in the form $x < k$, which are vertical lines that are shaded on the right or left.)

Several inequalities can be graphed together on the same standard (x, y) coordinate plane to model the constraints placed on a real-world situation. It is common for the test questions to ask you to draw conclusions based on these illustrations.

Consider the following figure, which shows the constraints the management has for their non-profit animal shelter, which takes in homeless dogs and cats and seeks to find them permanent homes. The management has a minimum number of dogs and cats that they want at all times, as well as a maximum number of animals they can house at once. Try to answer the following questions before looking at the solutions that follow them.

1. What is the lowest number of dogs the shelter wishes to have at all times?
2. What is the lowest number of cats the shelter wishes to have at all times?
3. What is the fewest and the greatest number of animals the shelter can house at any single time?
4. If the shelter has 12 cats on a given day, what are all the possible numbers of dogs it may have?

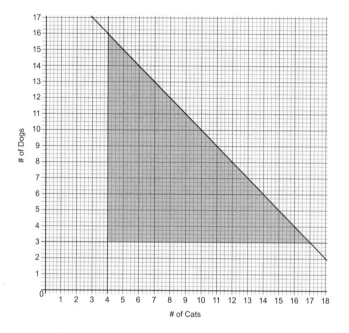

1. Since *# of Dogs* is on the y-axis, the constraint $y \geq 3$ represents the shelter's dogs. They wish to house at least 3 dogs at all times.
2. Since *# of Cats* is on the x-axis, the constraint $x \geq 4$ represents the shelter's cats. They wish to house at least 4 cats at all times.
3. Since the shelter plans on housing at least 3 dogs and 4 cats at all times, the fewest number of animals they would have at any time would be 7. The diagonal line corresponding to the inequality $y < 20 - x$ has the equation $y = 20 - x$ since the y-intercept is 20 and the slope is -1. The inequality illustrates that the greatest number of animals they can shelter at one time is 20.
4. If the shelter has 12 cats on a given day, it may have anywhere from 3 to 8 dogs, based on the constraints represented in the graph.

HEART OF ALGEBRA PRACTICE

Complete the following problems. Answers and explanations follow on page 128.

1 If $\dfrac{3x+1}{y} = 2$ where $y \neq 0$, then what is the value of $-2(3x - 2y)$?

  A. −2
  B. −1
  C. 1
  D. 2

2 For $P = 2(x^2 - 1)(x + 3)$ and $Q = 5x + 5$ where $x \neq -1$, which expression is equivalent to $\dfrac{P}{Q}$?

  A. $\dfrac{2}{5}(x^2 - 3)$

  B. $\dfrac{2}{5}(x^2 + 3)$

  C. $\dfrac{2}{5}(x^2 + 2x - 3)$

  D. $\dfrac{2}{5}(x^2 + 4x + 3)$

3 If $-\dfrac{2}{3}(x + 5) - 8 = -\dfrac{1}{2}x$, then what is the value of $x + 4$?

  A. −64
  B. −43
  C. −39
  D. −24

4 A business purchases 5 computer systems at a cost of $\$p$ each and 8 conference systems at a cost of $\$q$ each. Due to its long-standing relationship with the supplier, the business receives a discount of 10% on the order. If the sales tax charged on this purchase is 5%, then which expression represents the total cost of the order, after tax?

  A. $0.045(5p + 8q)$
  B. $0.945(5p + 8q)$
  C. $1.365(p + q)$
  D. $12.285(p + q)$

5 For $i = \sqrt{-1}$, which of the following is equivalent to the product $i^3(3 + 4i)(-2 + i)$?

  A. −10
  B. $10i$
  C. $10 + 5i$
  D. $-5 + 10i$

6 To find the current, measured in amp, I, in a resistor, the formula $I = \dfrac{V}{R}$ is used. In this formula, V represents the voltage in volts and R the resistance in ohms. If both the voltage and resistance are increased by a factor of 4, what happens to the current?

- **A.** The current increases by a factor of 2.
- **B.** The current increases by a factor of 4.
- **C.** The current increases by a factor of 16.
- **D.** The current does not change.

7 Which expression is equivalent to $\dfrac{m-4}{5} - \dfrac{1}{3m-2}$?

- **A.** $\dfrac{m-3}{7-3m}$
- **B.** $\dfrac{3(m^2+1)}{5(3m-2)}$
- **C.** $\dfrac{3m^2-14m+3}{5(3m-2)}$
- **D.** $\dfrac{m^2-11m+18}{5(3m-2)}$

8 Given the system of equations, what is the value of $x+y$?

$$\frac{2}{3}x - y = 3$$

$$\frac{1}{2}x = 2y$$

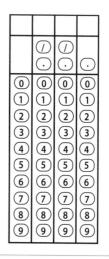

9 What is the smallest positive integer solution to the inequality $\left|2x - \dfrac{1}{3}\right| > 5$?

10 For what value of *s* does the system of equations have multiple solutions?

$$3a + 6b = \frac{1}{5}$$
$$2a + 4b = s$$

Answer Key and Explanations

1. D	3. A	5. D	7. C	9. 3
2. C	4. B	6. D	8. 9	10. $\dfrac{2}{15}$

1. **The correct answer is D.** First, cross-multiply to get $2y = 3x + 1$. Now subtract $2y$ and 1 from both sides. The result is $-1 = 3x - 2y$. Multiplying by -2 gives the needed value: $2 = -2(3x - 2y)$. Choice A is the value of $-2(2y - 3x)$. Choice B is the value of $3x - 2y$, and choice C is the value of $2y - 3x$.

2. **The correct answer is C.** Factor and then simplify, if possible:

$$\frac{P}{Q} = \frac{2(x^2 - 1)(x + 3)}{5x + 5}$$
$$= \frac{2\cancel{(x+1)}(x - 1)(x + 3)}{5\cancel{(x+1)}}$$
$$= \frac{2(x - 1)(x + 3)}{5}$$

Now FOIL to match the form of the answers:

$$\frac{2(x - 1)(x + 3)}{5}$$
$$= \frac{2(x^2 + 2x - 3)}{5}$$
$$= \frac{2}{5}(x^2 + 2x - 3)$$

You may get choice A if you correctly factor and cancel, but then do not apply FOIL to expand the new denominator. Similarly, choice B is the result of the same mistake if you first canceled $x - 1$ instead of $x + 1$ when simplifying. If you make this same canceling mistake but then correctly apply FOIL, you may get choice D.

3. **The correct answer is A.** Clear fractions and then solve the resulting linear equation to find the value of x. Then, add 4 to find the value of $x + 4$:

$$6\left(-\frac{2}{3}(x + 5) - 8\right) = 6\left(-\frac{1}{2}x\right)$$
$$-4(x + 5) - 48 = -3x$$
$$-4x - 20 - 48 = -3x$$
$$-68 = x$$
$$-64 = x + 4$$

If you do not correctly distribute the 4 in the second step, the result is -43 for the value of x (choice B) and -39 for the value of $x + 4$ (choice C). Choice D is the value of $x + 4$ if you forget to multiply the 8 on the left-hand side of the equation by 6 when clearing fractions.

4. **The correct answer is B.** The before-tax cost of the computers is $5p$, and it is $8q$ for the conference systems. This would give a total of $5p + 8q$ dollars. After the discount is applied, the price would then be:

$$(5p + 8q) - 0.1(5p + 8q) =$$
$$0.9(5p + 8q)$$

The tax is then added onto that giving a final total of

$$0.9(5p + 8q) + 0.05(0.9(5p + 8q))$$

$$= 0.9(5p + 8q) + 0.045\ (5p + 8q)$$

$$= 0.945(5p + 8q)$$

Notice how the tax is added on to the discounted price to find the overall total. The tax itself is choice A, so make sure to read the question carefully to know you need to find more than this! Choices C and D are based on the incorrect before-discount and before-tax cost of $13(p + q)$. To correctly represent this cost, the price of each individual item must be multiplied by the number of items of that type purchased. This can't be simplified further.

5. **The correct answer is D.** Recall that $i^2 = -1$. Therefore, $i^3 = i \times i^2 = -i$. Using this value, you can now FOIL, distribute the $-i$, and then simplify:

$$i^3(3 + 4i)(-2 + i) = -i(3 + 4i)(-2 + i)$$

$$= -i(-6 - 5i + 4i^2)$$

$$= -i(-6 - 5i + 4(-1))$$

$$= -i(-6 - 5i + -4)$$

$$= -i(-10 - 5i)$$

$$= 10i + 5i^2$$

$$= 10i + 5(-1)$$

$$= -5 + 10i$$

If you don't FOIL but perform all the other mathematics operations correctly, the result will be choice B. If you don't FOIL and also forget to distribute i^3, then the result is choice A. Choice C results from incorrectly using -1 as the value of i^3.

6. **The correct answer is D.** To determine the change, replace both values 4 times their original value (since the increase was "by a factor of 4").

$$I = \frac{4V}{4R} = \frac{V}{R}$$

Both fours are canceled out, so you can conclude that the current stays the same. The other answer choices are based on trying to read into the problem without applying the mathematics to answer it (for example, in choice C, assuming the changes will be multiplicative).

7. **The correct answer is C.** The common denominator is $5(3m-2)$. Use this to rewrite each fraction and then subtract:

$$\frac{m-4}{5} - \frac{1}{3m-2}$$

$$= \left(\frac{m-4}{5}\right)\left(\frac{3m-2}{3m-2}\right) - \left(\frac{1}{3m-2}\right)\left(\frac{5}{5}\right)$$

$$= \frac{(m-4)(3m-2)}{5(3m-2)} - \frac{5}{5(3m-2)}$$

$$= \frac{3m^2 - 14m + 8}{5(3m-2)} - \frac{5}{5(3m-2)}$$

$$= \frac{3m^2 - 14m + 3}{5(3m-2)}$$

The quadratic in the numerator is not factorable, and so this is the final simplified answer.

Choice B is the result of not applying FOIL in the second step and instead multiplying the first and last terms, and choice D is the result of not using the correct common denominator.

8. **The correct answer is 9.** It is helpful to first clear all fractions in each equation:

$$3\left(\frac{2}{3}x - y\right) = 3(3)$$

$$2\left(\frac{1}{2}x\right) = 2(2y) \;\Rightarrow$$

$$2x - 3y = 9$$

$$x = 4y$$

The second equation gives the value of x in terms of y, making substitution a good method to use:

$$2(4y) - 3y = 9$$
$$8y - 3y = 9$$
$$5y = 9$$
$$y = \frac{9}{5}$$

Given this, you can now find the value of x and $x+y$:

$$x = 4y = 4\left(\frac{9}{5}\right) = \frac{36}{5}$$

$$x + y = \frac{9}{5} + \frac{36}{5} = \frac{45}{5} = 9$$

9. **The correct answer is 3.**

If the absolute value of a number is more than 5, that means it is more than 5 units away from 0 on the number line. Therefore it must be smaller than –5 or larger than 5.

Mathematically:

$$\left|2x - \frac{1}{3}\right| > 5 \;\Rightarrow\; 2x - \frac{1}{3} > 5 \text{ or}$$

$$2x - \frac{1}{3} < -5$$

Since the question asks about positive integers, you need to worry only about the first inequality.

$$2x - \frac{1}{3} > 5$$

$$2x > \frac{16}{3}$$

$$x > \frac{16}{6} = \frac{8}{3} = 2\frac{2}{3}$$

The smallest integer that is larger than $2\frac{2}{3}$ is 3.

10. The correct answer is $\dfrac{2}{15}$.

For the system to have multiple solutions, one equation must be a multiple of the other. Checking the coefficients for *a:*

$$(3a) \times \text{constant} = 2a$$
$$\text{constant} = \frac{2a}{3a} = \frac{2}{3}$$

You can verify that this is the correct constant by also checking the coefficients for *b*. Therefore:

$$s = \frac{2}{3}\left(\frac{1}{5}\right) = \frac{2}{15}$$

SUMMING IT UP

- There are four main content areas the SAT® Math Test will cover: The Heart of Algebra, Problem Solving and Data Analysis, Passport to Advanced Math (advanced functions and equations), and Additional Topics in Math (geometry, trigonometry, and complex numbers).

- About 80 percent of the SAT® Math Test questions are multiple-choice questions, and about 20 percent are grid-in questions for which you must come up with your own answer.

- About 33 percent of SAT® Math Test questions fall into the Heart of Algebra category, which covers linear equations and systems, and includes topics like manipulating numbers and expressions, translating word problems, creating and solving linear equations and inequalities, solving and graphing systems of linear equations and inequalities, and working with absolute values.

- The hardest questions on the SAT® Math Test include multiple steps—if you look closely, the individual steps will usually involve basic math; you'll just have to perform three to four steps correctly to solve.

- When faced with a radical expression, your first step should be to look for a way to simplify. Once your numerator and denominator are factored, cancel like factors before you solve.

- A complex number is a number of the form $a + bi$, where a and b are both real numbers and $i^2 = -1$.

- Knowing the following pattern will help you answer questions involving high powers of i. Find the closest multiple of 4 that is no bigger than the exponent. Subtract that multiple from the exponent, and find the value of i to that power for your answer:
  - $i = \sqrt{-1}$
  - $i^2 = -1$
  - $i^3 = i^2 \times i = -i$
  - $i^4 = i^2 \times i^2 = -1 \times -1 = 1$

- The denominator of a fraction must always be a rational number—your goal is to make it rational before you calculate. Multiply the numerator and denominator by the conjugate of the denominator. (The conjugate of a complex number $a + bi$ is $a - bi$.)

- If an equation involves fractions, the first thing you should do is multiply both sides of the equation by the least common denominator of all fractions appearing in the equation to clear them and make calculations easier to work with.

- For any real number a, the *absolute value of a*, denoted $|a|$, is the distance between a and 0:

$$|a| = \begin{cases} a, \text{ if } a \geq 0 \\ -a, \text{ if } a < 0 \end{cases}$$

- If the absolute value portion of an equation is mixed with other terms, the first step is always to isolate the absolute-value expression.

- When solving a system of linear equations, identify ordered pairs (x, y) that satisfy *both* equations. There are only three possibilities that can occur:

  ○ The graphs of the lines in the system are parallel = 0 solutions

  ○ The graphs of the lines in the system intersect in a single point = 1 solution

  ○ The graphs of the lines in the system are the same = Infinitely many solutions

- In linear equations, y = starting point + (rate of change)x. The starting point is the number that doesn't get influenced when other factors change. The rate of change is a factor that will cause an increase or decrease in the final value of a relationship as one of the conditions changes.

CHAPTER 6:
PROBLEM SOLVING
AND DATA ANALYSIS

OVERVIEW

- Problem Solving and Data Analysis: An Overview
- Ratios and Proportional Relationships, Percentages, and Units
- Sneaky Averages
- Representing Quantitative Data
- Probabilities
- Problem Solving and Data Analysis Practice Questions
- Summing It Up

PROBLEM SOLVING AND DATA ANALYSIS: AN OVERVIEW

Approximately 29 percent (17 of 58) of the questions on the SAT® Math Test will assess your knowledge of Problem Solving and Data Analysis. These multiple-choice and open-response questions will be on the Calculator section of the exam. Pay attention; the topics covered in this category of the SAT® Math Test will be the most practical and widely used skills you'll encounter in both your personal life as well as in a variety of different careers.

As you practice with questions on the SAT® Math Test, you'll notice that many of the questions in the problem-solving section deal with real-life topics and data. For instance, you might see questions that deal with science-related topics such as experimental research or social studies situations like population studies. These types of questions are more authentic and exemplify the efforts made to create a test format that better reflects real life.

RATIOS AND PROPORTIONAL RELATIONSHIPS, PERCENTAGES, AND UNITS

A ratio is a comparison of two different quantities, and a proportion is any equation that sets two ratios equal to one another. Problems on the SAT® Math Test will often ask you to solve for a missing value using ratios or proportions. You will need to integrate skills you have learned in algebra in order to solve and manipulate these equations (refer back to Chapter 5 if you need a refresher on the toughest algebra concepts).

Let's look at an example of a question testing your knowledge of proportions.

Example:

The ratio of *easy : moderate : difficult* exam questions on a particular standardized test is 3:7:2. On one version of this exam, there are 30 more moderate than difficult items. How many total questions are on this exam?

Solution:

One method that can be used to solve this problem is to set up an algebraic equation to represent the total number of items using the ratio provided:

Total # of items = 3x (easy) + 7x (moderate) + 2x (difficult)

We are given a fact about the relationship between items, so let's write down what we know. Because there are 30 more moderate than difficult questions, we can create the following equation:

7x (moderate) = 2x (difficult) + 30

Then, solve the equation:

$$7x = 2x + 30$$
$$x = 6$$

Substituting $x = 6$ in the ratio $3x : 7x : 2x$ gives us 18 easy, 42 moderate, and 12 difficult questions. Thus, there are a total of $18 + 42 + 12 = 72$ exam items.

Look for Ways to Simplify

You likely know that cross-multiplying is a way to simplify a proportion. (To cross-multiply $\frac{a}{b} = \frac{c}{d}$, compute $ad = bc$.) Whenever possible, always make sure to reduce each side of the equation before cross-multiplying. This will not only save you time later but also reduce the chances of computation errors. It is more efficient to solve for x in the simplified proportion $\frac{2x}{13} = \frac{x-4}{1}$ than it is to solve the equivalent proportion $\frac{6x}{39} = \frac{4x-16}{4}$.

In some problems, all you will need to do is creatively manipulate ratios and proportions. In these cases, you aren't looking for a numerical solution, but rather an equivalent expression or equation. For instance, consider the following example:

If $\dfrac{x+y}{y} = \dfrac{4}{5}$, which of the following is also true?

A. $\dfrac{x}{y} = -\dfrac{1}{5}$

B. $\dfrac{x}{y} = \dfrac{1}{5}$

C. $\dfrac{x-y}{y} = \dfrac{2}{5}$

D. $\dfrac{x+y}{x} = 4$

Cross-multiplying would give you:

$5(x + y) = 4y$	Distribute
$5x + 5y = 4y$	Combine like terms
$5x = -y$	

Continue to rearrange the equality so that you have both variables, x and y, on the same side. To do this, you can divide both sides by x to get $\dfrac{-y}{x} = 5$ and then divide both sides by -1 to get $\dfrac{y}{x} = -5$. Then find the reciprocal: $\dfrac{x}{y} = -\dfrac{1}{5}$. **The correct answer is A.**

Another method of solving this problem would be to consider alternative ways to write the initial equation. The fraction $\dfrac{x+y}{y}$ can be written equivalently as $\dfrac{x}{y} + \dfrac{y}{y}$, which simplifies to $\dfrac{x}{y} + 1$. Now in this proportion, we have $\dfrac{x}{y} + 1 = \dfrac{4}{5}$. Subtract 1 from both sides to get $\dfrac{x}{y} = -\dfrac{1}{5}$. So, $\dfrac{y}{x} = -5$.

NOTE: Perhaps the simplest way of solving a multiple-choice question that involves variables is to select and substitute values for x and y that make the proportion true:

$$\frac{x+y}{y} = \frac{4}{5}$$

Always choose the simplest values possible. In this proportion, setting y equal to 5 appears to be the simplest substitution. From there, you can quickly determine from $x + 5 = 4$ that $x = -1$, and a quick scan of the answer choices will reveal the correct answer choice.

Here is another example of a tough ratio question that is a little harder than it might initially seem.

If the ratio of a to b is 2 to 5 and the ratio of a to c is 8 to 3, what is the ratio of b to c?

A. 3:20

B. 7:11

C. 20:3

D. 11:7

As always, start solving by writing down *all* the given information first. Set up proportions to represent these ratios:

$$\frac{a}{b} = \frac{2}{5} \quad \text{and} \quad \frac{a}{c} = \frac{8}{3}$$

Is there a way to manipulate the ratios $a:b$ and $a:c$ so that we can see the relationship $b:c$?

$$\frac{a}{b} \times \frac{c}{a} = \frac{c}{b}$$

Now, substitute the values given values for a, b, and c:

$$\frac{2}{5} \times \frac{3}{8} = \frac{6}{40}, \text{ or } \frac{3}{20}$$

Thus, the ratio c to b is 3:20.

But you're not done! Note that the question asks for the ratio of b to c, so the correct solution is 20:3, which means **the correct answer is C**.

 ALERT: It would have been very easy to do all of the work correctly and then carelessly select choice A for the answer because you didn't answer exactly what the question asked. Don't waste your hard work by making a careless mistake at the end!

UNITS

Knowing how to deftly convert from one unit to another will likely come in handy on the SAT® exam. Familiarity with basic unit conversions, like hours to seconds, miles to feet, etc., is important, but the hardest questions go a step beyond these typical calculations by asking you to combine several conversions in several steps.

Take a look at the following sample problem.

Example:

A race car can accelerate from 0 miles per hour to 70 miles per hour in 45 seconds. What is the acceleration expressed in feet per minute^2?

Solution:

Remember that acceleration is the rate of change of velocity of an object with respect to time: $a = \frac{\Delta v}{\Delta t}$.

In this example, you are provided with the change in velocity, 70 mph – 0 mph, and the change in time, 45 seconds – 0 seconds.

In order to change the units from miles, hours, and seconds to feet and minutes, identify the conversion factors:

$$1 \text{ mile} = 5,280 \text{ feet}$$

$$1 \text{ hour} = 60 \text{ minutes}$$

$$1 \text{ minute} = 60 \text{ seconds}$$

Let's start with the velocity. We want to convert the miles/hour to feet/minute:

$$\frac{70 \text{ miles}}{1 \text{ hour}} \times \frac{5,280 \text{ feet}}{1 \text{ mile}} \times \frac{1 \text{ hour}}{60 \text{ minutes}} = \frac{6,160 \text{ feet}}{\text{minute}}$$

Then convert the time from seconds to minutes:

$$\frac{45 \text{ seconds}}{1} \times \frac{1 \text{ minute}}{60 \text{ seconds}} = 0.75 \text{ minute}$$

Placing this back into the acceleration formula, we get:

$$a = \frac{\Delta v}{\Delta t} = \frac{\dfrac{6,160 \text{ feet}}{1 \text{ minute}}}{0.75 \text{ minute}} = 8,213 \text{ feet/minute}^2$$

The SAT® exam will assess your ability to apply unit conversions to the concept of area. For example, in the following question, notice the dimensions of the room are given in feet but the carpet is sold in square yards:

Example:

The living room in Tabitha's home is 18 feet long by 14 feet wide. The carpet she will install costs $16 per square yard. What will be the total price of the carpeting for Tabitha's living room?

Solution:

Always start by sketching a simple diagram that illustrates what you are given:

14 ft.

18 ft.

$l = 18$ ft.
$w = 14$ ft.

price of carpet = $16/sq. yd.

Then, convert the dimensions of Tabitha's living room to yards, and calculate the area and the corresponding price.

Convert the length from feet to yards:

$$\frac{18 \text{ ft.}}{1} \times \frac{1 \text{ yd.}}{3 \text{ ft.}} = 6 \text{ yd.}$$

Convert the width from feet to yards:

$$\frac{14 \text{ ft.}}{1} \times \frac{1 \text{ yd.}}{3 \text{ ft.}} = \frac{14}{3} \text{ yd.}$$

Calculate the area and total cost:

$$\text{Total Area} = 6 \text{ yd.} \times \frac{14}{3} \text{ yd.} = 28 \text{ yd.}^2$$

$$\text{Total Cost} = 28 \text{ yd.} \times \frac{\$16}{\text{yd.}^2} = \$448$$

At \$16 per square yard, 28 square yards of carpeting will cost Tabitha \$448.

Another approach to solving this problem is to calculate the area of the living room first, and then convert the resulting area of square feet to square yards.

What is the area of Tabitha's living room?

Since $A = LW$, we have $A = (18 \text{ ft.})(14 \text{ ft.}) = 252 \text{ ft.}^2$

Remember that 1 yard = 3 feet, so 1 square yard will be equal to a square that is 3 feet by 3 feet:

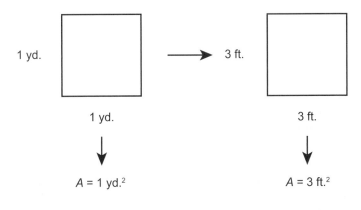

$$1 \text{ yd.}^2 = 9 \text{ ft.}^2$$

Therefore, a square yard is equivalent to 9 square feet, which can be used to make the conversion ratio $\dfrac{1 \text{ yd.}^2}{9 \text{ ft.}^2}$.

Multiply the area of 252 square feet by the conversion ratio to change the square footage into square yards:

$$\frac{252 \text{ ft.}^2}{1} \times \frac{1 \text{ yd.}^2}{9 \text{ ft.}^2} = 28 \text{ yd.}^2$$

Finally, at $16 per square yard, 28 square yards of carpeting will cost Tabitha $448.

Here is an example of another unit rates conversion problem that requires you to apply your knowledge of unit rates and percentages to exchange rates.

Example:

A toy company in the United States purchases its plastic parts from a manufacturing company in China. For one batch of parts, the manufacturing company charges a set price and then adds a 12 percent transportation fee. If the toy company pays $675 for the batch, what was the original price charged without the transportation fee in Chinese yuan? (1 yuan = 0.14 dollar)

Solution:

Let x = price of the batch in yuan.

Then $x + 0.12x$ = the total price that the manufacturing company charged in yuan, including the 12 percent transportation fee.

Use the given conversion factor of 1 yuan = 0.14 dollars:

$$\frac{(x + 0.12x) \text{ yuan}}{1} \times \frac{0.14 \text{ dollars}}{1 \text{ yuan}} = 675$$

$$(1.12x)(0.14) = 675$$

Solving for x gives us x = 4,304.85. The manufacturing company in China charged 4,304.85 yuan for the batch.

PERCENTAGES

Problems involving percentages are commonplace on the SAT® Math Test. While it's true that you can use your calculator for many, there are some basic rules to remember when working with percentages. (We covered these back in Chapter 5.) Now, let's dig a little deeper.

One concept that is often deceptive is what happens when a number is increased and then decreased by the same percentage (or vice versa). For example, at first glance, one might think that if a stock drops 20 percent on Monday and then increases by 20 percent on Tuesday, it is back at 100 percent of its Monday starting price. This is not the case! When you need to use two or more percentage manipulations to determine a final percentage value, use a starting point of 100 as your sample to work with. This way the final result translates easily into a percentage, since you'll be comparing it to the initial value of 100.

Say the stock had a value of 100 on Monday morning. It dropped by 20 percent on Monday, so it had a value of 80 on Tuesday morning. It is this new Tuesday morning value of 80 that is increased by 20 percent; in other words, $(0.20)(80) = 16$. So, its value is then $80 + 16 = 96$, or 96 percent of its Monday starting price.

 TIP When you need to use two or more percentage manipulations to determine a final percentage value, use a theoretical starting point of 100.

You may also find it helpful to represent this change in percentage algebraically:

Let x = starting value on Monday morning.

$x - 0.2x$ = starting value on Tuesday morning after the 20% drop

$x - 0.2x + 0.2(x - 0.2x)$ = value after the 20% increase on Tuesday's value

$x - 0.2x + 0.2(x - 0.2x)$

$$x - 0.2x + 0.2(x - 0.2x)$$

Monday Morning

Tuesday Morning

Wednesday Morning

Here is another question asking for a similar type of calculation.

Example:

Starting at 9 a.m., the temperature increases by 30 percent until 2 p.m., then drops by 40 percent until 9 p.m. The temperature at 9 p.m. is what percentage of the morning temperature at 9 a.m.?

Start this question by assuming that the starting temperature was 100°F. After a 30 percent increase during the day, the temperature would be 130°F. A 40 percent decrease in the evening would mean a drop of 52°F (40% of 130 is 52). Subtracting 52° from 130° yields 78°. Since the starting temperature we chose was 100°, the final temperature of 78° is 78 percent of the original temperature.

In other words, $x + 0.3x - 0.4 (0.3x + x) = 0.78x$.

Using the starting value of 100, we can see that:

$$100 + 0.3(100) - 0.4((0.3)(100)+100) = 78$$

Another percentage concept that can be tricky deals with a compounding percentage increase or decrease. For example, if a population drops by 10 percent four years in a row, one might initially think it will experience a 40 percent decrease. However, this is not the case. Instead, a 10 percent decrease every year to a population of p people will be 90 percent of the previous year's population. The expression that would represent the population each successive year would look like this:

Years	Population After 15% Decrease
0	p
1	$0.90p$
2	$0.90(0.90p) = 0.81p$
3	$0.90(0.81p) = 0.729p$
4	$0.90(0.729p) = 0.6561p$

So after 4 years, the population is 65.6 percent of the starting population—not just 60 percent of the initial population.

SNEAKY AVERAGES

Finding the average, or mean, of a list of numbers is a pretty simple concept, but there are a few different types of sneaky average questions that often trip up even the shrewdest students. Be on the lookout for questions that blend finding averages with a bit of algebra. Merging two different concepts or skill sets is very, very common on the SAT® exam. Students often find this difficult because you often learn skills one at a time and may not synthesize and use these skills *together*, especially to solve applied problems like the following.

Example:

Parker is performing in a gymnastics meet where her competition score will be the average of her scores on high beam, uneven bars, vault, and floor. After receiving the following scores, what must she score on her floor routine in order to have a competition score of 9.2?

Event	Score
High beam	8.9
Uneven bars	9.3
Vault	9.1
Floor	

Solution:

When asked to find the number needed to arrive at a particular average, many students make a common mistake of taking the average of the given data and then weighing that average equally with the missing data point. *Do not* start this problem by taking the average of 8.9, 9.3, and 9.1. This approach would weigh her floor performance as equally important as the other three events combined, which is incorrect. Instead, set up an average equation with 4 events, allowing f to be her score on the floor event, and then solve for *f*:

$$\frac{8.9+9.3+9.1+f}{4}=9.2$$

Solving for *f*, you should get 9.5.

 ALERT: When finding the last value needed to arrive at a desired average, do *not* first take the average of the known values. Instead, set up an equation to calculate the mean and solve for the missing variable.

Here is another example that requires you to understand and apply the concept and formula for the mean of a set of data as well as integrate your knowledge of algebraic equations and solving for unknown variables.

Example:

Cider Mill Farm regularly collects data on the weight of apples that grow in its orchards. Based on a sample of 50 apples, Cider Mill proclaimed that the average weight of its apples was 92 grams. After examining the data again, it was discovered that one of the apples was actually a small pumpkin! After removing the outlier, the new average weight was 11 grams less than their original claim. What was the weight of the small pumpkin masquerading as an apple?

Solution:

To solve this problem, remember how means are calculated:

$$\frac{\text{sum of apple weights}}{\text{numbers of apples weighed}} = \text{average weight of apples}$$

In this example, we know that the average weight of the 50 apples (including the one pumpkin) is 92. Therefore, $\frac{\text{sum of apple weight}}{50} = 92$.

By cross-multiplying, we find that the sum of apple weight $= 50 \times 92 = 4{,}600$ grams.

Now, we can set up a new equation equal to the corrected average:

$$\frac{\text{sum of apple weight} - \text{weight of baby pumpkin}}{\text{numbers of apples weighed} - 1 \text{ baby pumpkin}} = 92 - 11$$

$$\frac{4{,}600 - x}{49} = 81$$

Cross-multiplying, we get $(49)(81) = 4{,}600 - x$, and solving for x gives us 631. The baby pumpkin weighed 631 grams.

Another tricky problem type involves weighted averages. Consider the following example.

Example:

Guests at Sierra's Serene Urban Oasis rate their hotel experience on a starring system that ranges from 1 to 7 stars. What is the average number of stars Sierra's Serene Urban Oasis received on Monday, to the nearest 0.1 stars?

Number of Stars	Number of Reviews with These Stars
1	0
2	2
3	3
4	5
5	7
6	12
7	8

Solution:

The math in this type of problem is very simple. It's the setup, and then the many calculations within, where errors can easily sneak in. Don't just take the average of the numbers in the left- or right-hand columns. First, add an additional column to the right side of the table and use that column to record the products of each row: (*number of stars*) × (*number of reviews*). This takes into account the relative weight of each star rating.

Number of Stars	Number of Reviews with These Stars	Subtotals of Stars Earned:
1	0	$1 \times 0 = 0$
2	2	$2 \times 2 = 4$
3	3	$3 \times 3 = 9$
4	5	$4 \times 5 = 20$
5	7	$5 \times 7 = 35$
6	12	$6 \times 12 = 72$
7	8	$7 \times 8 = 56$

The sum of the right-most column shows us that 196 stars were earned in total. The sum of the middle column indicates that there were 37 total reviews. Now divide the 196 number of stars earned by the 37 reviews to determine that the average review was 5.3 stars.

NOTE: Weighted averages are calculated by taking into account the relative weight of each value in a set. These weightings determine the importance of each value on the overall average. In the previous example, the star ratings influence on the overall average star rating depended on the frequency of reviews, as shown in the middle column of the table.

Tough questions involving mean might also ask about other statistical measures of central tendency, like the median and mode, and measures of variation like range and standard deviation of a set of data. Here is one example of a question testing your knowledge of these different values.

An investor records the average value of his stock each month over the course of a year. The monthly averages values remained relatively steady, except in the month of December, when the stock plummeted dramatically. None of the months had the exact same stock value as another. The investor then calculates the median, range, mean, and standard deviation of all of his monthly averages. He also calculates these same measures without including the average for the month of December. Which of the following can the investor conclude from his two data sets?

A. The mean and median will be equal in the data set that does not include December.

B. The standard deviation will be greater for the set that does not include December.

C. The mean will be less than the median in the set that includes December's data.

D. The median will not be affected by the removal of December from the data set.

This question does not require you to perform any calculations, but it does require you to understand the concepts of mean, median, range, and standard deviation and how outliers impact them. Let's look at each choice one by one:

Choice A: The mean and median will likely be similar in the data set that does not include December, since the problem states that the months were relatively consistent. Without seeing the exact values, we would be unable to determine the exact value of the mean and median to confirm that they are equivalent.

Choice B: The standard deviation is a measure of the amount of variation in the data set. December's stock value will increase the standard deviation because it introduces greater variability in the stock values overall.

Choice C: This is the correct answer. Like the standard deviation, means are greatly affected by outliers. December's low stock values will draw the mean down but will not affect the median greatly, because the median is based on the middle value when the stock values are arranged in sequential order from least to greatest.

Choice D: Instead of calculating the median of 12 values, the investor would calculate the median based on 11 values (without December), which would change the value of the median since none of the months have the same stock value.

For problems that do not provide numerical values and require you to think conceptually about the meaning of values and formulas, it may be helpful to create a small subset of data to experiment with. In the previous example, you could create a set of 12 imaginary and simple stock values arranged in order from lowest to greatest: 1, 6, 7, 8, 9, 10, 11, 12, 13, 14, 15, 16, where 1 would be the low outlier of December. You could then calculate the mean, median, range, and standard deviation of the set of data, and then recalculate with the value of 1 removed. This will allow you to see the pattern of the measures of central tendency and variation and enable you to draw valid conclusions.

REPRESENTING QUANTITATIVE DATA

Quantitative data is often represented using graphs and charts to create a visual of the data from which to analyze and draw conclusions. For the SAT® Math Test, you should know how to work with the basic types of visual representations and understand how to interpret them. The summary below gives you a quick review of some of the common representations used on the test.

DATA TABLES

Data tables show a summary of data points in a linear way. Tables use rows (horizontal) and columns (vertical) where each cross-section represents a data value.

The two-way table below represents a survey of undergraduate, graduate, and continuing education students in a state university that asked where participants received the majority of their world news. Results were counted for each age group of students.

	TV	Internet	Newspaper
18–22	12	51	2
23–49	44	33	17
Over 50	24	7	17

From data tables like this, you should be able to answer questions like the following:

- How many students responded to the survey?
- What proportion of students surveyed were undergraduate students?
- What proportion of students surveyed reported receiving their world news from the Internet?
- What proportion of those aged 50 or over surveyed received their news from TV?
- Is there a relationship between age group and preference for world news sources?

In order to calculate these values, fill in the margins of the table with the total number of students surveyed in each age group.

	TV	Internet	Newspaper	Total
18–22	12	51	2	**65**
23–49	44	33	17	**94**
Over 50	24	7	17	**48**
Total	**80**	**91**	**36**	**207**

- There were 207 total students who responded to the survey.
- Undergraduate students, shown as the 18–22 age group, made up $\frac{65}{207}$, or 31.4 percent, of the survey responses.
- $\frac{91}{207}$, or 43.9 percent, of the students surveyed reported receiving their world news from the Internet.
- $\frac{24}{48}$, or 50 percent, of those aged 50 or over received their news from TV.

In order to determine if there is a relationship between age group and news source, calculate the relative proportions for each age group. Looking only at the numbers in the table can be deceiving. As an example, if you look only at the numbers in the Newspaper column, you may think that there is no difference between students over 50 and students in the 23–49 age range in terms of their preference for the newspaper as their world news source. If you calculate the relative proportions however, $\frac{17}{94}$ students versus $\frac{17}{48}$ of those over 50, it is clear that a greater proportion of older adults (over 50) prefer the newspaper than do the young to middle-aged adults (23–49).

> When examining data tables, pay careful attention to the variables in question, the subtotals for each row and column, and the relative proportions.

When working through a problem for which the data is organized tabularly, the key is to understand what each data value represents. In the example below, you can read the table across starting with the number of children. By reading across each row of the table, you can form a "story" of the data. What does each column and each row of the table tell you?

A researcher chose 200 adult households at random from two counties: Greenwood County and Indigo Lake County. Both counties were part of a 10-year experiment to reduce birth rate. Each county took different measures in the past

10 years to reduce birth rate, including educational programs, parent groups, and other incentives. The researcher asked each adult the number of children under the age of 10 in their household. The results are shown in the table below.

Number of Children (Under 10 Years)	Greenwood County	Indigo Lake County
0	32	19
1	31	27
2	22	41
3	11	12
4	4	1

There are a total of 1,200 adult households in Greenwood County and 2,100 adult households in Indigo Lake County. Based on the data collected by the researcher, which of the following best describes the expected number of households with 3 or more children (under the age of 10) in each county?

A. The total number of households with 3 or more children is expected to be equal for the two counties.

B. The total number of households with 3 or more children in Greenwood County is expected to be 93 more than in Indigo Lake County.

C. The total number of households with 3 or more children in Indigo Lake County is expected to be 93 more than in Greenwood County.

D. The total number of households with 3 or more children in Greenwood County is expected to be 2 more than in Indigo Lake County.

In this example, the researcher is using the data from a sample of 200 households to predict the expected number with 3 or more children in each county. If you add up the totals in each column, you will see that the researcher surveyed exactly 100 households from each county.

In Greenwood County, $\dfrac{(11+4)}{100}$ households had 3 or more children.

In Indigo Lake County, $\dfrac{(12+1)}{100}$ households had 3 or more children.

This gives us the relative proportions $\dfrac{15}{100}$ and $\dfrac{13}{100}$, respectively.

We can use this relative proportion to calculate the expected total number of households with 3 or more children in each county:

$$\text{Greenwood County: } \dfrac{15}{100} \times 1{,}200 = 180$$

$$\text{Indigo Lake County: } \dfrac{13}{100} \times 2{,}100 = 273$$

We would therefore expect Indigo Lake County to have approximately 93 more households with 3 or more children under 10 than Greenwood County. **The correct answer is C.**

TAKING PREDICTION SKILLS ONE STEP FURTHER

Does this mean that Greenwood Lake used better birth rate reduction methods? Examine the other values in the table and think about how you could determine if there is a significant difference between the two counties in terms of the distribution of the number of children in each household.

Always remember that when a random survey is mentioned in a question, it means that you can use the survey's results to mirror the larger population. So, for instance, if in a sample, a% of the sample behaves a certain way, this holds for the larger population because the small sample is representative of the larger population.

To illustrate: Suppose you are baking a batch of cupcakes for a large party. Three hundred cupcakes need to be frosted. The cupcake frosting consists of cream cheese, butter, chocolate chips, and sprinkles. You mix the frosting thoroughly to get rid of any lumping of ingredients and then taste a small spoonful to make sure the consistency and distribution of chocolate and sprinkles is appropriate. This should give you a good idea of how the rest of the frosting tastes. You don't need to taste all of the frosting—you don't even need to take a larger spoonful. A small spoonful is enough to make a judgment about the overall frosting.

This is the same for a population. If you want to find out about a large population, take a random sample (this is equivalent to mixing the frosting and then taking a spoonful) and use the data you collect to draw conclusions about the larger population. If the sample is not random, you may end up with biased results. If the frosting in the cupcake batch was not mixed well, you might end up with a spoonful without any sprinkles!

Tips for tackling survey data questions on the SAT® Math Test:

- Read the data carefully and define what each variable and its associated values mean.
- Identify minimum and maximum values.
- Remember that survey results from a small sample can be used to represent the larger population.

LINE GRAPHS

Line graphs show the relationship between two variables. Pay attention to the scale used on each axis—the scale can often be used to distort the graph to exaggerate or minimize a potential relationship between the two variables. In the following scatterplot, draw a line to connect each point for the sets of data points. Use the relative slopes to compare the rate of change in growth between the two treatment groups.

A laboratory is experimenting with two different types of artificial lights and their effect on plant growth in the absence of natural sunlight. Two seeds from the same plant are placed in separate pots with soil, and one pot is assigned Light A and the other Light B. All other factors (like watering) are held constant. The height of each plant (in cm) is measured over a period of 16 weeks. Which of the following statements correctly compares the rate of growth under the two different light treatments?

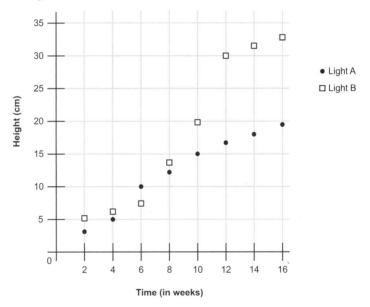

A. The average rate of change over the 16-week period is approximately the same for the plants under both light conditions.

B. The rate of change for both plants was greatest between the 10th and 12th week.

C. The plant with Light A treatment experienced a greater rate of growth than the plant with Light B treatment in the first 6 weeks, and the plant with Light B treatment experienced a greater rate of growth in weeks 6 to 12.

D. The plant with Light B treatment experienced a greater rate of growth than the plant with Light A treatment in the first 6 weeks, and the plant with Light A treatment experienced a greater rate of growth from weeks 12 to 16.

Examine the relative slopes between each set of points (Light A versus Light B). Use the data points to determine more closely the rates of change. You will notice that while the plant under Light A treatment experiences an overall gradual growth, with its greatest change in growth between the 4th and 6th week, the plant under Light B treatment experiences slow growth for the first 6 weeks and then a rapid increase between weeks 6 and 12 (choice C). In some problems, you may be asked to calculate the exact rate of change between two values. For example, the plant under Light A experienced a growth of 5 cm between week 4 and 6, which is a rate of $\frac{5}{2}$ = 2.5 cm/week, whereas the plant under Light B experienced a growth of 10 cm between weeks 10 and 12, which is a rate of $\frac{10}{2}$ = 5 cm/week.

SCATTERPLOTS

Scatterplots show potential relationships between two variables. With scatterplots, note the pattern of the points. Ask yourself whether they are close together, far apart, clustering around a region of the graph, or show a distinct linear or other pattern.

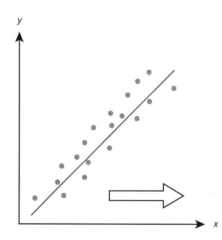

For this scatterplot, the x- and y-variables show a positive correlation—as the x-values increase, the y-values also increase. The line is considered a line of best fit (or trend line) because it shows the best representation of the linear pattern of the data. A line of best fit may pass through all, some, or none of the actual points.

Scatterplots with a negative correlation show that as the x-value increases, the y-value decreases.

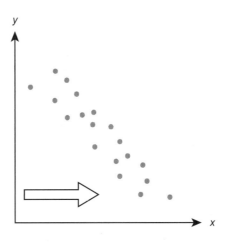

Let's see how questions using scatterplots might be presented on the test.

A fitness center is examining the relationship between different types of exercises among its participants. The center randomly selects seven of its members and records the maximum number of consecutive pull-ups the member can perform in one minute and the maximum number of jump ropes the member can perform consecutively in one minute. The scatterplot below shows each member's performance. Use this scatterplot to answer the questions that follow.

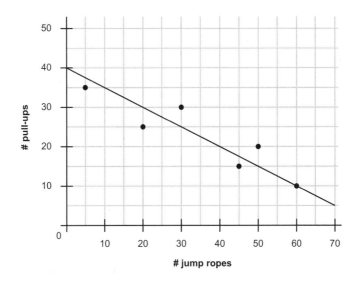

1. Describe the correlation between the variables.

    There appears to be a negative correlation between number of pull-ups and number of consecutive jump ropes that can be completed in one minute. The points are relatively close to the line of best fit, indicating a strong relationship.

2. Use the line of best fit to predict the number of consecutive jump ropes that a member would be able to do if they can complete 50 pull-ups in one minute. Interpret this prediction.

    Calculate the line of best fit by identifying two points on the line and calculating the slope and y-intercept. Two easily identifiable points on the line of best fit are (0, 40) and (60, 10). This gives us a slope of $\frac{(10-40)}{(60-0)} = \frac{-30}{60} = \frac{-1}{2}$. Since the y-intercept happens to be one of the points (0, 40) we selected, the line of best fit is $y = -\frac{1}{2}x + 40$. If we substitute the value $y = 50$ into the equation, we get $50 = -\frac{1}{2}x + 40$. Solving for x gives us –20. The equation predicts that a member who can complete 50 pull-ups would be able to complete –20 jump ropes. This prediction obviously does not make sense, since one cannot do a negative number of jump ropes. This problem illustrates one of the dangers of extrapolation from a very small sample size. The line of best fit would be better used to predict the expected number of pull-ups or jump ropes *within* the range of sample values.

3. Interpret the slope and y-intercept of the line of best fit.

    The slope of $-\frac{1}{2}$ indicates that for every additional jump rope that a member can complete, the number of pull-ups that the member can complete decreases by a factor of $\frac{1}{2}$. The y-intercept of (0, 40) indicates that if a member could not do any jump ropes, he or she would be expected to be able to complete 40 pull-ups. This may not be realistic but is what this particular sample of seven fitness members reveals.

HISTOGRAMS

Histograms display a distribution of quantitative and continuous data. Though similar to bar graphs, histograms are unique in that they show data continuously; in other words, they allow you to visually represent frequencies for intervals and not just categorical data. Histograms also allow you to see the overall distribution of the graph. In the following example, we see the distribution of physicians at Meadowbrook General Hospital by experience, or years of active practice.

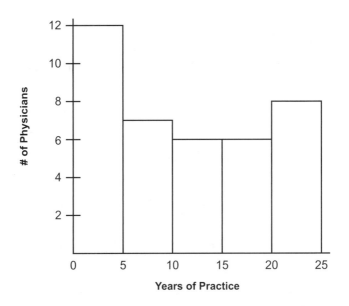

Use this histogram to answer the following questions:

1. How many physicians are practicing at Meadowbrook General Hospital?

Add up the frequencies in the histogram to determine the total number of practicing physicians: $12 + 7 + 6 + 6 + 8 = 39$ physicians.

2. What is the median number of years of active practice for the physicians at this hospital?

The median is the middle value of a set of values ordered from least to greatest. Since there are 39 values, the median should lie at the 20th value. This would fall in the third "bin" of the histogram, or between 10 and 15 years of active practice.

3. Describe the relationship between the mean and the median of this data.

Without having the actual data values, we cannot identify the exact value of the mean or median. We can however tell that the distribution of data is relatively symmetric with no outliers. This indicates that the mean and median will be relatively close in value. Remember that the median is relatively resistant to outliers while the mean is typically pulled in the direction of outliers.

> **TIP:** The median of a data set is usually resistant to outliers. The mean of a data set can easily be pulled in the direction of outliers.

BOX-WHISKER PLOTS

Box-whisker plots provide basic statistics for a set of data. They also allow you to see the general distribution of values: where data is concentrated, the overall range, median, and potential outliers. The following plot displays scores on a recent statistics exam.

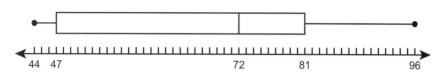

From the given box-whisker plot, we can create a Five-Number Summary:

Minimum	1st Quartile	2nd Quartile	3rd Quartile	Maximum
44	47	72	81	96
Least value (the left-most dot of the graph)	25% of the data is less than this value (the left-most line of the graph)	50% of the data is greater than this value; also the median of the data set (the middle line of the graph)	25% of the data is greater than this value (the right-most line of the graph)	Greatest value (the right-most dot of the graph)

If a student scores a 74 percent, what does this tell you about their performance in relation to the rest of the class?

A student scoring 74 percent would be between the 2nd and 3rd quartile. They would have performed better than 50 percent of their peers.

You may also be asked to compare two or more box-whisker plots, as shown in the following example.

The box plot below shows the speed of light calculated in five different experiments, as compared to the true speed of light.

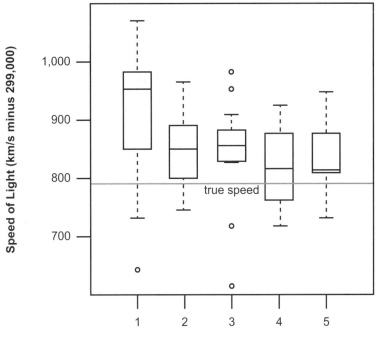

Use the graphical summary to answer the following questions:

1. Which experiment showed the greatest range of values? Which experiment showed the most consistent spread of values?

   Experiment 1 has the greatest range of values in speed of light. The minimum value, not including the outlier is around 750 and the maximum is close to 1,500! The range would be approximately 750. If you ignore outliers, Experiment 3 has the smallest range and most consistent set of values, ranging from around a low of 850 to a high of 900, a range of 50.

2. Which experiment had a median value that was closest to the true speed of light?

   The median value is represented by the dark line within each "box." Referencing the graph, we see that the median value in Experiment 5 is closest to the true speed of light.

3. If one of the values for the speed of light was 800 km/s, how does its value compare to the other values in Experiment 4?

   A value of 800 km/s would be between the 1st and 2nd quartile in Experiment 4, meaning that its value is greater than 25 percent of the other values but still within the bottom 50 percent of the data set.

PROBABILITIES

Probabilities are values between 0 and 1 that represent the chance of an event occurring. Probabilities can be represented as decimals, fractions, or percentages. By definition, the probability of a simple event is calculated by dividing the event (or outcome) by the number of total outcomes:

$$\frac{event}{\#of\ total\ outcomes}$$

Let's look at an example of a probability question.

A random group of patients who recently had their annual check-up were surveyed and asked whether or not they received a flu shot this past year and whether they came down with the flu in the subsequent year. The table below shows a summary of the data collected. If one of the surveyed patients who received a flu shot is chosen at random for a follow-up check-up, what is the probability that the patient was afflicted by the flu?

	Flu Afflicted	Not Flu Afflicted
Flu Shot	17	15
No Flu Shot	21	11

A. $\dfrac{17}{32}$

B. $\dfrac{21}{38}$

C. $\dfrac{17}{32}$

D. $\dfrac{21}{32}$

It is often helpful to first calculate the row and column totals, as shown here:

	Flu Afflicted	Not Flu Afflicted	Total
Flu Shot	17	15	32
No Flu Shot	21	11	32
Total	38	26	64

The question asks for the probability that a randomly selected patient who received a flu shot still came down with the flu.

The event = the patient was flu afflicted

Total possible outcomes = the surveyed patients who received the flu shot

$$\frac{\text{event}}{\text{\# of total outcomes}} = \frac{17}{32} \text{ (choice C)}$$

Consider the incorrect answer choices and the probabilities they represent:

- Choice A $\left(\dfrac{17}{38}\right)$ represents the probability of randomly selecting a patient who received a flu shot from among those flu afflicted.

- Choice B $\left(\dfrac{21}{38}\right)$ represents the probability of randomly selecting a patient who did not receive a flu shot from among those flu afflicted.

- Choice D $\left(\dfrac{21}{32}\right)$ represents the probability of randomly selecting a patient who was flu afflicted from among those who did not receive a flu shot.

A compound probability is a probability associated with a compound event, or one that is formed using unions, intersections, etc. of two or more simple events.

- If A and B are two events, then the event "A and B" consists of outcomes that belong to *both* A and to B.

Event	Description	Probability
A	the probability of selecting a red card from a deck of cards	$\dfrac{26}{52}$, or $\dfrac{1}{2}$
B	the probability of selecting a 4 from a deck of cards	$\dfrac{4}{52}$, or $\dfrac{1}{13}$
A and B	the probability of selecting a card that is both red and a 4	$\dfrac{2}{52}$, or $\dfrac{1}{26}$

- If A and B are two events, then the event "A or B" consists of outcomes that belong to *either* event A or event B, or *both*.

- If A and B have no outcomes in common, then P(A or B) = P(A) + P(B).

Event	Description	Probability
A	the probability of rolling a die and landing on a 6	$\dfrac{1}{6}$
B	the probability of rolling a die and landing on a 5	$\dfrac{1}{6}$
A or B	the probability of rolling a die and landing on a 5 *OR* a 6	$\dfrac{2}{6} = \dfrac{1}{3}$

- If A and B have outcomes in common, then we must account for the overlap when computing the probability. So, P(A or B) = P(A) + P(B) − P(A and B).

Event	Description	Probability
A	the probability of selecting a red card from a deck of cards	$\dfrac{26}{52}$, or $\dfrac{1}{2}$
B	the probability of selecting a 4 from a deck of cards	$\dfrac{4}{52}$, or $\dfrac{1}{13}$
A or B	the probability of selecting a red card OR a 4 **Note:** There are two cards that are both red and a 4 that must be accounted for in the calculation of probability.	$\dfrac{26}{52} + \dfrac{4}{52} - \dfrac{2}{52} = \dfrac{28}{52}$, or $\dfrac{7}{13}$

- If A and B are two events that are *independent* of each other (i.e., the fact that event B has occurred has no effect on the probability of A occurring, AND the fact that A has occurred has no effect on the probability of B occurring), then the compound probability P(A and B) = P(A) × P(B). (This type of event is often cast in the context of some experiment (like selecting a ball or a card at random) done "with replacement.")

Event	Description	Probability
A	the probability of drawing a blue marble from a bag	$\frac{2}{10}$, or $\frac{1}{5}$
B	the probability of drawing a red marble from a bag	$\frac{3}{10}$
A and B	the probability of selecting a blue marble followed by a red marble, if the blue marble is placed back in the bag before the second drawing	$\frac{1}{5} \times \frac{3}{10} = \frac{6}{100} = \frac{3}{50}$

Use the rules of compound probabilities to solve the following problem.

A group of students who either attend a public school, or a private school, or are home schooled are surveyed to identify their meal preferences. The data collected is shown in the following two-way table. If a student is chosen at random to receive a free meal, what is the probability the student will be a vegetarian public school attendee OR a non-vegetarian homeschooler?

	Vegetarian	Non-Vegetarian
Homeschooled	12	3
Public School	15	28
Private School	7	19

A. $\frac{3}{14}$

B. $\frac{11}{84}$

C. $\frac{10}{21}$

D. $\frac{11}{21}$

The key word in this problem is "OR." If we let event A = the probability the selected student is a vegetarian and attends public school and let event B = the probability the selected student is a non-vegetarian and is homeschooled, we can use the union of probabilities: P(A or B) = P(A) + P(B). Events A and B have no outcomes in common since the selected student cannot be both vegetarian and non-vegetarian and both attend public school and be homeschooled.

Of the 84 students surveyed, 15 attend public school and are vegetarian (event A), and 3 are homeschooled and non-vegetarian (event B). Thus the P(A or B) = $\frac{15}{84} + \frac{3}{84} = \frac{18}{84}$, or $\frac{3}{14}$ (choice A), once simplified.

FINDING MISSING INFORMATION

Occasionally, you will be provided the margins of a table and asked to determine the missing information. Sometimes, the level of difficulty increases when computing probabilities requires the use of algebraic techniques. For instance, consider the following example.

Example:

A popular coffee chain documents its customer orders one morning as part of a study to determine whether the business should continue to market its caffeine-free options. Fifty customer orders are randomly selected from all orders during a particular weekend morning. The data reveals that female customers ordered 8 more decaffeinated drinks than male customers, and that male customers ordered 5 less than double the number of caffeinated drinks that female customers ordered.

Solution:

Use the following partial data table given and the information provided above to determine the probability that a randomly selected customer purchased a decaffeinated beverage.

Gender	Coffee Type		
	Caffeinated	**Decaffeinated**	
Female			27
Male			
			TOTAL:

Before you start to make any kind of calculations, fill in all the values you know.

If we let x = the number of male customers that purchased a decaffeinated drink, then we know that $x + 8$ = the number of female customers that purchased a decaffeinated drink.

Similarly, if we let y = the number of female customers that purchased a caffeinated drink, then we know that $2y - 5$ = the number of male customers that purchased a caffeinated drink.

We also know from the original problem that there were 50 total customers, so if 27 are female, we know that 23 are male:

Gender	Coffee Type		
	Caffeinated	Decaffeinated	
Female	y	$x + 8$	27
Male	$2y - 5$	x	23
			TOTAL: 50

From the table, we can create a system of equations and then solve for each variable using substitution or elimination. Revisit Chapter 5 to refresh your knowledge of these methods.

$$y + x + 8 = 27$$
$$2y - 5 + x = 23$$

Simplify the two equations so that both variables are on the same side of the equation:

$$x + y = 19$$
$$x + 2y = 28$$

Let's use elimination since the x-variable will cancel out quite easily by subtracting one equation from the other:

$$\begin{array}{r} x + y = 19 \\ -\quad x + 2y = 28 \\ \hline -y = -9 \\ y = 9 \end{array}$$

Substitute $y = 9$ into one of the equations:

$$x + y = 19$$
$$x + 9 = 19$$
$$x = 10$$

If we substitute these values into the original data table, we get:

	Coffee Type		
Gender	Caffeinated	Decaffeinated	
Female	$y = 9$	$x + 8 = 18$	27
Male	$2y - 5 = 13$	$x = 10$	23
	22	28	**TOTAL: 50**

Now we can return to the original question to determine the probability that a randomly selected customer had ordered a decaffeinated beverage.

Calculating the column totals, we see that 28 customers ordered a decaffeinated beverage, so the probability would be $\frac{28}{50}$, or 0.56.

PROBLEM SOLVING AND DATA ANALYSIS PRACTICE

Complete the following problems. Answers and explanations follow on page 174.

1 A florist is creating a storefront display of roses and has already used 125 red roses and 96 white roses in a giant wreath. The florist just received a gift of 140 additional white roses to use in the display. How many more red roses should the florist add to the display so that $\frac{2}{3}$ of the total number of roses used is red?

A. 347
B. 280
C. 32
D. 229

SHOW YOUR WORK HERE

2 A kiddie train ride at the carnival travels 20 meters in 11.2 seconds. If the train goes at the same speed throughout the ride and takes 10 minutes to take its passengers in one large loop around the carnival, how long is the loop in feet? (1 meter = 3.28 feet)

A. 1,070 feet
B. 3,500 feet
C. 123 feet
D. 17.9 feet

SHOW YOUR WORK HERE

3 A rectangular flower garden is undergoing alterations in positioning and use of space. The landscaping company is planning to increase the length of the garden by 15 percent and decrease its width by a different percentage. If these changes decrease the area of the rectangle by 10%, what was the percentage change in the width?

A. 10%
B. 15%
C. 25%
D. 22%

4 A waiter at a local restaurant is curious as to whether the amount of time his patrons spend at the restaurant during the meal will affect his tips. The following scatterplot shows the percent tip the waiter received for 8 different customers and the approximate time (in minutes) each of these patrons spent at the restaurant for a meal. The time did not include time spent waiting to be seated.

SHOW YOUR WORK HERE

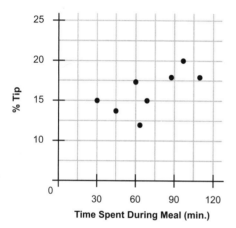

Time Spent During Meal (min.)

Based on the graph, which of the following could be the line of best fit for these points?

A. $y = -\dfrac{1}{2}x + 20$

B. $y = 6x + 11$

C. $y = \dfrac{1}{6}x + 10$

D. $y = 2x - 5$

5 To determine if Vitamin D is helpful in patients with mild to moderate depression, a research center conducted an experimental study with a group of 200 patients selected randomly from a pool of patients diagnosed with depression. One hundred participants were assigned a daily supplement of Vitamin D and the other 100 patients were assigned a placebo that looked like a vitamin supplement. The data collected revealed that the participants in the first group reported significant improvement in mood and daily functioning as compared to the group that only received the placebo. Based on the results and design of this study, which of the following can the researchers conclude?

A. Vitamin D is likely to improve mood and cognitive functioning in patients with mild to moderate depression.

B. Vitamin D improves mood and cognitive functioning in depressed patients more than other prescribed treatments.

C. Vitamin D will improve mood and cognitive functioning in all adults who take it.

D. No conclusions can be drawn because the study design is flawed.

6 A research lab is exploring whether prior training in mazes will help rats navigate subsequent but very different mazes. Some laboratory rats are randomly assigned to two groups. Group A receives prior training with one type of laboratory maze. Group B receives no training. Rats from each group are then placed into a new and more difficult maze and timed to see how long it takes them to escape. The results of the study are summarized in the box-plots below.

Rat Maze Times

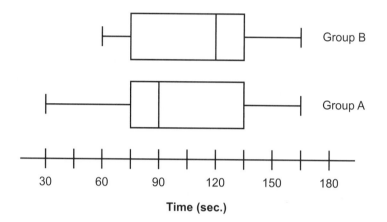

Time (sec.)

In comparing Group A to Group B, which of the following MUST be true?

A. A larger percentage of rats in Group A finished in 150 seconds or more compared to Group B.

B. There were more rats in Group A than Group B.

C. A rat that completed the maze in 105 seconds would have performed better relative to its peers if it came from Group A than from Group B.

D. A rat that completes the maze in 60 seconds must come from Group B.

7 The wingspan of a sample of monarch butterflies are measured each year at the insectarium. The butterflies are housed in two separate sections of the facility. The 14 butterflies living in Exhibit A had an average wingspan of 9.3 cm and the 19 butterflies living in Exhibit B had an average wing span of 10.1 cm. However, one of the butterflies had been moved from Exhibit A to Exhibit B during this period and its wingspan was counted in both exhibits. After correcting for this error, the insectarium workers calculated the average wingspan of all the monarch butterflies from both exhibits to be 9.7 cm. What was the wingspan of the monarch butterfly that was erroneously counted twice? (Enter your answer in the grid below.)

8 The following table shows the number of employees at a travel insurance company in 2016 that can speak one, two, three, or four or more languages, categorized by the number of countries visited. Based on the data, if an employee is selected at random from this group, what is the probability that he/she can speak 3 or more languages OR has visited 6 or more different countries?

SHOW YOUR WORK HERE

		Number of Languages Spoken			
		1	2	3	4+
Number of Countries Visited	1 or 2	12	14	4	0
	3–5	5	2	7	1
	6–9	2	7	7	1
	10+	0	1	0	1

A. 25%

B. 50%

C. 33%

D. 67%

---

9 James's starting salary at the graphic design company is $45,000. After the first year, he receives a 15% raise and each succeeding year, he is scheduled to receive a 5% raise. What will James's approximate salary be at the start of his 4th year at the company?

A. $57,000

B. $56,000

C. $59,000

D. $60,000

A local charity has four different drop-off locations for donations. Each location collects a specific category of items (clothing, toys and games, non-perishable food items, or books). The following pie chart summarizes the percentages of total donations in each category last year. One bag/box of goods is counted as a single donation item.

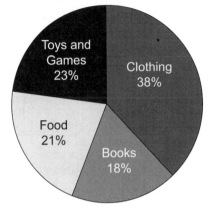

This year, the charity received 19 more donation items than last year. The number of items of clothing increased by 15% and the number of toy & game items, as well as book items, both decreased by 7%. If the number of non-perishable food items received was 13 this year, how many clothing donations were received *last year*? (Enter your answer in the grid below.)

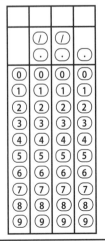

1. A	3. C	5. A	7. 11.7	9. A
2. B	4. C	6. C	8. B	10. 17

1. **The correct answer is A.** If $\frac{2}{3}$ of the total number of roses must be red, the ratio of red : white roses must be 2:1. Therefore:

$$\frac{125+x}{96+140} = \frac{2}{1}$$

Cross-multiply to get $125 + x = 472$ and $x = 347$.

Choice B ignores the roses already used in the display and calculates the number of red roses needed to create a 2:1 ratio with only the 140 white roses. Choice C calculates the proportion with the ratio 2:3 used, and choice D uses the ratio 3:2 in the proportion.

2. **The correct answer is B.** For this question, we need to convert the meters to feet and the seconds to minutes.

$$20 \text{ meters } \times \frac{3.28 \text{ feet}}{1 \text{ meter}} = 65.6 \text{ feet}$$

$$11.2 \text{ seconds } \times \frac{1 \text{ minute}}{60 \text{ seconds}} = 0.187 \text{ minutes}$$

We can now use a proportion to solve for the missing distance:

$$\frac{65.6 \text{ feet}}{0.187 \text{ minutes}} = \frac{x \text{ feet}}{10 \text{ minutes}}$$

Cross-multiply to get $0.187x = (65.6)(10)$. Solving for x to get an answer of $x \approx 3,508$ feet. The closest answer is 3,500 feet, which is choice B. Choices A, C, and D are miscalculations.

3. **The correct answer is C.** Sketch a diagram and label it with the adjusted length and width.

$W - xW$

$L + 0.15L$

New length = $1.15L$

New width $- (1 - x)W$

Original area = $A = LW$

New area = $A - 0.10A =$
$(1.15L)(1 - x)W$

We can now solve this equation for x:

$0.9A = 1.15(1 - x)(L)(W)$

Since $A = LW$, we can eliminate those variables from both sides of the equation:

$$0.9 = 1.15(1 - x)$$

$0.7826 = 1 - x$

$$x = 0.217$$

Thus, the width of the garden was decreased by approximately 22 percent (choice D).

4. **The correct answer is C.** First, identify whether the points have a generally positive or negative correlation. As time spent during the meal increases, there seems to be a general increase in percent tip, indicating a positive slope. This rules out choice A. Sketch a line through these points, trying to get as close to as many points as possible. You will notice that the y-intercept should be around 10 to 12. A y-intercept of -5 would create too steep a best-fit line to approximate the points on this plot, ruling out choice D. To take it further, calculate the slope of your best fit line. Remember to use the scale. A single unit box on the graph represents 5% for the y-variable and 15 minutes for the x-variable, so $\frac{1}{6}$ should be the best approximation of the slope among these answer choices.

5. **The correct answer is A.** The design of the study is appropriate as patients were selected randomly from a pool of depressed patients and were randomly assigned to two treatment groups. The group that did not receive a Vitamin D supplement took a placebo to control for a potential placebo effect. Because of this, the results of this small study can be generalized to the larger population of mild to moderately depressed patients, but not to the entire population of adults.

6. **The correct answer is C.** A rat that completed the maze in 105 seconds would have fallen below the median in Group B, and in the second quartile, but in Group A, the same rat would be above the median in the third quartile of rat times. Read through the other answer choices to confirm that they are false.

Choice A: This would mean that the distance from the fourth quartile to the maximum value should be greater for Group A than Group B, but the box-plot reveals that the last quartile is roughly equivalent for both groups. About 25 percent of the rats from both groups took more than 150 seconds to complete the maze.

Choice B: A box-whisker plot, unlike a scatterplot or histogram, does not tell you how many results are in the study, only a summary of the overall results. We cannot assume that there were more rats in one group or the other.

Choice D: A rat that completes the maze in 60 seconds could have come from either group. We know that a rat in Group B completed the maze in 60 seconds since the minimum value for Group B is 60, but there may have been one or more rats in Group A that also completed the maze in 60 seconds.

7. **The correct answer is 11.7.** Set up an equation using the information provided.

Exhibit A:

$$\frac{\text{sum of wingspans}}{14} = 9.3 \text{ cm}$$

sum of wing spans for Exhibit A = 130.2 cm

Exhibit B:

$$\frac{\text{sum of wingspans}}{19} = 10.1 \text{ cm}$$

sum of wing spans for Exhibit B = 191.9 cm

Note: The total number of butterflies should be 14 + 19 − 1 (to take into account the monarch that was counted twice).

Exhibits A and B:

$$\frac{\text{sum of wingspans}}{32} = 9.7 \text{ cm}$$

sum of wingspans for Exhibit A and B = 310.4 cm

The sum of the wingspans for Exhibit A and Exhibit B should equal the sum of the wingspans calculated for both in the corrected average. However, because of the monarch that is counted twice, there will be a discrepancy.

130.2 + 191.9 versus 310.4

130.2 + 191.9 − 310.4 = 11.7

Thus, the wingspan of the monarch counted twice is 11.7 cm.

8. **The correct answer is B.** Remember that the probability of two events that *share* events in common is P(A or B) = P(A) + P(B) − P(A and B).

Let A = the employee speaks 3 or more languages

Let B = the employee has visited 6 or more countries

A and B = the employee speaks 3 or more languages AND has visited 6 or more countries

Calculate the row and column totals and the overall total to the find the number of employees at the travel insurance company:

		Number of Languages Spoken				
		1	2	3	4+	Total+
	1 or 2	12	14	4	0	30
Number	3–5	5	2	7	1	15
of	6–9	2	7	7	1	17
Countries						
Visited	10+	0	1	0	1	2
	Total	19	24	18	3	64

To find the P(A), look at the subtotals for the employees that speak 3 languages or 4+ languages: $18 + 3 = \dfrac{21}{64}$.

To find P(B), look at the subtotals for the employees that have visited 6–9 countries or 10+ countries: $17 + 2 = \dfrac{19}{64}$.

To find the P(A and B), look at the intersection of events A and B. The relevant values are italicized in the table above: $7 + 0 + 1 + 1 = \dfrac{9}{64}$

P(A or B) = P(A) + P(B) − P(A and B).

$\text{P(A or B)} = \dfrac{31}{64}, \dfrac{21}{64} + \dfrac{19}{64} - \dfrac{9}{64} = \text{which is closest to 50 percent.}$

9. **The correct answer is A.** Remember to take successive percentages of the new salary for each year:

$$45,000 + 0.15(45,000) + 0.05(0.15)(45,000) + 0.05(0.05)(0.15)(45,000) \approx \$57,000.$$

10. **The correct answer is 17.** Here is a simple table to organize what we know about the relative proportion of donations in each category:

	Last Year	This Year
Clothing	0.38	0.38 + 0.15 = 0.53
Toys & Games	0.23	0.23 − 0.07 = 0.16
Food	0.21	
Books	0.18	0.18 − 0.07 = 0.11

If we add up the percentages from this year, we get 0.53 + 0.16 + 0.11 = 80 percent. This means that this year's relative percentage of food donations should be 20 percent (a 1 percent decrease from last year).

Since we know that the number of food donations was 13 this year, we know that 20 percent of the total donations = 13. In other words, $0.20x = 13$. Solving for x gives us 65. If there were 65 total donations this year, there were 65 − 19 = 46 donations total last year.

To determine the number of clothing donations last year, we can calculate $0.38(46) = 17.48$, which we can round down to 17 since the charity cannot receive a partial donation.

SUMMING IT UP

- Approximately 29 percent of SAT® Math Test questions will test your knowledge of Problem Solving and Data Analysis; questions in this section often deal with real-life topics and data.

- When solving questions that test real-life scenarios, take a moment to translate the problem into mathematical language, extract all known information and draw a diagram, and keep careful track of units and relationships between variables.

- Reduce each side of the equation before cross-multiplying to save you time and reduce the chance of computation errors.

- One way to solve a multiple-choice question that involves variables is to substitute values for a and b that make the proportion true, then check in every answer choice.

- Acceleration is the rate of change of velocity of an object with respect to time: $a = \dfrac{\Delta v}{\Delta t}$.

- 1 yard = 3 feet, so 1 square yard will be equal to a square that is 3 feet by 3 feet: $1 \text{ yard}^2 = 9 \text{ feet}^2$.

- When a number is increased and then decreased by the same percentage, you cannot simply add and then subtract the same value—the starting value changes after the first calculation. When you need to use two or more percentage manipulations to determine a final percentage value, use a starting point of 100 as your sample to work with.

- When asked to find the number needed to arrive at a particular average, do not take the average of the given data and then weigh that average equally with the one missing data point. Instead, set up an equation to calculate the mean and solve for the missing variable.

- Calculate weighted averages by taking into account the relative weight of each value in a set—every value in these problems will have a different level of representation. These weightings determine the importance of each value on the overall average.

- The **median** is the middle value when values are arranged in sequential order from least to greatest.

- **Standard deviation** is a measure of the amount of variation in the data set. Standard deviation and mean are greatly affected by outliers.

- When working with a data table, don't rush through until you have a good sense of what each part of the table represents. Before you answer questions, read across each row of the table and down each column and ask yourself what information each portion gives you.

- When presented with any kind of data (either numerical values or variables), read the data carefully and define what each variable and its associated values mean.

- When given a **line graph**, pay attention to the scale used on each axis, which can distort the graph to exaggerate or minimize a potential relationship between variables. If possible, you should look to calculate the slopes of any given lines, which will let you compare rates of change in growth.

- When you see a **scatterplot**, the first thing to do is note the pattern of the points. In a positive correlation, as the x-values increase, the y-values also increase. In a negative correlation, as the x-value increases, the y-value decreases. A line of best fit shows the best representation of the linear pattern of the data.

- **Histograms** visually represent frequencies for intervals and not just categorical data; they also allow you to see the overall distribution of a sample set. To find the total number of items/people in a sample set when given a histogram, you must add up the frequency of each given value.

- When given a **box-whisker plot**, create a Five-Number Summary. Find the minimum (the least value), the 1st quartile (25 percent of the data is less than this value), 2nd quartile (the median of the data set), 3rd quartile (25 percent of the data is greater than this value), and maximum (greatest value).

- **Probabilities** are values between 0 and 1 that represent the chance of an event occurring; a simple event probability is calculated by dividing the $\dfrac{\text{event}}{\text{\# of total outcomes}}$.

- **Compound probability** questions ask about unions or intersections of two or more simpler events.
  - If A and B are two events, then the event "A and B" consists of outcomes that belong to both A and to B.
  - If A and B are two events and A and B have no outcomes in common, then P(A or B) = P(A) + P(B). If A and B do have outcomes in common, then P(A or B) = P(A) + P(B) – P(A and B).
  - If A and B are two events *independent* of each other (i.e., the fact that event B has occurred has no effect on the probability of A occurring, AND the fact that event A has occurred has no effect on the probability of B occurring), then P(A and B) = P(A) × P(B).

CHAPTER 7: PASSPORT TO ADVANCED MATH

PASSPORT TO ADVANCED MATH: AN OVERVIEW

Approximately 28 percent (16 of 58) of the questions on the SAT® Math Test will cover skills in the Passport to Advanced Math category. These questions are all on the tough side, as they ask you to recognize and manipulate more complex equations and expressions and perform operations involving polynomials. You will find these questions on both the Calculator and No Calculator sections.

In this chapter, we'll quickly review the basics for each subtopic within Passport to Advanced Math, and work you step by step through problems that test these concepts. The best way to prep for the toughest SAT® exam questions is to see how they'll be presented in test-like language. It's one thing to know how to do the math—it's another to recognize what math you're being asked to do when it's contained within a problem.

Let's start with one of the trickiest concepts you'll see on the SAT® exam: functions.

FUNCTIONS

Let's quickly review the basics of functions. Function notation takes the form $f(x) = y$, with x as the *independent* variable and y as the *dependent* variable. That is, the value of y depends on the value of x. For instance, if $f(x) = -3x^2 + 2x - 5$ and x is -2, then $y = f(-2)$ would be:

$$f(-2) = -3(-2)^2 + 2(-2) - 5$$
$$= -3(4) - 4 - 5$$
$$= -12 - 4 - 5$$
$$= -21$$

Once you have that concept down, you'll be ready to face the more complex functions questions the SAT® exam will throw at you. These questions will ask you to manipulate two or more functions, and interpret their meaning, both visually and in the context of real-world problems. If you have two functions like $f(x)$ and $g(x)$, then you can form a composite function, $f(g(x))$.

For instance, if you are given the two functions $f(x) = 4x$ and $g(x) = 5x^2$ and are asked to find $f(g(x))$ or $g(f(x))$, start with the innermost function and work your way out:

$$f(g(x)) = 4(5x^2) = 20x^2$$

and

$$g(f(x)) = 5(4x)^2$$
$$= 5(16x^2)$$
$$= 80x^2$$

As always, the toughest SAT® Math Test questions will take it an additional step. Here is another example of a similar pair of functions where you are asked to calculate a composition of functions with additional operations outside of the composition.

Example:

If $f(x) = 2x$ and $g(x) = 7x^2$, evaluate $-2g(f(3)) + 1$.

Solution:

$-2g(f(3)) + 1 =$

$$-2g\underbrace{\left(2 \cdot 3\right)}_{=f(3)} + 1 =$$

$$-2g(6) + 1 =$$

$$-2\,(7(6)^2) + 1 =$$

$$-2 - 7(36) + 1 =$$

$$-503$$

Try another problem, which once again asks you to combine your knowledge of functions with more basic algebra for one of those multi-step problems you'll often find on the SAT® exam.

Example:

If $f(x) = 7 - x$ and $g(x) = x^2 - 3x + 9$, what is an equivalent expression to $g(f(m-1))$?

Solution:

This question is first asking for the expression $m - 1$ to be put into the $f(x)$ function. This will create $f(m-1) = 7 - (m-1)$, so $f(m-1) = 8 - m$. Next, input the expression for $f(m-1)$ into all of the x terms in the $g(x)$ function:

$$g(x) = x^2 - 3x + 9 \text{ and } f(m-1) = 8 - m$$

$$g(f(m-1)) = (8-m)^2 - 3(8-m) + 9$$

Now expand and simplify like terms:

$$g(f(m-1)) = 64 - 16m + m^2 - 24 + 3m + 9$$

$$g(f(m-1)) = m^2 - 13m + 49$$

KEY FEATURES OF FUNCTIONS AND GRAPHS

Some of the toughest questions on the SAT® Math Test require you to manipulate, construct, or evaluate functions of various kinds, and often you are not provided with an actual algebraic rule for the function. You should be familiar with how to identify when a function is increasing or decreasing on given intervals and how to determine relative (or absolute) maximum (highest) points and relative (or absolute) minimum (lowest) points on a graph.

Let's see how these concepts translate to a graphical SAT® Math Test problem.

The following shows the graphs of two functions, $f(x)$ and $g(x)$. At which of the following values of x is $f(x) - g(x) = 3$?

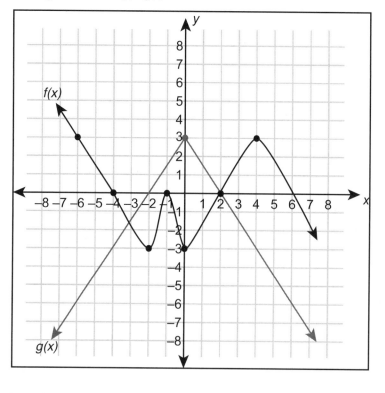

A. −2

B. 0

C. 2

D. −4

In this example, you can look at the points on the graph to evaluate each of the four possible values for x in the equation $f(x) - g(x)$ and see which difference gives you 3:

Choice A: $f(-2) - g(-2) = -3 - 0 = -3$
Choice B: $f(0) - g(0) = -3 - 3 = -6$
Choice C: $f(2) - g(2) = 0 - 0 = 0$
Choice D: $f(-4) - g(-4) = 0 - (-3) = 3$

Choice D is the only one that works, so **the correct answer is D**.

Another way to visually come to the same answer is by looking for a height difference between the two graphs of 3 units. This occurs at $x = -4$ and -2. But for $x = -2$, $f(-2) - g(-2)$ would give you $-3 - 0 = -3$.

Now use this same graph of functions $f(x)$ and $g(x)$ to determine the value of $f(g(0))$.

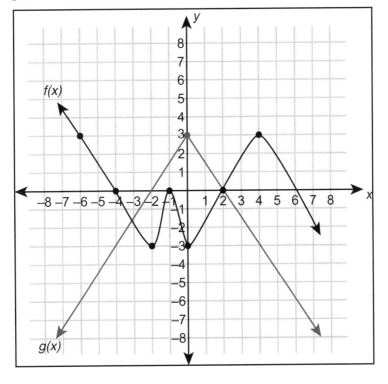

A. -3
B. 0
C. 2
D. 6

The correct answer is C. To find $f(g(0))$, first find the y-value of the function $g(x)$ when $x = 0$. We find that $g(0) = 3$. Now, we can find the y-value for the function $f(x)$ when $x = 3$. We find that $f(g(0)) = f(3) = 2$.

Another concept that often appears on the SAT® Math Test is calculations involving average rates of change.

The average value of a function $y = f(x)$ on an interval from $x = a$ to $x = b$ is defined by $\frac{f(b) - f(a)}{b - a}$. Graphically, this is the slope of the line segment connecting $(a, f(a))$ to $(b, f(b))$. Taking this one step further, you will likely need to interpret these qualitative characteristics within a real-world context.

Let's see what such a question would look like on the exam.

Amy is making dinner for her family and decides to use the oven to bake a casserole and then a dessert of pumpkin pie. The following graph shows the temperature of the oven between 2:30 and 6:30 p.m. During which time period is the average rate of change in oven temperature the largest?

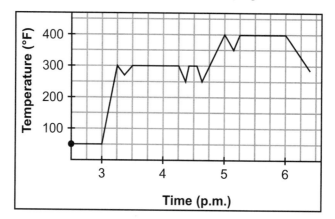

- **A.** 3:00 to 3:30 p.m.
- **B.** 3:30 to 4:00 p.m.
- **C.** 4:30 to 5:00 p.m.
- **D.** 5:30 to 6:00 p.m.

The correct answer is A. The temperature is increasing most rapidly between 3:00 and 3:15 p.m., so the 3:00 to 3:30 p.m. period likely has the greatest average rate of change since there is only a small negative rate of change between 3:15 and 3:30 p.m. Between 3:30 and 4:00 p.m., there is no change in temperature at all, so we have an average rate of change of 0. This is the same for 5:30–6:00 p.m. Between 4:30 and 5:00 p.m., the rate of change is 0, then negative, and then positive, but the positive slope is not as steep as the increase between 3:00 and 3:15 p.m., making choice A the best answer.

Even though a definition like average rate of change *could* involve a calculation, take a step back and see if it is truly necessary to work out the math, or if you can reason more conceptually. This can save valuable seconds, or even minutes!

TRANSFORMATIONS

A concept that might come up when asked to analyze graphs of functions is recognizing how graphs can transform (shift and rotate), and how this changes function notation. **Vertical shifts** occur when a constant is added or subtracted to the entire function: $f(x) + k$ will shift the graph of $f(x)$ *up* k units if $k > 0$ and will shift a graph *down* if $k < 0$. For example, given an original function $g(x) = \dfrac{2}{x+4}$, we could determine that $g(x) + k = \dfrac{2}{x+4} + k$ will shift the graph vertically by k. **Horizontal shifts** occur when a constant is added or subtracted into *within* a function, represented by $f(x + k)$. Here, the graph of $f(x)$ will shift *left* k units if $k > 0$ and will shift *right* k units if $k < 0$.

Horizontal shifts seem a little counterintuitive—when you're adding, you move left; when you're subtracting, you move right.

For example, given an original function $h(x) = \sqrt{13 - 4x}$, the function $h(x + k) = \sqrt{13 - 4(x + k)}$ will shift the graph to the left by k units when $k > 0$ and to the right by k units when $k < 0$.

The following table summarizes these rules; assume c > 0:

$f(x + c)$	shifts a graph to the **left** c units
$f(x - c)$	shifts a graph to the **right** c units
$f(x) + c$	shifts a graph **up** c units
$f(x) - c$	shifts a graph **down** c units
$-f(x)$	reflects a graph about the x-axis; y-values all turn negative
$f(-x)$	reflects a graph about the y-axis; x-values all turn negative

Internalize these before you take your test, so you're not stuck trying to remember which type of addition moves up and down, and which moves left and right. Saving precious seconds on test day is key; not only will you be able to confidently answer your question and move on, you also won't be plagued by self-doubt that might derail your mindset.

Any opportunity you have to boost your confidence is one you should take—knowing tough but manageable rules like these are key to your success.

As you know by now, it's one thing to understand the math mechanics; it's another (and one key to SAT® success) to understand the math mechanics when presented in an applied context. Let's work through a series of questions that can really help you visualize how these manipulations of function graphs work.

This question isn't as difficult as some you will face on test day (and it doesn't come with four choices to select from), but we want to make sure you really understand how to translate test language into math and know precisely how to use your skills to lead to the right answer.

Example:

After running for 18 minutes, Angelika is 2 miles away from her house. After running for 1 hour and 26 minutes, Angelika is 10 miles from her house. Write a linear equation to model the relationship between time (t) spent running and Angelika's distance (d) from her house during her training run.

TIP When you know two points on a line, you can find its slope:
$$m = \frac{y_2 - y_1}{x_2 - x_1}$$

Solution:

This question is simply asking you to write a linear equation given two points: 1 hour and 26 min. = 86 min. We can use the points (18, 2) and (86, 10) to represent two different (t, d) values.

The slope of this line would be:

$$m = \frac{d_2 - d_1}{t_2 - t_1} = \frac{10 - 2}{86 - 18} = \frac{8}{68} = \frac{2}{17}$$

Thus, the equation of the line is $d = \frac{2}{17}t + b$. Since we don't know if Angelika actually started running from her house, we will substitute one of data points to find the y-intercept.

Let's use (18, 2):

$$d = \frac{2}{17}t + b$$

$$2 = \frac{2}{17}(18) + b$$

$$2 = \frac{36}{17} + b$$

$$-\frac{2}{17} = b$$

The linear equation that models the relationship between time spent running and Angelika's distance from her house is $d = \frac{2}{17}t - \frac{2}{17}$.

Let's build upon this question to analysis that is more representative of one of the toughest concepts on the SAT® Math Test.

Example:

If we assume that $\frac{2}{17}$ of a mile for every minute run is a good estimate of Angelika's average rate, and we learn that Angelika walked 1 mile from her house before starting to run, how would our linear model change?

Solution:

The original linear equation we generated, $d = \frac{2}{17}t - \frac{2}{17}$, indicates a rate of change of $\frac{2}{17}$ and that Angelika's starting position was $\frac{2}{17}$ of a mile in the opposite direction of her course, as indicated by the negative sign. If Angelika actually started 1 mile away from her house and in the direction of her course, the new y-intercept would be (0, 1). At time $t = 0$, her position would be $d = 1$ mile from her house. The new linear equation would be $d = \frac{2}{17}t + 1$.

Therefore, visually, the linear model would have shifted up by $1\frac{2}{17}$ units.

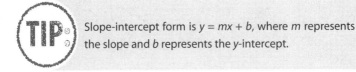

TIP Slope-intercept form is $y = mx + b$, where m represents the slope and b represents the y-intercept.

See Chapter 8 for more in-depth information about slope and equations of lines.

QUADRATIC FUNCTIONS AND PARABOLAS

The graph of a quadratic function in the form $f(x) = ax^2 + bx + c$ either increases, reaches a high point (called a **maximum**), and then decreases, or starts off decreasing, reaches a low point (called a **minimum**), and then increases. The graph of a quadratic is called a **parabola**. The **vertex** is the point at which the minimum or maximum occurs.

For a parabola in the form $f(x) = ax^2 + bx + c$, the x-value of the vertex can be found by calculating $x = -\dfrac{b}{2a}$. The actual vertex point is then $\left(-\dfrac{b}{2a}, f\left(-\dfrac{b}{2a}\right) \right)$. The parabola will have symmetry across the vertical line passing through the vertex; that is, the parabola will be exactly the same size and shape but reversed on either side of the vertex.

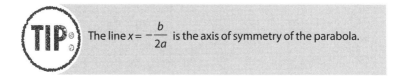

TIP The line $x = -\dfrac{b}{2a}$ is the axis of symmetry of the parabola.

If (h, k) is the vertex of a parabola, then the standard form for its equation is as follows:

$$y = a(x - h)^2 + k.$$

PARABOLA SHAPE

When looking at its general shape, the U-shaped parabola is in the form $f(x) = ax^2 + bx + c$ (where $a > 0$), and an upside-down U-shaped parabola is in the form $f(x) = ax^2 + bx + c$ (where $a < 0$).

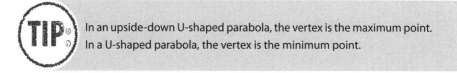

TIP In an upside-down U-shaped parabola, the vertex is the maximum point. In a U-shaped parabola, the vertex is the minimum point.

A parabola in the form of $f(x) = ax^2 + bx + c$ crosses the x-axis at its x-intercepts (also called zeros) in the form $(p, 0)$ where p is a real number. These intercepts are found by solving the equation $ax^2 + bx + c = 0$. There are three possibilities for the type of solutions to such an equation:

1. **Two different real solutions p and q**: in such a case, the quadratic expression $ax^2 + bx + c$ actually factors as $(x + p)(x + q)$. In turn, the graph of the parabola has two x-intercepts at $x = -p$ and $x = -q$. Graphically, this occurs only if the vertex lies above the x-axis and the parabola opens downward (so the coefficient of x^2 is negative), or if the vertex lies below the x-axis and the parabola opens upward (so the coefficient of x^2 is positive).

2. **One repeated real solution p**: in such a case, the quadratic expression $ax^2 + bx + c$ actually factors as $(x - p)^2$. In turn, the graph of the parabola has only one x-intercept, namely at $x = p$. Graphically, this occurs only if the vertex lies on the x-axis.

3. **Two complex conjugate solutions:** in such a case, the parabola does not cross the x-axis. This can happen one of two ways: either the vertex is above the x-axis and the parabola has a minimum at the vertex, or the vertex lies below the x-axis and the parabola has a maximum at the vertex.

 Any time you are presented with a graph for a function that is not a line, you should consider the zeros. While the zeros represent the solution of the function's equation, visually, they represent where the curve crosses the x-axis on the graph.

The following problem also requires you to interpret a quadratic function in context.

Example:

A diver's path after leaving the diving platform can be modeled by the equation $h = -10t^2 + 11t + 6$, where t is the time in seconds after the diver leaves the platform and h is the height in feet of the diver above the water. How long will it take the diver to hit the water? What is the greatest height she will reach?

Solution:

As always, before you dive in, translate what you are given and what you know. Sketch a graph of the diver's path:

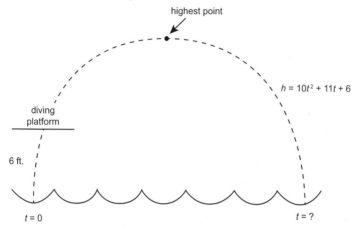

The key to solving the first part of this problem is knowing the height of the diver when she hits the water. At ground level, the height of the water is 0 feet. So, substitute 0 for h and factor the resulting quadratic expression:

$$0 = -10t^2 + 11t + 6$$

$$0 = -(10t^2 - 11t - 6)$$

$$0 = (5t + 2)(2t - 3)$$

$$5t + 2 = 0 \text{ or } 2t - 3 = 0$$

$$t = -\frac{2}{5} \text{ or } t = \frac{3}{2}$$

Reject the negative time, and we find that the diver will hit the water after $t = 1.5$ seconds.

The second question asks us the greatest height the diver will reach. This is the same as the *maximum* value of our parabolic function. Use the fact that the axis of symmetry of a parabola can be found using the equation $x = -\frac{b}{2a}$ to find the time when the diver will reach her greatest height. In this case, $t = -\frac{11}{2(-10)} = \frac{11}{20} = 0.55$ seconds.

If we substitute $t = 0.55$ seconds into the original quadratic, we get the following:

$$h = -10t^2 + 11t + 6$$

$$h = -10(0.55)^2 + 11(0.55) + 6 = 9.025$$

The diver's greatest height reached was 9.025 feet.

Let's look at another example that requires you to manipulate an equation and solve for roots.

Consider the equation $-3(8 - 4x) = 2x(x + 6)$. What is the product of the two solutions of this equation?

A. $12i$
B. 12
C. $-2\sqrt{3}$
D. -12

The correct answer is B. First, apply the distributive property on both sides of the equation. Then, bring all terms involving an x to the right side and the constant term to the left side:

$$-3(8-4x) = 2x(x+6)$$
$$-24+12x = 2x^2 +12x$$
$$-24 = 2x^2$$
$$-12 = x^2$$

Now, to solve for x, take the square root of both sides:

$$x = \pm\sqrt{-12} = \pm i\sqrt{12} = \pm 2i\sqrt{3}$$

Identifying the two solutions as $-2i\sqrt{3}$ and q as $2i\sqrt{3}$, we see that

$$\left(-2i\sqrt{3}\right)\left(2i\sqrt{3}\right) = -4i^2(3) = (4)(3) = 12.$$

Choice A is incorrect because $i^2 = -1$, not i. Choice C is incorrect because $\sqrt{3} \cdot \sqrt{3} = 3$ and not $\sqrt{3}$. Finally, choice D is incorrect because this is the opposite of the correct answer. Remember, $i^2 = -1$, not 1.

Go back to Chapter 5 for a review of complex numbers if this multiplication was confusing for you!

EXPONENTS AND EXPONENTIAL FUNCTIONS

Remembering your basic rules of exponents is crucial for solving more complicated problems involving exponents and exponential functions. These rules help you manipulate exponents to simplify expressions. You should be very comfortable using these rules—don't skip over this review, even if you think you know them. The most common errors are also the most careless. You don't want to get a problem wrong because you've made a mistake on the basics!

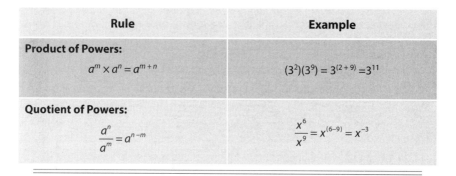

Rule	Example
Product of Powers: $a^m \times a^n = a^{m+n}$	$(3^2)(3^9) = 3^{(2+9)} = 3^{11}$
Quotient of Powers: $\dfrac{a^n}{a^m} = a^{n-m}$	$\dfrac{x^6}{x^9} = x^{(6-9)} = x^{-3}$

NOTE: The bases must be the same to use the product of powers and quotient of powers properties.

Rule	Example
Zero Exponent Property: $a^0 = 1$	$256^0 = 1$
Power of a Product Property: $a^n b^n = (ab)^n$	$(3^4)(6^4) = (3 \times 6)^4 = 18^4$
Power of a Quotient Property: $\dfrac{x^n}{y^n} = \left(\dfrac{x}{y}\right)^n$	$\dfrac{5^3}{r^3} = \left(\dfrac{5}{r}\right)^3$

NOTE: Use the power of a product and quotient properties when the bases are different, but the exponent is the same.

Rule	Example
Negative Exponent Property: $$a^{-n} = \frac{1}{a^n}$$	$$\frac{x^6}{x^9} = \frac{1}{x^3} = x^{-3}$$
Power of a Power Property: $$(a^n)^m = a^{n \times m}$$	$$(x^3)^5 = x^{(3)(5)} = x^{15}$$
Rational Exponent Property: $$a^{\frac{c}{b}} = \sqrt[b]{a^c}$$	$$\sqrt[2]{x^5} = x^{\frac{5}{2}}$$

Zero Exponent Property is an example of a Math Test-type question that requires solid knowledge of the rules of exponents. As you approach this question, remember one key part of test-taking success we've highlighted throughout the math section of this book—ask yourself, "How can I simplify this problem? How can I make it more manageable to deal with? How can I make it so that it's easier to combine its separate parts?"

Find the value of a if $3^{-a} \times \left(\dfrac{1}{27}\right)^{-2a} = \sqrt{3}$

A. -1

B. $\dfrac{1}{5}$

C. $\dfrac{1}{10}$

D. $\dfrac{1}{2}$

The correct answer is C. Apply the rules of exponents to simplify the equation:

$$3^{-a} \cdot \left(\frac{1}{27}\right)^{-2a} = \sqrt{3}$$

$$3^{-a} \cdot (27^{-1})^{-2a} = 3^{\frac{1}{2}}$$

$$3^{-a} \cdot 27^{2a} = 3^{\frac{1}{2}}$$

$$3^{-a} \cdot (3^3)^{2a} = 3^{\frac{1}{2}}$$

$$3^{-a} \cdot 3^{6a} = 3^{\frac{1}{2}}$$

$$3^{5a} = 3^{\frac{1}{2}}$$

$$5a = \frac{1}{2}$$

$$a = \frac{1}{10}$$

EXPONENTIAL FUNCTIONS

Exponential functions arise in real-world contexts, and these frequently appear on the SAT® Math Test. Building an exponential function, which has the general form $f(x) = A \cdot b^x$, requires that you be able to identify the two parameters A and b.

- A is the initial value of $f(x)$ (that is, $f(0)$), or the initial amount present (e.g., of a substance, an initial population, a principal investment, etc.) when $x = 0$.

- $b > 0$ is the growth/decay rate. If b is larger than 1, then the function grows exponentially, while if $0 < b < 1$, the function decays toward zero exponentially fast.

- The variable x typically denotes time and occasionally spatial position.

NOTE: Don't get confused when different letters are used for a variable. For instance, if the variable used is t, don't automatically assume it represents time. The contextual meaning of a variable depends on the scenario being modeled.

Consider the following problem.

Example:

Andy and Theresa open two different bank accounts on January 1, 2017, and each deposit $200. Andy's account earns 1.5% compounded annually, and Theresa's account earns 2% compounded annually. After 3 years, how much more money will Theresa have in her account? (Round your answer to the nearest thousandth.)

Solution:

Here, you must build two exponential functions using the format $f(x) = A \cdot b^x$, evaluate them at the same time, and subtract the respective values. The initial investment for both is $A = \$200$. A percent interest rate of 1.5% yields a b value of $b = 1.015$. Likewise, a percent interest rate of 2.5% yields $b = 1.02$.

One common mistake test-takers often make is incorrectly using $b = 0.015$ (and 0.02) instead of 1.015 (and 1.02). For instance, if you earn 1.5% on $200 annually, then after one year, you would have $200 + (0.015)(\$200)$, which is equivalent to (1.015) ($200) (by factoring out $200). Assuming you allow the amount to keep rolling over, year after year, you have the following amounts after years 2 and 3:

Year 2: $(1.015)(\$200) + (0.015)[(1.015)(\$200)] = (1.015)[(1.015)(\$200)] = (1.015)^2(\$200)$

Year 3: $(1.015)^2 (\$200) + (0.015) [(1.015)^2 (\$200)] = (1.015)[(1.015)^2 (\$200)] = (1.015)^3(\$200)$

Going back to the original problem, Andy's account worth at time t years is $200(1.015)^t$, and Theresa's is $200(1.02)^t$.

Instead of expanding out the increase each year as shown above, you can also substitute the values for A, the initial investment, and b, the rate of increase:

After 3 years, Andy's account will have $200(1.015)^3 = \$209.136$.

After 3 years, Theresa's account will have $200(1.02)^3 = \$212.242$.

Theresa will earn $212.242 - 209.136 = \$3.11$ more than Andy.

POLYNOMIALS

Let's first review some basics, the building blocks of answering SAT® Math Test questions that involve polynomials.

1. Any two terms of an algebraic expression are like terms if their variable parts are identical; otherwise, they are unlike terms.
2. To combine like terms, add the coefficients and write the same variable part: $6x + 4x = 10x$; $125r^{46} - 3r^{46} = 122r^{46}$. You cannot, however, add $b^{34} + b^4$. These are unlike terms. The answer is not b^{38}! This seems like an easy concept,

especially if you are an advanced student, but when under the pressure of an important test like the SAT® exam, you would be surprised by how many students make errors they *know* are wrong. Work quickly, but work intelligently and double-check even the simplest of calculations.

3. Sometimes, you may have to multiply various expressions before you can combine like terms. Doing so requires the use of the distributive property, which says that $a(b + c) = ab + ac$.

 ALERT: If using the distributive property when there is simply a negative sign in front of the parentheses, it is understood that the negative sign really stands for –1. So, for instance, $-(x - 4)$ is written as $-1(x - 4)$, which is equal to $-1(x) -1(-4) = -1x + 4$.

FACTORING POLYNOMIALS

The following table summarizes the different types of factoring that you may need to use throughout the SAT® Math Test.

Factoring Method	Factoring Examples
GCF (greatest common factor)	$3x^4 + 9x$ factors to $3x(x^3 + 3)$
FOIL (first-inner-outer-last)	$x^4 + 4x^2 + 3$ factors to $(x^2 + 3)(x^2 +1)$
Difference of Squares	$(a + b)(a - b) = a^2 - b^2$
Difference of Cubes	$(a - b)(a^2 + ab + b^2) = a^3 - b^3$ $(a + b)(a^2 - ab + b^2) = a^3 + b^3$

Occasionally, you will encounter a problem that requires you to divide polynomials. When faced with these problems, use long division to arrive at $\dfrac{P}{Q} + \dfrac{r}{Q}$, where P is the original polynomial, Q is the divisor, and r is the remainder. For example, consider the following question.

Which of the following expressions is equivalent to $\dfrac{7x+2}{x-9}$?

A. $\dfrac{7+2}{-9}$

B. $7-\dfrac{2}{9}$

C. $7+\dfrac{65}{x-9}$

D. $7-\dfrac{61}{x-9}$

The correct answer is C. Simplifying $\dfrac{7x+2}{x-9}$ using long division will work here since the

degree of the numerator is greater than or equal to the degree of the denominator:

remainder

$$
\begin{array}{r}
7 \\
x-9 \overline{\smash{)}7x+2} \\
-(7x-63) \\
\hline
65
\end{array}
+ \dfrac{65}{x-9}
$$

The 65 becomes a remainder. Therefore, we conclude that $\dfrac{7x+2}{x-9}$ is equal to $7+\dfrac{65}{x-9}$.

Look Out for Undefined Values!

You might be asked to identify values that render a rational expression, such as the one in the previous sample question, as undefined. If you have a rational expression of the form $R(x)=\dfrac{p(x)}{q(x)}$, then any value of x that makes $q(x)=0$ would result in a division by zero. Thus, such x-values render $R(x)$ undefined and are excluded from its domain.

For instance, the values $x=1$ and $x=-2$ make the rational expression $\dfrac{x}{(x-1)(x+2)}$ undefined.

 Any time you arrive at an answer, if the original question has variables in its denominator, take a moment to check that your answer does not lead to an undefined result.

Often, questions about polynomials will require a bit more conceptual thinking involving factors, zeros, and polynomials. For instance, consider this problem:

For a polynomial $g(x)$, $g(-1) = 4$. Which of the following must also be true?

A. $g(4) = -1$

B. -1 and 4 are roots of the function $g(x)$.

C. $\dfrac{g(x)}{x+1}$ results in a remainder of 4.

D. $(-1, 4)$ is a local maximum of the function $g(x)$.

For problems like this, it is easier to use a process of elimination since we need to focus on the answers and figure out which one is true. Choice A is incorrect because we do not know if $(4, -1)$ is a point that satisfies $g(x)$ simply because we know $(-1, 4)$ lies on the graph of $g(x)$. Choice B is incorrect since we know that $(-1, 4)$ is a point on the graph of $g(x)$, so $(-1, 0)$ cannot be a root. The point $(4, 0)$ could possibly be a root, but we aren't provided any information that would confirm/suggest this. Choice D is also incorrect because there is no information to suggest that $(-1, 4)$ is a maximum/minimum value.

The correct answer is C. So, this leaves choice C. If the remainder of $\dfrac{g(x)}{x+1}$ is 4, that means the result of the division is a quotient plus the remainder, which is $q(x) + \dfrac{r}{x+1}$.

The remainder would be a real number. We can write the entire problem as

$$\frac{g(x)}{x+1} = q(x) + \frac{r}{x+1}.$$

Clear the denominators by multiplying both sides by $(x+1)$:

$$g(x) = (x+1)q(x) + r$$

Given that $g(-1) = 4$, let's test this by substituting $x = -1$ into $g(x) = (x+1)q(x) + r$:

$$g(-1) = (-1 + 1)q(x) + r$$

$$g(-1) = r$$

We know that $g(-1)$ is 4, so r must equal 4. Hence, it follows that when $g(x)$ is divided by $x+1$, the remainder is 4.

Problems of this conceptual nature can also be stated graphically instead of algebraically. Consider this problem dealing with the graph of a third-degree polynomial $p(x)$:

Which of the following is NOT true of the given graph?

A. The graph of p has two x-intercepts.
B. The remainder when $p(x)$ is divided by $(x + 3)$ is 0.
C. $p(0)$ is a positive number.
D. $(x - 4)^2$ is a factor of $p(x)$.

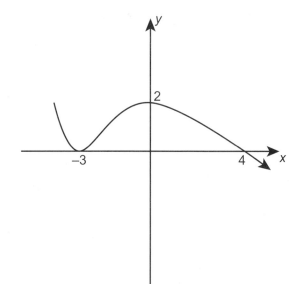

The correct answer is D. The graph of the polynomial is not tangent to the x-axis at $x = 4$, but it is tangent at $x = -3$. The only way the graph of a polynomial can simply cross through the x-axis at $x = a$ without being tangent to it is for $(x - a)$ to be a distinct factor, meaning it cannot occur more than once in the factored form of the polynomial. Likewise, the only way a graph of a polynomial can be tangent to the x-axis at $x = a$ is for $(x - a)$ to be a factor with multiplicity greater than 1.

Since we are given that the graphed polynomial has degree 3, meaning the sum of the powers of all of its factors equal 3, we conclude that the power of $(x - 4)$ must be 1 and the power of $(x - (-3))$ must be 2. Thus, the function must be of the form $A(x - 4)^1 (x + 3)^2$, where A is some nonzero real number, so choice D cannot be true.

Choice A is incorrect because the graph touches the x-axis at two distinct places, ($x = -3$ and $x = 4$). Choice B is incorrect because this is a true statement. In fact, $(x + 3)^2$ is a factor of $p(x)$ because the graph is tangent to the x-axis at $x = -3$. Since $p(0) = 2$, which is positive, this statement is true. Choice C is incorrect.

PASSPORT TO ADVANCED MATH PRACTICE

Complete the following problems. Answers and explanations follow on page 208.

1 For the functions $f(x)$ and $g(x)$ shown below, which of the following *would* change if we replaced the original function $f(x)$ with $f(x) + 2$ and the function $g(x)$ with $g(x) + 2$?

SHOW YOUR WORK HERE

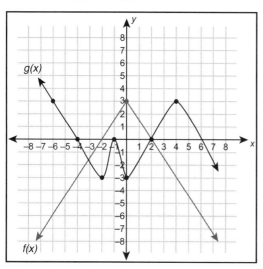

A. The rate of change of $f(x)$ at $x = 2$

B. The rate of change of $g(x)$ at $x = 2$

C. The difference between $f(x)$ and $g(x)$ at $x = 2$

D. The value of $f(x)$ and $g(x)$ at $x = 2$

2 For the following functions $f(x)$ and $g(x)$, find the value of $2f(g(-2)) - g(f(5))$.

x	−10	−2	0	5	9
$f(x)$	−4	−1	17	3	−1

x	−2	−1	0	3	5
$g(x)$	9	−5	0	−10	2

A. −12
B. −9
C. 8
D. 16

3 Coulomb's Law, $F = k\dfrac{q_1 q_2}{r^2}$, is a formula that describes the forces that interact between electrically charged particles. In this formula, k is Coulomb's constant, q_1 and q_2 are the magnitudes of the charges, and r is the distance between the charges. How would the force change if the distance between the two particles is halved and the magnitude of one of the charges is tripled?

A. The force would increase by a factor of $\dfrac{3}{2}$.

B. The force would decrease by a factor of $\dfrac{2}{3}$.

C. The force would increase by a factor of 12.

D. The force would decrease by a factor of $\dfrac{3}{4}$.

4 Which expression is equivalent to

$$\left(\frac{-2x^0 y^{-3}}{3\sqrt{xy^2}}\right)^{-1}?$$

A. $-\dfrac{3}{2}x^{\frac{1}{2}}y^5$

B. $\dfrac{2y^5}{3\sqrt{x}}$

C. $-\dfrac{2y}{3\sqrt{x}}$

D. $\dfrac{3\sqrt{x}}{2y^5}$

SHOW YOUR WORK HERE

5 Scientists are studying the decline in population of four sample ecosystems. Which of the following populations will be the smallest in 5 years?

A. A population of field mice that is currently at 540 and decreasing at an annual rate of 5%.

B. A population of snowshoe hares that is currently at 420 and decreasing at an annual rate of 0.025%.

C. A population of meerkats that is currently at 902 and decreasing at an annual rate of 12%.

D. A population of turtles that is currently at 450 and decreasing at an annual rate of 1%.

6 For the equation $-rx^2 = r - \dfrac{2}{3}qx$,

where q and r are constants, find the solutions of x expressed in terms of r and q.

A. $x = \dfrac{2q}{3r} - 1$ and $x = -1$

B. $x = \dfrac{q \pm \sqrt{(q^2 - 9r^2)}}{3r}$

C. $x = -\dfrac{2}{3}r$ or $x = -6$

D. $x = \dfrac{-2q \pm \sqrt{2q^2 - 36r^2}}{6r}$

7 The graph of a quadratic function has real roots at −3 and 5. What could be the possible vertex of this parabola?

A. $(3, -4)$

B. $(1, -16)$

C. $(2, -15)$

D. $(-1, 16)$

8 The following graph shows a polynomial function $h(x)$. Which of the following statements must be true
about this function?

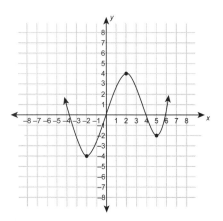

  A. The absolute maximum of $h(x)$
      is 5.
  B. The absolute minimum of $-h(x)$
      is -3.
  C. The equation of this poly-
      nomial is $h(x) = x(x + 3)(x - 4)$
      $(x - 6)$.
  D. $h(-3) = h(0) = h(4) = h(6)$

9 If $r(x)$ is a sixth-degree polynomial
where $r(-2) = r(0) = r(7) = 0$ and
$\dfrac{r(x)}{x^2 - 3} = 0$, which of the following is a
possible equation of $r(x)$?

  A. $r(x) = -x(x - 2)(x + 7)(x^2 - 3)$
  B. $r(x) = 7x(x + 2)^2(x - 7)(x - 3)^2$
  C. $r(x) = -3x^2(x + 2)(x - 7)(x^2 - 3)$
  D. $r(x) = x(x + 2)(x - 7)(x^2 - 3)$

10 For which of the following values of x is the function $f(x)$ undefined?

$$f(x) = \frac{12(x-1)(4x+9)}{12(x-1)+4(x-1)^2+9}$$

A. $1, -\dfrac{9}{4}$

B. 1

C. $-\dfrac{1}{2}$

D. $12, 4, 9$

Answer Key and Explanations

1. D	3. C	5. A	7. B	9. C
2. C	4. A	6. B	8. D	10. C

1. **The correct answer is D.** The function $f(x) + 2$ shifts all of the original points of the function $f(x)$ up two units, and the function $g(x) + 2$ shifts all of the original points of the function $g(x)$ up two units. Thus, the values of $f(2)$ and $g(2)$ would change, but the difference between the two values would stay the same because both graphs shift upwards by the same amount. The rate of change would also stay the same.

2. **The correct answer is C.** Work from the inside out, and first find $g(-2)$ and $f(5)$ using the tables provided. Remember that $g(-2)$ is asking you to identify $g(x)$, or the y-value when $x = -2$. Similarly, $f(5)$ is asking you for $f(x)$, or the y-value associated with $x = 5$. Since $g(-2) = 9$ and $f(5) = 3$, we can substitute back into the original equation to get $2f(9) - g(3)$. Using the tables again, we find that $f(9) = -1$ and $g(3) = -10$. We can simplify to get our answer: $2(-1) - (-10) = 8$.

3. **The correct answer is C.** If we manipulate the formula by multiplying one of the charges (q) by a factor of 3 and multiply the distance r by $\frac{1}{2}$, we get:
$$F = k\frac{3(q_1)q_2}{\left(\frac{1}{2}r\right)^2} = k\frac{3q_1q_2}{\frac{1}{4}r^2}$$

If we simplify the coefficients, we get $3 \div \frac{1}{4} = 12$. In other words, the force will increase by a factor of 12, if the distance is halved and one of the charges triples.

4. **The correct answer is A.** This question calls upon your knowledge of the exponent rules. In order to simplify, work from the outside in. To get rid of the negative 1 exponent on the outside, simply switch the values in the numerator and denominator:
$$\left(\frac{-2x^0y^{-3}}{3\sqrt{x}y^2}\right)^{-1} \text{ becomes } \left(\frac{3\sqrt{x}y^2}{-2x^0y^{-3}}\right)^1.$$

Now, we can work on simplifying the variables. We know that $x^0 = 1$ and that the square root of x can also be written raised to a fractional exponent of $\frac{1}{2}$. The y^{-3} in the denominator can be moved to the numerator to join y^2.

In other words, $\frac{3x^{\frac{1}{2}}y^2}{-2y^{-3}} = -\frac{3}{2}x^{\frac{1}{2}}y^5$.

5. **The correct answer is A.** Calculate the population in 5 years by substituting values into the exponential equation $P = A(1 - r)^t$, where A is the starting population, r is the rate of decrease, and t is the time in years.

If we calculate this for each group, we get approximately:

A: $P = 540(1 - 0.05)^5 \approx 417$ field mice

B: $P = 420(1 - 0.00025)^5 \approx 419$ snowshoe hares

C: $P = 902(1 - 0.12)^5 \approx 476$ meerkats

D: $P = 450(1 - 0.01)^5 \approx 427$ turtles

6. **The correct answer is B.** First, rewrite the equation in standard form:

$-rx^2 = r - \dfrac{2}{3}qx$ becomes

$rx^2 - \dfrac{2}{3}qx + r = 0$

Multiply the equation by 3:

$3rx^2 - 2qx + 3r = 0$

So, $a = 3r$, $b = -2q$, and $c = 3r$.

Using the quadratic formula, we can substitute the values for a, b, and c:

$x = \dfrac{-b \pm \sqrt{b^2 - 4ac}}{2a}$

$x = \dfrac{2q \pm \sqrt{(-2q)^2 - 4(3r)(3r)}}{2(3r)}$

$x = \dfrac{2q \pm \sqrt{4q^2 - 36r^2}}{6r}$

$x = \dfrac{2q \pm \sqrt{4(q^2 - 9r^2)}}{6r}$

$x = \dfrac{2q \pm 2\sqrt{(q^2 - 9r^2)}}{6r}$

$x = \dfrac{q \pm \sqrt{(q^2 - 9r^2)}}{3r}$

7. **The correct answer is B.** Since the roots are -3 and 5, we can write $f(x) = (x + 3)(x - 5)$. If we multiply the binomials, we get $x^2 - 2x - 15$.

If we then complete the square to write the function in vertex form, we will get:

$x^2 - 2x - 15 = 0$

$x^2 - 2x = 15$

$x^2 - 2x + 1 = 15 + 1$

$(x - 1)^2 = 16$

Now we can rewrite this equation as $f(x) = (x - 1)^2 - 16$. A possible minimum value of this quadratic is $(1, -16)$.

8. **The correct answer is D.** Evaluating the function $h(x)$ at $x = -3, 0, 4$, and 6 all give you a y-value of 0. They are all real roots of the polynomial function. Choice A is incorrect because the function $h(x)$ has no absolute maximum since the end behavior of the function is increasing to infinity as x decreases and as x increases. There is only a local maximum value of 5. Choice B is incorrect, because $-h(x)$ is the reflection of the function $h(x)$ over the x-axis. The absolute minimum of $h(x)$ would be 3, but $-h(x)$ would have no absolute minimum value as its end behavior would be decreasing to infinity. Choice C is incorrect because even though the equation $h(x) = x(x + 3)$ $(x - 4)(x - 6)$ shows the four real roots, there are an infinite number of polynomial equations that would share these same roots. Substitute any non-zero coordinate pair from the graph of $h(x)$, and you will see that it will not satisfy the equation shown here.

9. **The correct answer is C.** Since $r(x)$ is a sixth-degree polynomial where $r(-2) = r(0) = r(7) = 0$ and $\dfrac{r(x)}{(x^2 - 3)} = 0$, we know that $(x + 2)$, x, and $(x - 7)$ are factors of $r(x)$ and that $(x^2 - 3)$ is likely another factor of $r(x)$. We can eliminate choices A and D because both are fifth-degree polynomials. Choice B's last factor is incorrect. Choice C is correct because it reflects the correct factors; it has an additional factor of x, indicating a double root at $x = 0$.

10. **The correct answer is C.** When determining the values for x where a function is undefined, always set the denominator equal to 0. You do not have to worry about the numerator values at all. In this case, we are looking at $12(x - 1) + 4(x - 1)^2 + 9 = 0$. Rewrite this equation into quadratic form, $4(x - 1)^2 + 12(x - 1) + 9 = 0$. Notice that the quadratic function is a *perfect square* that looks very much like the perfect square $4x^2 + 12x + 9 = 0$. Factoring this equation would give us $(2x + 3)(2x + 3) = 0$ or $(2x + 3)^2 = 0$. If we apply the same factoring technique to the equation $4(x - 1)^2 + 12(x - 1) + 9 = 0$, we get $(2(x - 1) + 3)^2 = 0$. Take the square root for both sides to get $2(x - 1) + 3 = 0$. When you solve for x, you should get $x = -\dfrac{1}{2}$.

SUMMING IT UP

- Approximately 28 percent of the questions on the SAT® Math Test cover skills in the category Passport to Advanced Math. These questions will ask you to work with more complex equations and expressions. The SAT® Math Test will assess your ability to perform all operations with polynomials: addition, subtraction, multiplication, and division.

- Function notation is $f(x) = y$, with x as the *independent* variable and y as the *dependent* variable.

- When solving problems that involve composite functions like $f(g(x))$, start with the innermost function and work your way outward.

- The average value of a function $y = f(x)$ on an interval from $x = a$ to $x = b$ is defined by $\dfrac{f(b) - f(a)}{b - a}$.

- Vertical shifts occur when a constant is added or subtracted to the entire function: $f(x) + k$ will shift the graph of $f(x)$ *up* k units if $k > 0$ and will shift a graph *down* if $k < 0$. Horizontal shifts occur when a constant is added or subtracted *within* a function, represented by $f(x + k)$: the graph of $f(x)$ will shift *left* k units if $k > 0$ and will shift *right* k units if $k < 0$.

- $-f(x)$ reflects a graph about the x-axis; y-values all turn opposite.

- $f(-x)$ reflects a graph about the y-axis; x-values all turn opposite.

- If you are having trouble understanding the scenario presented in a problem, it's worth your time to sketch a diagram to see all given information visually.

- Memorize all of your exponent rules; these are the trickiest to master:
  - $a^n b^n = (ab)^n$
  - $\dfrac{x^n}{y^n} = \left(\dfrac{x}{y}\right)^n$
  - $a^{-n} = \dfrac{1}{a^n}$
  - $(a^n)^m = a^{n \times m}$

- An exponential function has the general form $f(x) = A \cdot b^x$.
  - A is the initial value of $f(x)$, or the initial amount present when $x = 0$; $b > 0$ is the growth/decay rate.
  - If b is larger than 1, then the function grows exponentially; if $0 < b < 1$, the function decays toward zero exponentially fast.
  - x typically denotes time and occasionally spatial position.

- The graph of a quadratic function in the form $f(x) = ax^2 + bx + c$ either increases to reach a high point (a maximum) and then decreases, or starts off decreasing to reach a low point (a minimum) and then increases.

- For a parabola in the form $f(x) = ax^2 + bx + c$, the x-value of the vertex $= -\dfrac{b}{2a}$. The actual vertex point is then $\left(-\dfrac{b}{2a}, f\left(-\dfrac{b}{2a}\right)\right)$.

- If (h, k) is the vertex of a parabola, then the standard form for its equation is $y = a(x - h)^2 + k$.

- A parabola in the form of $f(x) = ax^2 + bx + c$ crosses the x-axis at its x-intercepts (also called **zeros**) in the form $(p, 0)$ where p is a real number. There are three solution types:
  - **Two different real solutions p and q**, where the quadratic expression factors as $(x + p)(x + q)$, and the graph of the parabola has two x-intercepts at $x = -p$ and $x = -q$.

  - **One repeated real solution p**, where the quadratic expression factors as $(x - p)^2$, and the graph of the parabola has only one x-intercept, $x = p$.

  - **Two complex conjugate solutions**, where the parabola does not cross the x-axis: either the vertex is above the x-axis and the parabola has a minimum at the vertex, or the vertex lies below the x-axis and the parabola has a maximum at the vertex.

- Here is a summary of the most difficult factoring methods:
  - Difference of Squares: $(a + b)(a - b) = a^2 - b^2$

  - Difference of Cubes: $(a - b)(a^2 + ab + b^2) = a^3 - b^3$ and $(a + b)(a^2 - ab + b^2) = a^3 + b^3$

- In the rational expression $R(x) = \dfrac{p(x)}{q(x)}$, any value of x that makes $q(x) = 0$ would result in a division by zero and thus be undefined.

CHAPTER 8: ADDITIONAL TOPICS IN MATH

OVERVIEW

- Additional Topics in Math: An Overview
- Lines, Angles, Triangles, and Circles
- Area, Volume, and Density
- Right Triangles, Circles, and Trigonometric Functions
- Analytic Geometry—Equations and Circles
- Additional Topics in Math Practice
- Summing It Up

ADDITIONAL TOPICS IN MATH: AN OVERVIEW

About 10 percent (6 of 58) of the questions on the SAT® Math Test will ask about topics that fall under an umbrella category called Additional Topics in Math. As the name suggests, these are the extras that don't fall under any of the other three test subjects. Topics covered include geometry, trigonometry, and complex numbers, and are in both the Calculator and Non-Calculator sections. While only a small portion of your test is dedicated to these questions, they can often be some of the toughest you'll face.

This chapter will focus on the most complex and tricky concepts you might face on test day, with sample problems involving lines, angles, triangles, and two- and three-dimensional shapes that you are likely to encounter. We're not going to review the most basic concepts—because this section is so small and we want to expose you to the language of the SAT® when it comes to Additional Topics in Math, we want to show you as many sample questions as possible so you can put your knowledge to use.

Throughout, we will review and then walk through geometry-related problems that will require sketching diagrams and applying your knowledge of various properties and theorems.

LINES, ANGLES, TRIANGLES, AND CIRCLES

The following definitions play an important role in many theorems and problems in geometry. You likely are familiar with the concepts, but you should make sure you have the vocabulary down cold before test day. It would be a shame to know the calculations you need to make but to be unsure of what exactly a question is asking.

- **Bisector line:** a line that divides a line segment into two congruent parts

- **Angle bisector:** a ray that divides an angle into two congruent sub-angles

- **Perpendicular bisector:** a line that divides a line segment into two congruent parts and intersects the line segment in a 90-degree angle

- **Vertical angles:** the non-adjacent angles formed when two lines or line segments intersect. Vertical angles are always congruent. In the following figure the vertical angle pairs are $\angle 1 \cong \angle 2$ and $\angle 4 \cong \angle 3$:

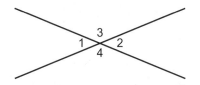

- **Transversal:** a line that intersects two or more lines. When a transversal intersects two parallel lines, it forms several pairs of congruent angles and also supplementary angles. All of the acute angles will be congruent and all of the obtuse angles will be congruent. Unless the transversal intersects the parallel lines at a right angle, there will be four obtuse and four acute angles formed. In the following figure, congruent obtuse angles are $\angle 1 \cong \angle 3 \cong \angle 5 \cong \angle 7$, and congruent acute angles are $\angle 2 \cong \angle 4 \cong \angle 6 \cong \angle 8$:

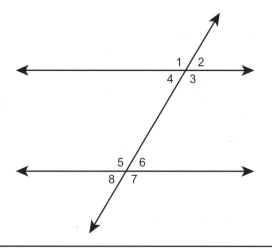

Often, you will need to formulate algebraic equations to solve the plane geometry questions on the SAT® Math Test. Let's look at a question.

Example:

In the following figure, m is parallel to n. What is the value of $x + y$?

Solution:

The line passing through the parallel lines m and n is a transversal. From the properties previously described, you can therefore conclude that the angles with measures 38° and $(y - 7)$° are congruent. This gives you the equation:

$$38 = y - 7$$
$$45 = y$$

The angles with measures $(2x)$° and $(y - 7)$° are adjacent and lie along the same line. These angles must have a total measure of 180°. But you already know that the angles with measures 38° and $(y - 7)$° are congruent. This gives a second equation, which you can use to find the value of x:

$$2x + 38 = 180$$
$$2x = 142$$
$$x = 71$$

Finally, the value of $x + y = 45 + 71 = 116$.

ALERT: Solving a parallel line question is more challenging when more than one transversal is shown. It's a good idea to use your pencil to darken *one* of the transversals and *both* of the parallel lines so that you can see the corresponding angles made by one of the transversals. Don't get those angles confused with the angles made by the *other* transversal.

Triangles

Similar triangles: Two triangles are similar if they are different sizes, their corresponding angles have the same measure, and their corresponding sides have the same ratio.

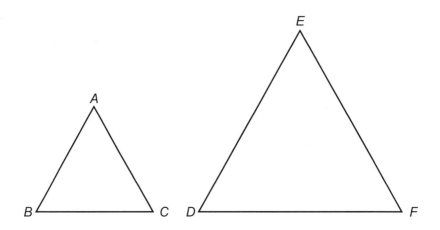

Congruent triangles: Two triangles are congruent if they have the same three angles AND the same three sides.

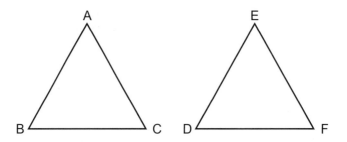

The **triangle inequality theorem** states that *the sum of any two sides of a triangle must be greater than the third side.* If that is something you're not already familiar with, make sure you understand how to work through the following problem.

Example:

In $\triangle ABC$, m $\angle A$ = m $\angle C$ and $AC = 5$. If $BC = a$, for positive integer a, then what is the smallest possible value for a?

Solution:

Given that m $\angle$ A = m $\angle$ C, the two sides opposite these angles, $\overline{BC}$ and $\overline{AB}$ must have equal length. That is, $\triangle ABC$ is an isosceles triangle with $AB = BC = a$.

Using the three side lengths and the triangle inequality theorem, you can write that $a + a > 5$ (other inequalities you can write for this triangle using this theorem aren't as useful). Solving this inequality for a gives you the statement that $a > \dfrac{5}{2} = 2.5$. The smallest integer that satisfies this inequality is 3.

CIRCLES

When a line is tangent to a circle, it intersects the circle at only *one* point and forms a 90° angle with the radius that terminates at that point. Use this definition to construct an illustration to model the information given in the following question.

Example:

A circle with a radius of *r* units is centered at point *M*. A line is tangent to the circle at point *P*, and point *N* lies along this line such that $PN = 4$. If $MN = 10$, what is the value of *r*?

Solution:

Given this information, you can sketch the following picture. Note that it isn't important to get each part of the image exactly to scale, but to translate the information to a figure that can help you understand the question. The 90° angle is added based on the triangle inequality theorem.

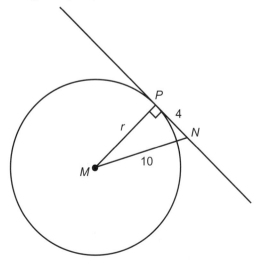

You can now see that the radius of the circle, r, is actually a leg of a right triangle formed by the points P, N, and M. Applying the Pythagorean theorem:

$$r^2 + 4^2 = 10^2$$
$$r^2 + 16 = 100$$
$$r^2 = 84$$
$$r = \sqrt{84} = 2\sqrt{21}$$

The radius of the circle is $2\sqrt{21} \approx 9.2$ units.

The following question also requires you to use your understanding of tangent lines, along with some other properties of circles.

Example:

In the figure below, lines m and n are tangent to the circle centered at point R at the points P and Q, respectively. What is the value of x?

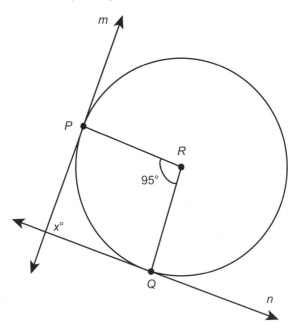

Solution:

Since the two lines are tangent at the points P and Q, you know that $m\angle P = 90° = m\angle Q$.

Further, since the points P, Q, and R are three vertices of a quadrilateral that would include x as the measure of an interior angle:

$$95 + 90 + 90 + x = 360$$
$$275 + x = 360$$
$$x = 85$$

The value of x is therefore 85.

An **inscribed angle** is formed from two secant lines, which are segments inside the circle that hit two points on the circle. There are several useful theorems concerning inscribed angles. For instance, the **inscribed angle theorem** states that an inscribed angle is half the measure of the central angle of the circle.

Example:

In the circle centered at the point O below, what is the value of x?

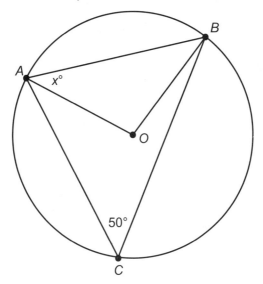

Solution:

With problems like this, it is a good idea to spend some time analyzing the given figure so that you can decide which theorem or theorems should be applied. This analysis here would lead you to note that $\angle ACB$ is an inscribed angle, and both $\overline{OA}$ and $\overline{OB}$ are radii. Two conclusions can then be drawn:

1. By the inscribed angle theorem, $m\angle AOB = 100°$.

2. $OA = OB$, so $m\angle OAB = m\angle OBA = x°$.

These conclusions lead to the following equation that is based on the interior angles of $\triangle OAB$:

$$x + x + 100 = 180$$
$$2x + 100 = 180$$
$$2x = 80$$
$$x = 40$$

Thus, the value of x is 40.

AREA, VOLUME, AND DENSITY

The area of a plane region is a measure of how much space the region takes up. On the SAT® Math Test, it is unlikely that you will be asked to simply compute the area of a region. Typically, the need to compute such an area will need to be teased out of a real-world problem, or you will need to probe more deeply into the notion of area of a plane figure and address slightly more conceptual questions.

For instance, the notion of similarity as it pertains to triangles is undoubtedly quite familiar to you, and we reviewed the basics earlier in the chapter. What may be less familiar is that general polygons can be similar as well, as long as their corresponding angles are equal and their corresponding side pairs are proportional.

Let's consider two similar shapes A and B. If shape A has side lengths that are twice as long as those in shape B, how will the perimeter and area of shape B be different from shape A?

- The perimeter of shape B will be *twice* as large as shape A.

- The area of shape B will be *four times* as large as shape A.

Since area requires you to *multiply* the length of two dimensions together, if *both* dimensions are twice as long, then $(2 \times length)(2 \times width)$ will result in an area that is $4 \times (length \times width)$.

Work carefully as you apply this awareness to the following question, which will work out the mechanics behind these facts and help you to better understand them.

Example:

Rectangle $ABCD$ is similar to rectangle $PQRS$, with $RS = \dfrac{CD}{5}$. If the area of $ABCD$ is a and the perimeter is p, then what are the perimeter and the area of $PQRS$ in terms of a and p, respectively?

Solution:

The statement $RS = \dfrac{CD}{5}$ combined with the fact that the rectangles are similar tells you that each side of PQRS is $\dfrac{1}{5}$ the length of the corresponding side in ABCD. Let's use the following notation:

$$AB = 1 \text{ (for length)}$$

$$CD = w \text{ (for width)}$$

Note that it doesn't matter which we call the length or the width, since, in the end, we are doing the same operation (addition/multiplication), but just switching the order.

This implies that:

$$PQ = \frac{1}{5}\ell = \frac{\ell}{5}$$

$$RS = \frac{1}{5}w = \frac{w}{5}$$

In ABCD, you are given the area is a. Using the notation above, $a = 1w$. Similarly, you are given that the perimeter is p, so $p = 2l + 2w$. Now you can find the area and perimeter of PQRS.

$$\textbf{Area: } \left(\frac{\ell}{5}\right)\left(\frac{w}{5}\right) = \frac{\ell w}{25} = \frac{a}{25}$$

$$\textbf{Perimeter: } 2\left(\frac{\ell}{5}\right) + 2\left(\frac{w}{5}\right) = \frac{2\ell + 2w}{5} = \frac{p}{5}$$

As expected, the area of the similar rectangle is $\dfrac{1}{25}$ the area of the original area, while the perimeter is $\dfrac{1}{5}$ the original perimeter.

ALERT: Consider two similar polygons that have a scale factor of k. The longer sides are each the product of their corresponding shorter sides × k. Although the *perimeter* of the larger polygon will be k times the perimeter of the smaller polygon, this is not true for the area. The area of the larger polygon will be k^2 times larger than the area of the smaller polygon.

It's likely that you'll need to use a good deal of algebraic modeling and equation solving when working with perimeter and area questions—no tough question on the SAT® Math Test is ever just testing one concept; it will contain layers within of, at minimum, algebra and geometry together.

Example:

Triangle *ABC* is equilateral with *AB* = *n*, for a nonzero real number *n*. If $\triangle ABC \cong \triangle DEF$ such that the perimeter of $\triangle DEF$ is $\dfrac{9n}{4}$, then what is *DE* in terms of *n*?

Solution:

The fact that *ABC* is an equilateral triangle means that not only is it true that *AB* = *n*, but it is also true that *BC* = *n* and *AC* = *n*. That is, the side lengths are all the same.

The notation $\triangle ABC \cong \triangle DEF$ indicates that the two triangles are similar. Automatically then, you know that *DEF* is also an equilateral triangle since each side length of *DEF* would then be a constant multiple of the corresponding side lengths of *ABC*.

You are told that the perimeter of *DEF* is $\dfrac{9n}{4}$. If each side of *DEF* has a length of *s*, then that means:

$$3s = \frac{9n}{4}$$
$$12s = 9n$$
$$s = \frac{9n}{12} = \frac{3n}{4}$$

Since, as indicated above, *DEF* is an equilateral triangle, each side has this length. Therefore, $DE = \dfrac{3n}{4}$.

Some geometry questions will require you to calculate the areas and perimeters of composite shapes. Often, the regions for which you will be asked to compute the area will be composites of other, more familiar regions. When faced with any figure on the SAT® Math Test, you should always keep in mind that you might have to add lines in order to break up information and properly answer the question. Also, as you will see in this example, many geometry questions will involve some algebra as well!

Example:

The image below shows two half-circles, each with a diameter of $3x + 7$, connected by two parallel line segments. In terms of x, what is the area of the resulting figure?

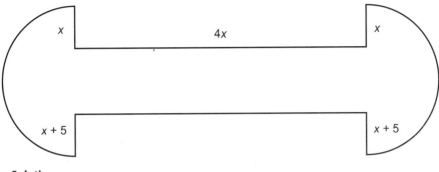

Solution:

Given that these are half-circles, you can draw lines to show their diameters as follows.

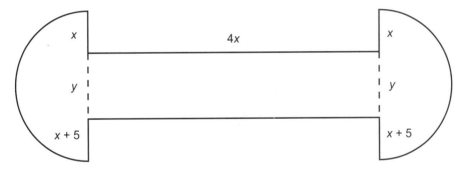

Here, we let the unknown side length be represented by y, though you could label it with any variable. This shows that there is a rectangle (since the two line segments are parallel) connecting the two half-circles, which has sides of length $4x$ and y. To find the area in terms of x, you will first need to find the value of y in terms of x.

For either half-circle, the diameter is $3x + 7$. Therefore:

$$x + y + x + 5 = 3x + 7$$
$$2x + y + 5 = 3x + 7$$
$$y = x + 2$$

The area of the rectangular portion of the figure is therefore:

$$4x(x + 2)$$

The area of each half-circle is found using the formula $\frac{1}{2}\pi r^2$, where r is the radius, which is half the diameter.

Area of each half circle: $\frac{1}{2}\pi\left(\frac{3x+7}{2}\right)^2 = \frac{1}{2}\pi\left(\frac{1}{4}\right)(3x+7)^2 = \frac{\pi}{8}(3x+7)^2$

Finally, by adding the areas of each individual piece of the composite figure, you will have the area of the entire figure.

Area of composite figure:
$$4x(x+2)+\frac{\pi}{8}(3x+7)^2+\frac{\pi}{8}(3x+7)^2 = 4x(x+2)+\frac{\pi}{4}(3x+7)^2$$

As with all questions like this, how you write the final answer would depend on the answer choices themselves. You may have to FOIL and collect like terms, or you might leave it in the form seen above.

Try another problem testing the same skills, this time using perimeter in a real-world context.

Example:

The diagram below shows a region around which fencing is to be installed, as indicated by the solid lines. Sections labeled "A" are to use wooden panels, at a cost of $15.50 per foot, while sections labeled "B" are to use plastic panels, at a cost of $8.90 per foot. To the nearest tenth, what will be the total cost of the fencing?

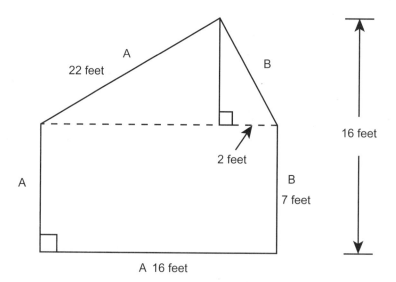

Solution:

The figure formed by the proposed fencing is a rectangle and a triangle, with one shared side that will not be fenced (the dashed line). There is already enough information to determine the cost of the fencing along the rectangular portion of the figure.

The side labeled B will have a cost of $8.90(7), while the opposite side, labeled A, will have a cost of $15.50(7). The long side on the bottom of the figure is also labeled A and will have a cost of $15.50(16). This gives a subtotal of:

$$\$8.90(7) + \$15.50(7) + \$15.50(16) = \$418.80$$

To find the cost of the top two sections of fence, you will need to do a little more work. Label the unknown side length x, as shown below.

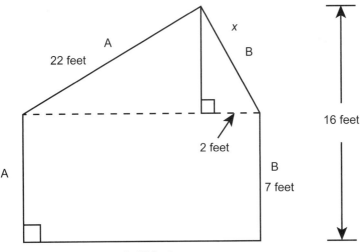

This is the hypotenuse of a right triangle with legs of length $16 - 7 = 9$ feet and 2 feet. Therefore:

$$2^2 + 9^2 = x^2$$
$$x^2 = 85$$
$$x = \sqrt{85}$$

The total cost of the upper two sections will then be $15.50(22) + $8.90($\sqrt{85}$) ≈ $423.05.

You now can calculate the total overall cost as: $418.80 + $423.05 = $841.85.

Notice how in the calculation, rounding the square root of 85 was avoided until the last part of that calculation. This is meant to limit rounding error. You should always try to round in the last possible step or use many more decimals than you need until the last possible step.

One last type of area problem is one that involves shapes nested within each other. You will be given information about one of the shapes and will be required to calculate the perimeter or area of the second shape. When attacking questions such as the one that follows, it's important that you label the given illustration as much as possible, which will help you make connections between the given information and the steps you need to take to answer the question.

Square *ABCD* has an area of 12 square units and is inscribed into circle *P*. Which of the following is the closest approximation of the area of circle *P*?

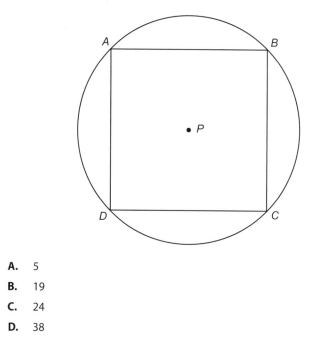

A. 5
B. 19
C. 24
D. 38

In order to find the area of circle *P*, we need to find its diameter or radius. Notice that the diagonal $\overline{DB}$ of square *ABCD* is also the diameter of the circle, so start with the information given about the square. If square *ABCD* has an area of 12, then $A = s^2 = 12$, and we can determine that $s = \sqrt{12}$. Use $\sqrt{12}$ in the Pythagorean theorem to find the square's diagonal:

$$a^2 + b^2 = c^2$$
$$\left(\sqrt{12}\right)^2 + \left(\sqrt{12}\right)^2 = \left(\overline{DB}\right)^2$$
$$24 = \left(\overline{DB}\right)^2$$
$$\sqrt{24} = \overline{DB}$$

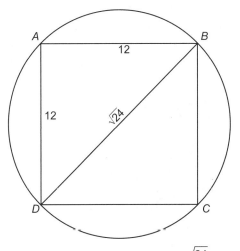

So, the diameter of circle P is $\sqrt{24}$ and thus, the radius is $\dfrac{\sqrt{24}}{2}$. Substitute this into the formula for area of a circle:

$$A = \pi r^2 = \pi \left(\frac{\sqrt{24}}{2} \right)^2 = \pi \left(\frac{24}{4} \right) \approx 18.84$$

The correct answer is B. Choice A is the approximate diameter of the circle. Choice C is incorrect because 24 is the radicand of the diameter of the circle, but it is not the area of this circle. Choice D is incorrect because it is the area of a circle that has a diameter of $\sqrt{12}$, and not $\sqrt{24}$.

The surface area of a figure is the total area that a surface occupies in space. For instance, to find the surface area of a cube, you would find the area of each face and then multiply by 6. Keep in mind that each face of a cube is a square, so you can simply find the length of an edge and square it.

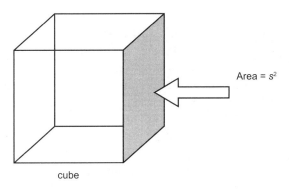

cube

ALERT: A common, careless error that students often make is calculating the *volume* of a figure when asked to calculate the surface area. We can't say it enough—slow down enough to make sure you know exactly what is being asked and that you've answered the correct problem.

As with most one-step concepts, surface area computations will be part of a larger problem on the SAT® Math Test. For instance, consider the following problem:

Example:

A rectangular prism has a length of 5 units, a width of *n* units, and a height of *n* units. If the surface area of this prism is 78 square units, then what is the value of *n*?

Solution:

Using this description, you can sketch the following to help you think about the dimensions of this rectangular prism.

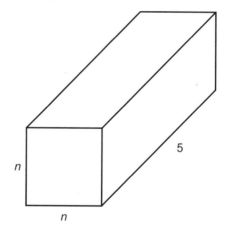

The surface area of 78 square units would have been calculated by finding the area of the two squares on either end of the prism and the areas of the four rectangles that make up the rest of the surface. The area of each of the square faces is n^2 units, and the area of each rectangular base is $5n$ units. Using this and the given surface area, you can write a formula to find *n*.

$$2n^2 + 4(5n) = 78$$
$$2n^2 + 20n - 78 = 0$$
$$n^2 + 10n - 39 = 0$$

This is a quadratic equation, so you could use factoring, completing the square, or the quadratic formula to solve it. This turns out to be nicely factorable, making this the best option.

$$n^2 + 10n - 39 = 0$$
$$(n-3)(n+13) = 0$$

The two solutions are $n = -13$ and $n = 3$. Since n is a side length, it cannot be negative; the correct answer is $n = 3$.

The measure of volume tells you how much space fills a 3D figure. On test day, you might face a question involving volumes of standard solids like cones, prisms, pyramids, cylinders, and spheres, as well as composite solids.

 Even though you are given the formulas for a cylinder and cube within the test, you should review those standard formulas and understand what each term represents.

Often, the information needed to compute the volume of a solid will be buried in a problem. For instance, consider the following question:

Example:

When the height of a cylinder is increased by 5 feet, the resulting cylinder has a volume of 135π ft.³. If the radius of the original cylinder is 3 feet, what is its volume, in cubic feet?

Solution:

Let h represent the height of the original cylinder. When this is increased by 5, the new height will be $h + 5$. The volume of a cylinder with this height and the same radius would be $V = \pi(3)^2(h + 5)$.

The problem states that this volume is 135π ft.³, which allows you to write an equation involving h. Knowing h will then allow you to find the volume of the original cylinder.

$$\pi(3)^2(h + 5) = 135\pi$$
$$9\pi(h + 5) = 135\pi$$
$$9\pi h + 45\pi = 135\pi$$
$$9\pi h = 90\pi$$
$$h = 10$$

Therefore, the volume of the original cylinder is: $V_{original} = \pi(3)^2(10) = 90\pi$ ft.³.

Some problems on the SAT® Math Test deal with weight (e.g., pounds), mass, and density. The **density** of an object (amount of matter in the volume) is equal to the mass of the object divided by the volume of the object: $d = \dfrac{m}{V}$.

Let's consider the following problem involving body weight, height, and BMI. These problems often involve unit conversions, which add another layer of complication.

Example:

The Body Mass Index (BMI) for a person is computed using the following formula:

$$BMI = \frac{\text{Weight of person (in kg)}}{\left(\text{Height of person (in m)}\right)^2}$$

If a 150-pound female athlete is 6 feet tall, what is her BMI? (Use: 1 kg = 0.454 lb. and 1 m = 39.4 in.)

Solution:

Typically, when you are provided with a conversion factor, you can most certainly count on the fact that you will need to manipulate it before you can use it. The person's weight is given in pounds and must be converted to kilograms for use in the formula, and her height is given in feet and must be converted to inches. To this end, it is more convenient to change the given conversion factors to the following equivalent ones, obtained by dividing both sides of each conversion factor by the number on the right side:

1 kg = 0.454 lb. is equivalent to 1 lb. = 2.2 kg.

1 m = 39.4 in. is equivalent to 1 in. = 0.025 m.

Thus, 150 pounds = 150(2.2) kg = 330 kg, and 6 ft. = 6(12) in. = 72 in. = 72(0.025) m = 1.8 m.

So, the BMI is given by:

$$BMI = \frac{330 \text{ kg}}{\left(1.8 \text{ m}\right)^2} = 101.852 \ \frac{\text{kg}}{\text{m}^2}$$

RIGHT TRIANGLES, CIRCLES, AND TRIGONOMETRIC FUNCTIONS

A right triangle has two legs adjacent to the right angle and a hypotenuse opposite the right angle. The Pythagorean theorem expresses the relationship between the sides of a right triangle, stating that $c^2 = a^2 + b^2$, where side c is the hypotenuse and the sides a and b are legs.

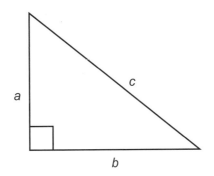

The triplet sets of numbers that satisfy this equation are called **Pythagorean triples.** It would be very beneficial for you to memorize some of them. The table below presents a few Pythagorean triples. Knowing these can speed up your computations as you take the test.

Common Pythagorean Triples
3, 4, 5
5, 12, 13
7, 24, 25
9, 40, 41

Right-triangle problems will also test your knowledge of trigonometric functions, so you should also be sure to remember your trusty trigonometric ratios. As you might have learned in class, you can easily remember them with the acronym SOH-CAH-TOA.

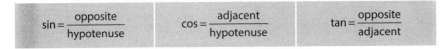

$$\sin = \frac{\text{opposite}}{\text{hypotenuse}} \qquad \cos = \frac{\text{adjacent}}{\text{hypotenuse}} \qquad \tan = \frac{\text{opposite}}{\text{adjacent}}$$

Let's look at an example of how questions on the SAT® Math Test will bring together lots of triangle concepts into one question.

Example:

The area of $\triangle ABC$, shown below, is $24\sqrt{14}$ square units. If cos A in triangle is $\dfrac{5}{9}$, then what is the value of tan C in triangle BDC?

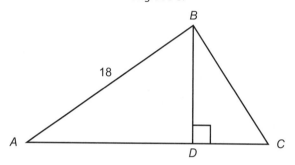

Solution:

In order to find tan C, you need to know the length of the side opposite this angle in triangle BDC (BD) and the side adjacent to this angle (DC). You will have to use the information given in the problem to find these two side lengths.

The value of cos A is the ratio of the side adjacent to $\angle A$ and the hypotenuse of triangle ADB. If this is $\dfrac{5}{9}$, it doesn't necessarily mean that these have lengths 5 and 9, respectively. Given the figure, you can therefore write:

$$\frac{5}{9} = \frac{AD}{18}$$

Solving this yields AD = 10.

Knowing this side now allows you to find one of the needed side lengths, BD, using the Pythagorean theorem:

$$10^2 + BD^2 = 18^2$$
$$BD^2 = 224$$
$$BD = \sqrt{224} = 4\sqrt{14}$$

To find *DC*, consider the given area of the large triangle *ABC*, $24\sqrt{14}$. Remember that the area is found using the formula $\frac{1}{2}bh$, which in this case would be $\frac{1}{2}(AC)(BD)$. Using the information you just found:

$$\frac{1}{2}(AC)(BD) = 24\sqrt{14}$$

$$\frac{1}{2}(AC)(4\sqrt{14}) = 24\sqrt{14}$$

$$(2\sqrt{14})(AC) = 24\sqrt{14}$$

$$AC = 12$$

Finally, remember that way back at the start of this problem, we found that *AD* = 10.

So, now we can say that $DC = 12 - 10 = 2$ and $\tan C = \dfrac{4\sqrt{14}}{2} = 2\sqrt{14}$.

If you face any trigonometry problems on the SAT® exam, you will need to apply your knowledge of angle types and trigonometric functions, along with some common trigonometric identities.

Remember your basics! We can't say it enough—even if you're sure you know some of these definitions, do every bit of prep you can to avoid careless and unnecessary mistakes on test day.

- **Complementary Angles:** two angles that have a sum of 90°. Adjacent complementary angles share a common side and form a right angle.

- **Supplementary Angles:** two angles that have a sum of 180°. Adjacent supplementary angles share a common side and form a straight angle.

- **Right Angle:** an angle that measures 90°, formed by two perpendicular line segments or lines.

- **Obtuse Angle:** an angle that measures more than 90°, but less than 180°.

- **Acute Angle:** an angle that measures less than 90°, but more than 0°.

- **Radian Measure:** a unit of measure for angles. One radian is the angle made at the center of a circle by an arc whose length is equal to the radius of the circle. You can convert an angle expressed using radians to an equivalent one whose measure is given in degrees by multiplying by $\dfrac{180°}{\pi}$.

- **Arc length:** the length S of the arc of a circle with radius r corresponding to a central angle θ is given by $S = 2\pi r\left(\dfrac{\theta}{360°}\right)$ when θ is expressed in degrees.

Two Useful Trigonometric Identities:

$$\sin^2 \theta + \cos^2 \theta = 1$$
$$\sin(\theta) = \cos(90° - \theta)$$

Example:

For a real number x and two acute angles, $\sin\left(\dfrac{\pi}{6} - x\right) = \cos\left(\dfrac{\pi}{4} - 2x\right)$. What is the value of x?

Solution:

The angles used in this problem are measured in radians. If the sine and cosine of the acute angles are equal, then you know from the second identity above that the angles are complementary. However, that is in terms of degrees. The angle measure of 90° is equivalent to $\dfrac{\pi}{2}$ radians (you should be able to verify this!). Thus:

$$\frac{\pi}{6} - x + \frac{\pi}{4} - 2x = \frac{\pi}{2}$$
$$\frac{\pi}{6} + \frac{\pi}{4} - 3x = \frac{\pi}{2}$$

To solve this, you can clear fractions using the common multiple of 12:

$$12\left(\frac{\pi}{6} + \frac{\pi}{4} - 3x\right) = 12\left(\frac{\pi}{2}\right)$$
$$2\pi + 3\pi - 36x = 6\pi$$
$$-36x = \pi$$
$$x = -\frac{\pi}{36}$$

ANALYTIC GEOMETRY—EQUATIONS OF LINES AND CIRCLES

SAT® Math Test questions will often ask you to determine the equation of a line given either algebraic or graphical information. Or, sometimes, you'll have to identify the correct graph when given the equation of a line.

Take a look at the following question.

Example:

In the (x, y) coordinate plane, line p has a slope of -4 and an x-intercept of 3. Line q passes through the points $(4, 9)$ and $(1, 3)$. If lines p and q intersect at the point (r, s), then what is the value of s?

Solution:

Lines in the (x, y) coordinate plane are represented by equations that can be written in the form $y = mx + b$, where m is the slope, and b is the y-intercept. The point at which two lines intersect represents the solution (x, y) to the system of equations created by the equations of the two lines.

Therefore, to answer this question, you must find the equation for each line and solve the resulting system of equations. The value of s will be the y-value from this solution.

Let's start with line p. We are given the slope, -4, and the x-intercept. The x-intercept is the value of x when $y = 0$. Since the x-intercept here is 3, you know the line passes through the point $(3, 0)$.

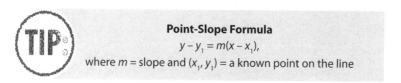

Point-Slope Formula
$$y - y_1 = m(x - x_1),$$
where m = slope and (x_1, y_1) = a known point on the line

Since you know the slope and a point through which the line passes, you can use the point-slope formula to find the equation of the line.

$$y - y_1 = m(x - x_1)$$
$$y - 0 = -4(x - 3)$$
$$y = -4x + 12$$

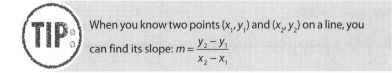

TIP When you know two points (x_1, y_1) and (x_2, y_2) on a line, you can find its slope: $m = \dfrac{y_2 - y_1}{x_2 - x_1}$

Now for line q, you were told in the problem that it passes through the points $(4, 9)$ and $(1, 3)$. Before you can apply the point-slope formula, you will need to calculate the slope using these two points. Let $(4, 9) = (x_1, y_1)$ and $(1, 3) = (x_2, y_2)$:

$$m - \frac{3-9}{1-4} = \frac{-6}{-3} = 2$$

Next, using the first point and the point-slope formula:

$$y - y_1 = m(x - x_1)$$
$$y - 9 = 2(x - 4)$$
$$y - 9 = 2x - 8$$
$$y = 2x + 1$$

The system of equations you need to solve is:

$$y = -4x + 12$$
$$y = 2x + 1$$

Recall that the question asks you to find s when the point of intersection is (r, s). That means you need to find the y part of the solution to this system. So, the fastest method would be to eliminate x by multiplying the second equation by 2.

$$
\begin{array}{l}
y = -4x + 12 \\
2y = 2(2x + 1)
\end{array}
\Rightarrow
\begin{array}{l}
y = -4x + 12 \\
\underline{2y = 4x + 2} \\
3y = 14 \\
y = \dfrac{14}{3}
\end{array}
$$

Thus, $s = \dfrac{14}{3}$.

Sometimes, you will be asked a slope question that requires you to blend algebra and coordinate geometry skills.

Line q contains points G (w, –4) and H (–6, $2w$). What is the value of the y-coordinate of point H if the slope of line q is $-\dfrac{6}{5}$?

A. −16

B. −8

C. 4

D. 8

Plug the given points into the slope formula:

$$\text{Slope} = \frac{y_2 - y_1}{x_2 - x_1} = \frac{-4 - 2w}{w - (-6)} = \frac{-4 - 2w}{w + 6}$$

Now set $\dfrac{-4 - 2w}{w + 6}$ equal to the given slope of $-\dfrac{6}{5}$ and solve for w:

$$\frac{-4 - 2w}{w + 6} = \frac{-6}{5}$$
$$-6w - 36 = -20 - 10w$$
$$4w = 16$$
$$w = 4$$

Don't stop there! Since $w = 4$ and H (–6, $2w$), the y-coordinate of H is 8. **The correct answer is D.** Choice A is what the value of the y-coordinate of point H would be if the slope of line q were $\dfrac{6}{5}$ instead of $-\dfrac{6}{5}$. Choice B is the opposite of the y-coordinate of point H. Choice C is the value of w, but not the value of the y-coordinate of H.

The midpoint between two coordinate pairs in the standard (x, y) coordinate plane is the point that is equal distance from the two given points. The **midpoint formula** should be easy for you to recall since the midpoint will always be the average of x-coordinates, followed by the average of y-coordinates:

The midpoint between (x_1, y_1) and $(x_2, y_2) = \left(\dfrac{x_1 + x_2}{2}, \dfrac{y_1 + y_2}{2} \right)$.

Although the **distance formula** looks rather intimidating, it is just an application of the Pythagorean theorem to the standard (x, y) coordinate plane. Take a look at how this calculates. Consider two points, say $P(x_1, y_1)$ and $Q(x_2, y_2)$, as shown:

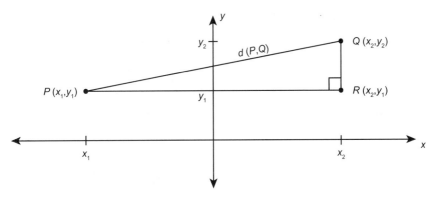

We seek to compute the distance between P and Q, denoted $d(P, Q)$. This distance coincides with the length of $\overline{PQ}$. Form the right triangle PRQ and observe that:

$$d(P, R) = \left| x_1 - x_2 \right| \text{ and } d(Q, R) = \left| y_1 - y_2 \right|$$

Hence, by the Pythagorean theorem, it follows that $[d(P, Q)]^2 = [d(P, R)]^2 + [d(Q, R)]^2$.

The distance between (x_1, y_1) and $(x_2, y_2) = \sqrt{\left(x_2 - x_1\right)^2 + \left(y_2 - y_1\right)^2}$.

You might be asked simply to find the distance between two points, or you may get a more challenging question such as the following one that requires you to apply the midpoint and distance formulas together.

The top floor of Tyler's hotel has a rooftop garden, a balcony, a pool, and a cupcake shop. In the figure below, each of these is represented on a standard (x, y) coordinate plane, using meters east of the entrance as the x-coordinates and meters north of the entrance as the y-coordinates. The hotel wants to build a fitness center halfway between the balcony at point B and the garden at point G. Approximately how many meters will the new fitness center be from the cupcake shop that is located at point C?

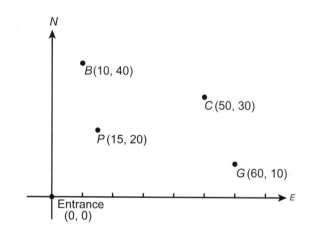

N

B(10, 40)

C(50, 30)

P(15, 20)

G(60, 10)

E

Entrance
(0, 0)

A. 10 meters

B. 16 meters

C. 18 meters

D. 21 meters

The correct answer is B. First, find the midpoint between points *B* (10, 40) and *G* (60, 10):

$$\text{Midpoint} = \left(\frac{x_1 + x_2}{2}, \frac{y_1 + y_2}{2} \right) = \left(\frac{10 + 60}{2}, \frac{40 + 10}{2} \right) = (35, 25)$$

The fitness center will have a location at (35, 25). To find out how far this will be from the cupcake shop at *C* (50, 30), use the distance formula:

$$d = \sqrt{(x_2 - x_1)^2 + (y_2 - y_1)^2} = \sqrt{(50 - 35)^2 + (30 - 25)^2} = \sqrt{225 + 25} = 15.8 \text{ m}$$

So the fitness center will be approximately 16 meters from the cupcake shop. Choice A is the difference between the coordinates of the location of the fitness center, which will be at (35, 25). Choice C is too large of an approximation since the actual distance was closer to 15.8 meters. Choice D is the approximate distance from the fitness center to the pool at point *P*.

All you need to know to represent a circle in standard form is the length of the radius and the coordinates of the center of the circle:

Standard form of a circle with center (*h*, *k*) and radius *r*:

$$(x - h)^2 + (y - k)^2 = r^2$$

Here's a sample test-like question about circles with a slight twist. It calls upon other concepts from this chapter, and as we keep driving home, is representative of the multi-step, difficult problems on the SAT® Math Test that ask you to draw on several pieces of knowledge. You know all the parts—you've prepped! Your job now is to recognize how and when to use them all together.

Example:

What is the equation for a circle for which the line segment with endpoints (2, 1) and (8, –3) is a diameter?

Solution:

We must compute the center and radius. First, find the radius by computing the length of this line segment using the distance formula, and taking $\frac{1}{2}$ of it:

$$d = \sqrt{\left(x_2 - x_1\right)^2 + \left(y_2 - y_1\right)^2} = \sqrt{\left(2-8\right)^2 + \left(1-(-3)\right)^2}$$
$$= \sqrt{36+16} = \sqrt{52} = 2\sqrt{13}$$

So, the radius equals $\sqrt{13}$. Next, the center is the midpoint of the given line segment:

$$\left(\frac{2+8}{2}, \frac{1+(-3)}{2}\right) = (5,-1)$$

Thus, the equation for the circle is $(x - 5)^2 + (y + 2)^2 = 13$.

 ALERT: Remember that the equation for the circle-radius form of a circle with center (h, k) and radius r, is the sum of squared *differences*, and *not* the sum of squared *sums*: $(x - h)^2 + (y - k)^2 = r^2$.

ADDITIONAL TOPICS IN MATH PRACTICE

Complete the following problems. Answers and explanations follow on page 248.

1. A storage tank with a diameter of x feet and a height of $2x$ feet is 75% full. Which expression represents the remaining capacity in terms of x cubic feet?

SHOW YOUR WORK HERE

   A. $\dfrac{3\pi x^3}{8}$

   B. $\dfrac{3\pi x^3}{2}$

   C. $\dfrac{\pi x^3}{2}$

   D. $\dfrac{\pi x^3}{8}$

2. The midpoint of $\overline{AB}$ in the xy-plane is $\left(\dfrac{3}{4}, \dfrac{21}{8}\right)$. If point A is located at $\left(-\dfrac{1}{2}, \dfrac{1}{4}\right)$, then what is the (x, y) coordinate of point B?

   A. $\dfrac{3}{2}$

   B. 2

   C. 5

   D. $\dfrac{21}{4}$

3 An artist plans to use wire, at a cost of $1.80 a foot, to make the pattern seen in the figure below. The pattern consists of four half-circles, where each half-circle section has a radius of 4 inches. To the nearest cent, what will be the total cost for the needed wire, in dollars?

SHOW YOUR WORK HERE

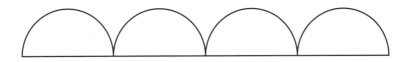

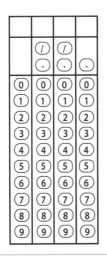

4 A circle with a radius of *x* units has an area of 18π. In square units, what is the area of an equilateral triangle with side lengths of *x* units?

A. 9

B. $\dfrac{3\sqrt{6}}{2}$

C. $\dfrac{9\sqrt{3}}{2}$

D. $3\sqrt{2}$

5 In the figure below, points *A*, *R*, and *B* lie along line *m*. If $m\angle PRQ = 105°$ and $\angle ARP \cong \angle QRB$, then what is the value of *x*? Round your answer to the nearest hundredth.

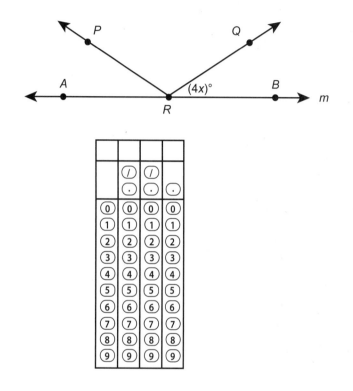

6 The side lengths of a square are increased by 60%. If the area of the original square was *A* square units and the area of the new square is *cA* square units, then what is the value of *c*?

7 For an acute angle θ, $\sin\theta = \dfrac{a}{b}$. What is the value of $\cos\theta$ in terms of *a* and *b*?

A. $\sqrt{b^2 - a^2}$

B. $\dfrac{\sqrt{b^2 - a^2}}{b}$

C. $\dfrac{a}{\sqrt{b^2 - a^2}}$

D. $\dfrac{1}{\sqrt{b^2 - a^2}}$

8 The angles with measure $\dfrac{3\pi x}{4}$ radians

and $\dfrac{\pi}{3}$ radians are supplementary.

What is the value of x?

SHOW YOUR WORK HERE

A. $\dfrac{2}{9}$

B. $\dfrac{8}{9}$

C. $\dfrac{10}{9}$

D. $\dfrac{16}{9}$

---

9 The surface area of a cube is $\dfrac{3}{2}$ square

meters. In cubic meters, what is the volume of the cube?

	$\oslash$	$\oslash$	
	$\odot$	$\odot$	$\odot$
⓪	⓪	⓪	⓪
①	①	①	①
②	②	②	②
③	③	③	③
④	④	④	④
⑤	⑤	⑤	⑤
⑥	⑥	⑥	⑥
⑦	⑦	⑦	⑦
⑧	⑧	⑧	⑧
⑨	⑨	⑨	⑨

10 The point (4, *a*) lies along the circumference of the circle in the (*x*, *y*) coordinate plane defined by the equation $(x - 4)^2 + (y + 1)^2 = 9$. If *a* is a positive integer, then what is the value of *a*?

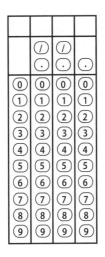

Answer Key and Explanations

1. D	3. 12.34	5. 9.38	7. B	9. $\dfrac{1}{8}$
2. C	4. C	6. 2.56	8. B	
				10. 2

1. **The correct answer is D.** The total volume of the storage tank is $V = \pi r^2 h$. You are given that the diameter is x, so the radius is therefore $\dfrac{x}{2}$. Applying the formula, you get:

    $$V = \pi \left(\frac{x}{2}\right)^2 (2x) = \pi \left(\frac{x^2}{4}\right)(2x) = \frac{\pi x^3}{2},$$

    which is answer choice C. However, you want to find the remaining capacity, which would be 25%, or $\dfrac{1}{4}$, this total volume. Thus, the final answer is $\dfrac{1}{4}V = \dfrac{1}{4}\left(\dfrac{\pi x^3}{2}\right) = \dfrac{\pi x^3}{8}$. Choice A is the result of finding 75%, or $\dfrac{3}{4}$, of the volume, while answer choice B is the result of doing the same but also using the diameter instead of the radius in the volume formula. Another way to get the incorrect answer choice C is to use the diameter instead of the radius, but correctly find $\dfrac{1}{4}$ of that volume.

2. **The correct answer is C.** Let the coordinates of point B be represented by (b_1, b_2). Then, using the midpoint formula, the value of the y-coordinate (b_2) can be found by solving $\dfrac{\frac{1}{4} + b_2}{2} = \dfrac{21}{8}$. Solving this equation:

    $$\frac{\frac{1}{4} + b_2}{2} = \frac{21}{8}$$

    $$\frac{1}{4} + b_2 = \frac{42}{8}$$

    $$\frac{1}{4} + b_2 = \frac{21}{4}$$

    $$b_2 = \frac{20}{4} = 5$$

    Choice D is one of the values you get as you solve this equation, and similarly, choice A is a value you would get when solving for the x-coordinate. Choice B is itself the x-coordinate, b_1.

3. **The correct answer is 12.34.** Since each half-circle is identical, you can first calculate the circumference of one of the half-circles and then add the diameter. Multiply this by 4 to find the total amount of wire needed in inches:

$$4 \times \left(2(4) + \frac{1}{2}(2\pi(4)) \right)$$
$$= 4 \times (8 + 4\pi)$$
$$= 32 + 16\pi \text{ inches}$$

The cost is $1.80 per foot, or $$\frac{1.80}{12}$$ per inch. Therefore, the total cost will be:

$$(32 + 16\pi) \times \$\frac{1.80}{12} \approx \$12.34$$

Be careful to try and round at the last possible step, or to more digits than you need, in order to ensure the most accuracy when working with applied problems requiring a rounded answer.

4. **The correct answer is C.** To answer the question about the triangle, you must first find the value of x. Given the area of a circle, you can write:

$$\pi x^2 = 18\pi$$
$$x^2 = 18$$
$$x = 3\sqrt{2}$$

Note that this is choice D, but you must work further to find what the question is asking for! It is helpful to sketch the described triangle and label the height, h.

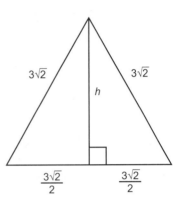

To find h, and then the area of the circle, you must notice that the height forms a right triangle with legs of length h, $\frac{3\sqrt{2}}{2}$, and a hypotenuse of length $3\sqrt{2}$. Apply the Pythagorean theorem:

$$h^2 + \left(\frac{3\sqrt{2}}{2} \right)^2 = \left(3\sqrt{2} \right)^2$$
$$h^2 + \frac{9(2)}{4} = 9(2)$$
$$h^2 + \frac{9}{2} = 18$$
$$h^2 = \frac{27}{2}$$
$$h = \frac{3\sqrt{3}}{\sqrt{2}} = \frac{3\sqrt{6}}{2}$$

This height is choice B, but you are trying to find the area. Apply the formula for the area of a triangle:

$$A = \frac{1}{2}bh = \frac{1}{2}\left(3\sqrt{2}\right)\left(\frac{3\sqrt{6}}{2}\right)$$

$$= \frac{9\sqrt{12}}{4} = \frac{9\left(2\sqrt{3}\right)}{4} = \frac{9\sqrt{3}}{2}$$

So, choice C is correct. Note that choice D is the result of using $x = 3\sqrt{2}$ as the height and base.

5. **The correct answer is 9.38.** The three described angles all lie along the same line, and so the sum of their measures is 180°. Since $\angle ARP \cong \angle QRB$, you can write:

$$4x + 4x + 105 = 180$$
$$8x + 105 = 180$$
$$8x = 75$$
$$x = \frac{75}{8} \approx 9.38$$

6. **The correct answer is 2.56.** If the side lengths of the original square were x units, then the area was $A = x^2$ square units. If the side lengths are increased by 60%, then the new side lengths are $x + 0.6x = 1.6x$ units. This gives an area of $(1.6x)^2 = 2.56x^2 = 2.56A$. Thus $c = 2.56$.

7. **The correct answer is B.** Since this is an acute angle, you can use a triangle to help you find the needed value. A quick sketch and application of the definition of sine gives the following.

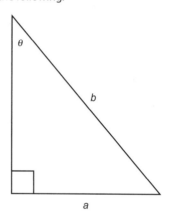

By the Pythagorean theorem, the side adjacent to θ (label this x) is:

$$x^2 + a^2 = b^2$$
$$x^2 = b^2 - a^2$$
$$x = \sqrt{b^2 - a^2}$$

Remember that you are not just finding this side length, so don't select answer choice A! From here, apply the definition for cosine:

$$\cos\theta = \frac{\text{adj}}{\text{hyp}} = \frac{\sqrt{b^2 - a^2}}{b}$$

Choice C is the tangent of this angle, and choice D is simply the reciprocal of choice A. The trig functions are not simply the reciprocal of any side length, but are ratios of a defined pair of side lengths.

8. **The correct answer is B.** If angles are supplementary, then their sum is $180°$ or π radians. Therefore:

$$\frac{3\pi x}{4} + \frac{\pi}{3} = \pi$$

$$12\left(\frac{3\pi x}{4} + \frac{\pi}{3}\right) = 12\pi$$

$$9\pi x + 4\pi = 12\pi$$

$$9\pi x = 8\pi$$

$$x = \frac{8}{9}$$

Choice A would be correct if the angles were complementary. Choice D is the result of treating the difference of the measures as equal to π, and choice C is the result of treating the difference as equal to $90°$, or $\frac{\pi}{2}$ radians.

9. **The correct answer is $\frac{1}{8}$.**

There are 6 faces to a cube, each with the same area. To find the volume, you will need to know the side lengths that make up each square face. Let x represent the side length. Then, given the surface area:

$$6x^2 = \frac{3}{2}$$

$$x^2 = \frac{3}{12}$$

$$x = \sqrt{\frac{3}{12}} = \frac{\sqrt{3}}{2\sqrt{3}} = \frac{1}{2}$$

The volume is then $V = \left(\frac{1}{2}\right)^3 = \frac{1}{8}$ cubic meters.

10. **The correct answer is 2.** The center of the circle is located at the point $(4, -1)$, and the radius is $\sqrt{9} = 3$. This means that along the line $x = 4$, the points $(4, -1-3)$ and $(4, -1+3)$ also lie along the circumference of the circle. Of these, only $-1 + 3 = 2$ is positive.

SUMMING IT UP

- About 10 percent of SAT® Math Test questions will cover skills in the Additional Topics in Math subsection; these questions will test skills in geometry, trigonometry, and complex numbers.

- **Vertical angles** are the nonadjacent angles formed when two lines or line segments intersect. Vertical angles are always congruent.

- A **transversal** is a line that intersects two or more lines. When a transversal intersects a pair of parallel lines, all of the acute angles will be congruent and all of the obtuse angles will be congruent.

- Two triangles are **similar** if they are different sizes, have the same angle measures, and their corresponding sides have the same ratio. Two triangles are **congruent** if they have the same three angles and the same three sides.

- The **triangle inequality theorem** states that the sum of any two sides of a triangle must be greater than the third side.

- When a line is tangent to a circle, it intersects the circle at only *one* point and forms a 90° angle with the radius that terminates at that point.

- An **inscribed angle** is formed when two secant lines hit two points on a circle. The inscribed angle theorem states that an inscribed angle is $\frac{1}{2}$ the measure of the central angle of the circle.

- If shape *A* has side lengths that are twice as long as those in shape *B*, the perimeter of shape *B* will be *twice* as large as shape *A* and the area of shape *B* will be *four times* as large as shape *A*.

- Take the time to label any given illustrations as much as possible with the information from the question stem.

- The **Pythagorean theorem** expresses the relationship between the sides of a right triangle: $c^2 = a^2 + b^2$, where side *c* is the hypotenuse and the sides *a* and *b* are legs.

- The triplet sets of numbers that satisfy the Pythagorean theorem are called **Pythagorean triples**. Here are some common triples you should memorize:
    - 3, 4, 5
    - 5, 12, 13
    - 7, 24, 25
    - 9, 40, 41

- Remember your trigonometric ratios with the acronym **SOH-CAH-TOA**:
  - $\sin = \dfrac{\text{opposite}}{\text{hypotenuse}}$

  - $\cos = \dfrac{\text{adjacent}}{\text{hypotenuse}}$

  - $\tan = \dfrac{\text{opposite}}{\text{adjacent}}$

- Useful trigonometric identities:
  - $\sin^2 \theta + \cos^2 \theta = 1$

  - $\sin(\theta) = \cos(90° - \theta)$

- One **radian** is the angle made at the center of a circle by an arc whose length is equal to the radius of the circle. Convert an angle expressed using radians to an equivalent one in degrees by multiplying by $\dfrac{180°}{\pi}$.

- The length S of the arc of a circle with radius r corresponding to a central angle θ is given by $S = 2\pi r \left(\dfrac{\theta}{360°} \right)$.

- **Point-slope formula**: $y - y_1 = m(x - x_1)$, where m = slope and (x_1, y_1) = a known point on the line.

- When given two points (x_1, y_1) and (x_2, y_2) on a line, its slope is $m = \dfrac{y_2 - y_1}{x_2 - x_1}$.

- The **Midpoint formula**: Between (x_1, y_1) and $(x_2, y_2) = \left(\dfrac{x_1 + x_2}{2}, \dfrac{y_1 + y_2}{2} \right)$.

- The **Distance formula**: Between (x_1, y_1) and $(x_2, y_2) = \sqrt{(x_2 - x_1)^2 + (y_2 - y_1)^2}$.

- The standard form of a circle with center (h, k) and radius r is $(x - h)^2 + (y - k)^2 = r^2$.

CHAPTER 9: EXPRESSION OF IDEAS QUESTIONS

OVERVIEW

- Expression of Ideas: An Overview
- Organization Questions
- Effective Language Use Questions
- Attacking Passages and Expression of Ideas Questions for a Perfect Score
- Expression of Ideas Practice
- Summing It Up

On your journey to achieving a perfect score on the SAT® exam, you'll encounter the Writing and Language Test, one of two tests that comprise the Evidence-Based Reading and Writing section. This is a 35-minute test, and you'll answer 44 questions that will task you with making qualitative editorial decisions designed to improve the writing passages included in the exam.

Be aware that 35 minutes is not a huge amount of time to tackle this test section, so you'll need to work quickly and wisely on test day in order to make efficient use of your time.

The key is to establish an effective test-taking pace *before* test day arrives! Use the practice in this book to establish a working pace that will help you achieve your perfect score goals. Students who show up on test day without having done this are at a real disadvantage.

The purpose of this test is to gauge your ability to read critically, recognize errors and weaknesses in writing, and make substantive fixes to improve written work—valuable and practical skills that will serve you well throughout your academic career and in your professional life after school.

The best strategic approach for mastering the SAT® Writing and Language Test is to analyze its two core measures. Questions in this test will fall into two categories:

- **Expression of Ideas:** Questions in this skill area will assess your ability to recognize and address key structural issues that impact the overall effectiveness of a piece of writing, including organization, development, and effective language use. Your ability to *effectively* express your ideas, both in written and verbal communication, will seriously impact how your ideas are understood and received—both in the classroom and in the world of work.

- **Standard English Conventions:** Questions in this skill area will test your ability to recognize—and fix—issues involving sentence structure, conventions of usage, and conventions of punctuation. You've undoubtedly learned during your academic career that your ability to use the core tenets of good grammar, punctuation, and sentence structure can seriously impact your grades—on tests, reports, projects, and term papers, to name just a few.

Within *each* of these two core skills areas, questions on the Writing and Language Test will measure your skill levels in the following categories:

- **Words in Context:** These questions will gauge your mastery of effective and appropriate word choice, based on context within the passages provided. Your vocabulary skills should be sharp for test day, and you'll need to be able to use available context clues to make decisions that impact tone, style, and syntax, with the goal of improving a given piece of writing.

- **Command of Evidence:** These questions are designed to test your ability to grasp how effectively a piece of writing conveys ideas and information, and to make critical improvements to enhance meaning, sharpen a claim or argument, and provide appropriate details and support.

- **Analysis in History/Social Studies and in Science:** These questions will measure your ability to critically read, comprehend, and analyze passages based on these important topic areas—and to make key decisions on how best to improve them.

This chapter will equip you with all the tools you need to master Expression of Ideas questions. Chapter 10 will focus on getting you ready to tackle Standard English Conventions questions. Together, these two chapters provide thorough, in-depth coverage of all the skill areas tested on the SAT® Writing and Language Test, and they will help bring your perfect score goal within reach.

EXPRESSION OF IDEAS: AN OVERVIEW

Questions that fall into the Expression of Ideas category on the SAT® Writing and Language Test measure your ability to analyze a written passage and make decisions regarding the author's use of organization, development, and effective language choices. You'll be tasked with making decisions about adding, deleting, moving, and revising words, sentences, and phrases within the passage, with the goal being to improve the readability, appropriateness, and effectiveness of the author's work.

These questions focus on core rhetorical skills, including the overall clarity and effectiveness of a piece of writing. They also involve making sure that the tone and mood of a piece of writing are consistent and appropriate, that the piece reflects effective organization, that the piece is free from off-topic and redundant details, that transitions between ideas are strong, that wordiness is avoided, and so on.

On your quest towards a perfect 1600 score, you'll be tasked with determining whether the author of each passage made appropriate choices to express his or her ideas at various points in the writing provided, as well as deciding if the alternative options provided among the answer choices for each question serve to enhance and improve the passage and more effectively express the ideas contained within.

Why are these skills such a key part of the SAT® exam? In order to effectively convey your intended meaning and craft an effective, compelling, and persuasive piece of writing, you'll need to properly utilize the core tenets of organization, development, and effective language use. As an elite student, you've certainly recognized that these skills are important tools for success in your academic career, and they will continue to remain essential skills for success—both in the classroom and after you graduate and embark upon your chosen professional career path.

Every decision you make on this section of the SAT® exam should accomplish the following goal: improve the quality and effectiveness of the written passages.

Your goal of achieving a perfect score on the SAT® exam is undoubtedly tied to a desire to gain acceptance into your target college or university—and possessing the skills required to effectively express your ideas in writing is critical for impressing admissions teams, who will be reading your application essays very carefully!

CAUTION

Proceed carefully. Compared to questions addressing standard English conventions, these issues can be a bit more challenging—even for elite students aiming for a perfect score—because the issues may not always be as immediately obvious as punctuation or spelling errors, for example. They are often more subtle and require a deeper level of reading analysis and comprehension. Factor in the pressure of the ticking clock on test day, and you'll quickly understand why it's in your best interest to come equipped with a proven set of test-taking strategies and plenty of advanced practice if you're going to achieve your perfect score goal.

Hopefully, it's now abundantly clear why you should devote a significant portion of your study plan to building and practicing your Expression of Ideas skills if you're aiming for a perfect score. We'll first take a brief look at each question type, and then delve deeper, with targeted analysis and practice. Let's move forward!

ORGANIZATION QUESTIONS

On the SAT® Writing and Language Test, you'll encounter a variety of Organization questions, which are designed to assess how well you can make decisions about effective grouping, distribution, and arrangement of ideas at the word, phrase, sentence, and paragraph levels. These will include the following question types: Logical Sequence and Introductions, Conclusions, and Transitions.

LOGICAL SEQUENCE QUESTIONS

These questions will test your ability to recognize if information provided in the passage—a word, phrase, sentence, or paragraph—is in the correct and most effective order. If it isn't, you'll be tasked with fixing it. A question can also introduce a new piece of text and ask you to determine where it best fits within the passage. This order can vary depending on a given passage and its intended purpose.

Always keep in mind that the goal of Logical Sequence questions is to make the information in the passage as cohesive and logical as possible. Here's an example of an Organization question that you may encounter on the SAT® exam:

> **[1]** First, get 6–10 tea bags and a large pitcher of water. **[2]** Boil the water, add the tea bags, and let steep for several hours. **[3]** Let's explore how you can make and enjoy iced tea at home. **[4]** Then add sweetener or lemon and ice, and enjoy your iced tea whenever you're feeling thirsty.

 To make this paragraph most logical, sentence 3 should be placed

- **A.** where it is now.
- **B.** before sentence 1.
- **C.** before sentence 2.
- **D.** after sentence 4.

This is a typical Logical Sequence question. You can see from this example how important organization is to ensure your ideas flow logically and that your audience can understand the thoughts you're trying to convey. Sentence 3 is an introductory sentence, designed to introduce the main topic of the paragraph—how to make iced tea. Therefore, it belongs before sentence 1, so **the correct answer is B.**

> **TIP** Some questions on the SAT® Writing and Language Test will focus on information in the passage that's correct as is. If the passage is correct as written, select choice A.

Introductions, Conclusions, and Transitions

These questions will test your ability to recognize the proper use and placement of information to introduce, conclude, and connect ideas within a passage and to effectively move between related ideas of the different paragraphs in a passage. Once again, this type of question can include moving, revising, adding, or deleting an underlined word, phrase, sentence, or paragraph within the passage, or it may ask you to consider introducing new text to the existing passage.

As you've undoubtedly realized during your academic career, solid introductions, conclusions, and transitions are essential tools for writing effective essays and papers. They help you engage with your audience, connect them with your ideas, and convince them that your thoughts and point of view are worth considering.

Here's an example of a question that falls under the introductions, conclusions, and transitions types that you may encounter on the SAT® exam:

Mice possess incredible speed and agility for their size. They are smart enough to evade a wide variety of traps. Mice even work together to warn each other of potential dangers. **2**

---

2 Which of the following sentences would make the most effective conclusion to this paragraph?

   A. Have you ever seen a mouse in your house?
   B. Cats love chasing—and—catching mice.
   C. Therefore, it's no wonder that mice are difficult to catch!
   D. It's well known that mice have a weakness for cheese.

When determining appropriate conclusion sentences for a paragraph or passage, a key strategy is to determine the main idea of the piece. Here, the preceding sentences all relate to how wily and cunning mice are—and how difficult to catch. Choices A, B, and D all relate to mice, but they fail to adequately sum up this core message. However, choice C captures this notion appropriately. **The correct answer is C.**

Be Careful Using the Answer-as-You-Go Approach!

Often, the best and brightest students like to work as fast as possible on the SAT® Writing and Language Test and tackle each question as they encounter the relevant number or underlined portion while reading a given passage for the first time.

This *can* be a good time-saving approach, but it's a strategy that's often more effective on Standard English Conventions questions, where context is usually less relevant.

On Expression of Ideas questions, the answer-as-you-go approach may *backfire*—particularly if there are carefully designed answer distracters that may *seem* correct until you've read and fully digested the passage and realize they were just cleverly designed traps. If you're on the hunt for a perfect score, you must be able to recognize and avoid such traps. Proceed with caution!

Questions Involving Opening Sentences

As we've mentioned, starting a piece of writing with a powerful and effective opening sentence is essential. The opening sentence sets the tone for the entire piece. It's also the sentence that can hook the reader's interest—or fail to do so. If you fail to capture a reader's attention early on, he or she may stop reading before reaching your key points.

On the Writing and Language Test, you may be tasked with identifying effective opening sentences for the writing passages provided. You'll typically be given a series of possible introductory sentences in a set of answer choices and will be asked to determine which is the most effective, given the context of the passage.

How can you identify effective opening sentences? They do the following:

- **Use engaging words to garner interest and capture attention.** (Example: *When Albert Einstein unveiled his ideas to the world, they rocked the field of physics to its core and changed mankind's understanding of the universe forever.*)

- **State the topic of the piece succinctly, confidently, and clearly.** (Example: *Without question, Albert Einstein's contributions to science have fundamentally changed mankind.*)

- **Ask an intriguing or provocative question.** (Example: *Can you think of someone whose ideas have fundamentally changed mankind forever?*)

- **Deploy a point-counterpoint structure.** (Example: *Most people think Albert Einstein is the most important thinker who has ever lived; however, ...*)

- **Use a surprising fact, theory, or bit of interesting trivia.** (Example: *Although Albert Einstein is widely considered to be one of the most brilliant scientific thinkers who has ever lived, did you know that he struggled to graduate high school?*)

- **If appropriate, uses a bit of humor.** (Example: *I understand that Albert Einstein was a brilliant scientific theorist, but why do I get dizzy every time I try to comprehend his scientific theories?*)

- **Start with a poignant quote.** (Example: *Albert Einstein once said "The difference between stupidity and genius is that genius has its limits."*)

Questions Involving Concluding Sentences

How you end a piece of writing is just as crucial as how you begin it. Remember, you want your writing to have two key impacts: an engaging first impression and a memorable final impression.

An effective conclusion serves to tie up your ideas and leave a lasting impression. It's the finishing touch on a piece of writing, and it should leave the reader feeling satisfied.

Not surprisingly, a strong conclusion should accomplish many of the same goals as a strong introduction:

- Present succinct, clear, and poignant message
- Reiterate key words or phrases from the passage
- Consider a memorable quote or question that encapsulates your main point(s)
- Redefine an important idea or detail in the passage
- Capture your perspective or point of view regarding the topic

Questions Involving Transition Words and Phrases

A key factor in effective writing and organization is how ideas connect to each other. The appropriate use of transition words and phrases in a piece of writing can make all the difference, and without them, a compelling piece with powerful ideas could turn into a rambling and incoherent mess that lacks authority. Sometimes, writers use entire sentences to transition between ideas—and you should be ready to encounter these on the SAT® exam.

As mentioned, transition words provide key context clues for answering questions on this section of the exam. Different transition words and phrases perform different functions, and your ability to recognize when transitions are being used correctly—and when they're not—will likely be put to the test on the SAT® exam. Review and master the following table, which will help you to be able to quickly and effectively tackle questions involving transitions on test day.

Function	Transitional Words and Phrases
Introduction	*to begin, first of all, to start with*
Addition	*also, furthermore, in addition, moreover, secondly*
Clarification	*in other words, that is to say, to put it another way*
Passage of time	*afterwards, later, meanwhile, next, subsequently*
Examples	*for example, for instance, to demonstrate, specifically, to illustrate*
Cause	*because, since*
Effect	*as a result, consequently, therefore*
Comparison	*comparatively, in comparison, in similar fashion, likewise, similarly*
Contrast	*at the same time, however, in contrast, nevertheless, notwithstanding, on the contrary, yet*
Conclusion	*in conclusion, in short, to conclude, to sum up, to summarize, ultimately*

Organization for Clarity and Effect

No passage, no matter how well written, can simply rest on a powerful introduction, memorable conclusion, and strong transitions. For a piece of writing to be fully effective, every sentence and paragraph needs to be on target and well organized.

Effectively tackling these sorts of questions on the SAT® Writing and Language Test begins even before you reach the questions. While you're reading each passage, keep your editorial instincts sharp. Note the type of organization the piece follows and get a sense of its structure and flow, which will help you identify any glaring inconsistencies or illogical organization.

Familiarize yourself with the following common organizational formats:

- **Chronological:** Information is organized by the time that the events occurred (can be forward or reverse).

- **Sequential:** Often used when describing a process, information is organized by the order in which the steps or parts occur.

- **Order of importance:** Information is organized by its relative value or importance (can be most to least important, or vice versa).

- **Compare and contrast:** Often used when writing about two or more things; first, one thing is discussed, and then another to compare it with, and so on.

- **Cause and effect:** Often used to describe a particular result and the events or reasons behind why that result occurred.

- **Issue/problem and solution:** A central dilemma is discussed, followed by strategies for addressing/fixing the problem.

Development Questions

On the SAT® Writing and Language Test, you'll encounter various questions regarding development, which will task you with identifying, revising, adding, and deleting key elements of the passages provided, in an effort to ensure that each piece of writing achieves its intended purpose.

On the test, you'll have to make important decisions about the following:

- **Proposition questions:** the main topic elements of each passage, including topic sentences, thesis statements, and core claims made by an author

- **Support questions:** the supportive elements of each passage, which include supportive information and details that bolster a writer's central ideas or claims made in a piece of writing

- **Focus questions:** the relevant elements of each passage, which requires you to make judgments regarding whether or not information presented supports, detracts, or is irrelevant to an author's purpose and central claims

- **Quantitative Information questions:** supplemental quantitative elements for a given passage; as previously mentioned, you'll encounter graphical information related to specific passages on the SAT® Writing and Language Test, and you'll need to make determinations regarding their purpose, accuracy, and level of effectiveness in relation to the passages. These graphical elements can take the form of graphs, charts, tables, illustrations, etc.

As you're likely aware, these core elements lie at the heart of every piece of writing and are essential tools for any author to effectively convey his or her intended meaning and message. This certainly holds true for the passages you'll encounter on the SAT® exam. For each of these elements, you'll need to make critical, analytical decisions, with the purpose of ensuring that each passage communicates its core points in the clearest and most effective way possible, with relevant support and a sharp focus.

PROPOSITION QUESTIONS

An effective writing passage contains a clear and compelling thesis statement, effective topic sentences, and compelling and relevant contextual claims—all designed to communicate and support the piece's intended meaning. On the SAT® exam, you'll be tasked with making decisions on adding, revising, and deleting material, as well as answering analytical and comprehension questions involving topic sentences, thesis statements, and core claims made by an author. These questions will test your ability to identify the main ideas of a passage and whether or not an author's attempt to convey his or her intended messaging was successful, or if revision is required.

As previously stated, you'll need to keep your "editor's hat" on at all times during the test, not only to identify each of these elements but also to determine if changes are needed. Let's take a closer look at each of these elements and how to effectively tackle related questions on the SAT® Writing and Language Test.

ALERT: If you're reading a passage and something seems wrong or irrelevant to you, make note of it. Chances are, it's *not* a coincidence and you'll come across it again when you're answering the questions. If you're already familiar with an issue and are ready for it, you'll likely save yourself some time finding the correct answer.

Check for a Stem

Proposition questions often—though not always—appear with a question stem, asking you to make a key decision about specific text, either currently within the passage, the question, or the answer choices. A typical question stem could be as follows:

Which of the following sentences should be deleted to reinforce the author's point of view that hippos are the most dangerous animals in the jungle?

Use this signal to help you quickly identify this question type and determine the best approach for getting the correct answer.

Thesis Statement

A thesis statement is a brief statement designed to succinctly convey an author's main point or claim. For example, a simple thesis statement for an essay might be as follows:

Thesis statement: *The hippopotamus is among the most formidable and dangerous animals in the jungle.*

The piece of writing that follows this thesis statement—if written well—should be designed to support this notion regarding the hippopotamus.

Whenever you begin a piece of writing, you should always have a thesis statement already in mind, as this will lie at the very core of why you're writing the piece in the first place.

Here's an example of a Proposition question similar to one you may encounter on test day and how to effectively attack it:

> Today, over 92 percent of Americans reportedly own cell phones and use them on a daily basis. More Americans now receive their news from websites than traditional newspapers. Americans can now handle a wide variety of daily responsibilities—from banking to paying bills—from the phones in their pockets. Even shopping for all the things they need can quickly and easily be handled without ever having to leave their homes. **3**

3 Which choice best reflects the main idea of the paragraph?

- **A.** Advances in technology have changed how average Americans live their lives.
- **B.** The average American no longer enjoys reading newspapers or shopping in stores.
- **C.** People all around the world have embraced modern technology in their daily lives.
- **D.** Americans are excited to see what the future has in store for modern technology.

In this question, we're on the lookout for a thesis statement that best summarizes all of the points in the paragraph. Perhaps you recognize a suitable answer immediately among the answer choices? If so, great—select it and move on to the next question. If you need more time, try eliminating incorrect answer choices to help you arrive at the correct answer. Choice B is incorrect because we aren't told in the paragraph whether or not the average American enjoys reading newspapers or shopping in stores. Choice C is incorrect because the paragraph focuses on Americans only, not people all over the world. Choice D is incorrect because the paragraph is focused on current technology, not the future of technology. That leaves us with choice A, which appropriately reflects the main idea of the paragraph: advances in technology have changed how average Americans live their lives. **The correct answer is A.**

When you run into trouble on a question, try eliminating as many incorrect answer choices as possible to help increase your chances of arriving at the correct answer.

Topic Sentences

Topic sentences can be considered the "thesis statements" of the paragraphs in which they appear—they communicate the main ideas of each of the paragraphs that make up a given piece of writing. Each paragraph—including the introduction, the body paragraphs, and the conclusion—will likely have an identifiable main idea designed to deliver its core point and purpose and support the piece as a whole.

Building on the thesis statement in the previous example, here's a sample topic sentence:

> **Thesis statement:** *The hippopotamus is among the most formidable and dangerous animals in the jungle.*
>
> **Topic sentence:** *The jaw of the hippopotamus is capable of almost unparalleled bite strength.*

Notice that the topic sentence directly supports the thesis statement. In essence, according to the author, one of the reasons why the hippopotamus is among the most formidable and dangerous animals in the jungle is because the jaw of the hippopotamus is capable of almost unparalleled bite strength.

Topic sentences often appear at the beginning or early on in a paragraph, with the material that follows designed to support the central claims made in these key sentences.

Core Claims

A core claim is a point or assertion that a writer is trying to make in his or her writing, which, when delivered effectively, relates directly back to both the topic sentence of the paragraph in which it appears as well as the thesis statement of the entire passage.

Claims can be found in persuasive, argumentative, and informative passages and can also take the form of a counterclaim, which is an opposing point of view or assertion to that of an author's. When handled effectively, directly addressing counterclaims in a piece of writing is an effective tool for providing a multifaceted, comprehensive analysis of an issue or argument.

Building on the thesis statement and topic sentence in the previous example, here's a sample claim:

Thesis statement: *The hippopotamus is among the most formidable and dangerous animals in the jungle.*

Topic sentence: *The jaw of the hippopotamus is capable of an almost unparalleled bite strength.*

Claim: *While defending themselves, hippos have been known to crush other dangerous predators—including alligators and crocodiles—using the pressure of their mighty jaws and large teeth.*

Notice how the claim made here directly supports both the topic sentence of the paragraph in which it would appear and the overall thesis statement.

Let's look at a possible counterclaim and how an author might address it within a paragraph.

Counterclaim: *Some scientists claim that tigers are the most formidable and dangerous animals in the jungle.*

Response to counterclaim: *However, there are numerous accounts of hippos successfully defending themselves from tiger attacks.*

A nuanced, well-developed essay will *not* shy away from directly addressing a counterclaim—it will not only mention it, it will also have a satisfying response to it.

Remember—you *don't* have to agree with the authors' core claims or revise your point of view to bring them into alignment—your job on test day is to determine if each author effectively communicated his or her intended point of view and to make revisions where needed in order to help ensure that this is done as well as possible.

SUPPORT QUESTIONS

Any passage worth the words that were used to write it will include sufficient support and details to bolster the author's point of view and claims. These are the subordinate ideas that lend credence and reinforcement to the larger central ideas in a piece of writing and can include relevant facts, research, details, data, figures, and examples.

On the SAT® Writing and Language Test, you'll be tasked with making decisions on adding, revising, and deleting supportive textual material, as well as answering analytical and comprehension questions involving relevant support, in an effort to bolster the points of view of the passage authors.

Let's take a look back at the hippopotamus and our previous core claim:

> **Thesis statement:** *The hippopotamus is among the most formidable and dangerous animals in the jungle.*

Here are a few examples of supportive claims for this main idea, as well as one claim that fails to support it. Can you identify the claim that fails to provide relevant support?

> **Support A:** *Hippos are extremely aggressive and unpredictable animals.*

> **Support B:** *Hippos possess a tremendous bite force.*

> **Support C:** *Hippos are largely herbivorous creatures.*

> **Support D:** *Hippos possess great strength and surprising speed and agility.*

As you might have guessed, choice C fails to support the core claim that hippos are dangerous and formidable jungle animals. Although this information *does* relate to the hippo and *does* provide an interesting contextual fact, the fact that hippos are largely vegetarians *does not* directly support the thesis statement that they are formidable and dangerous.

FOCUS QUESTIONS

Recognizing appropriate, effective, and necessary contextual information within a passage and eradicating the existence of irrelevant, tangential, or redundant information is a common question type on the SAT® Writing and Language Test. Remember, your goal on test day is to improve the passages you'll encounter, which includes text relevance and focus.

Every writer—and passage—has a focus, and information provided can either serve to support that focus or detract from it.

Let's refer back to our hippo example and take a look at how focus can come into play.

> **Thesis statement:** *The hippopotamus is among the most formidable and dangerous animals in the jungle.*

> **Topic sentence:** *The jaw of the hippopotamus is capable of an almost unparalleled bite strength.*

Let's concentrate on our topic sentence for a moment, which provides a core claim for one of the paragraphs within a passage whose core claim is as follows: The hippopotamus is one of the most formidable and dangerous animals in the jungle.

> **[1]** The jaw of the hippopotamus is capable of an almost unparalleled bite strength. **[2]** Using available technology, scientists have measured the sheer bite force of an adult hippo at a staggering 8,100 newtons. **[3]** Hippos have been known to crush other large and dangerous animals between their powerful jaws. **[4]** Other animals with powerful jaw strength include crocodiles and lions. **4**

---

4 Which of the following sentences in the paragraph should be eliminated to maintain the focus of the paragraph?

    A. Sentence 1

    B. Sentence 2

    C. Sentence 3

    D. Sentence 4

Were you able to determine the sentence that's a bit off focus? Sentence 4 is the best choice. The other sentences *directly* relate to the topic sentence (sentence 1) and maintain the focus of the paragraph. However, sentence 4 provides tangential information and should be deleted. **The correct answer is D.**

If you're aiming for a perfect score on test day, your ability to identify an author's purpose and focus and make sound judgments regarding text relevance will need to be super sharp. Bring your best editing eye on test day, and when you read each passage, make note of anything that seems off, including redundant words and phrases, and any information that seems completely off-topic or just barely related to the central ideas of the passage.

QUANTITATIVE INFORMATION QUESTIONS

As previously mentioned, some of the passages on the SAT® Writing and Language Test will be accompanied by an associated informational graphic, which will provide relevant quantitative information pertaining to the passage topic.

Let's refer back to our hippopotamus example. The informational graphic shown below might accompany a passage with the following thesis: The hippopotamus is among the most formidable and dangerous animals in the jungle.

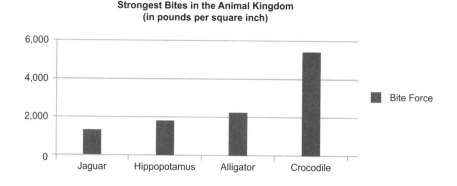

Strongest Bites in the Animal Kingdom
(in pounds per square inch)

The following question might appear in relation to this informational graphic:

[1] The hippopotamus is among the most formidable and dangerous animals in the jungle. [2] They possess an **5** unrivaled bite force, and a fearsome size and agility. [3] Wild hippos can be aggressive and unpredictable, and are best avoided when encountered by man or animal. [4] Hippos have been known to crush attacking predators between their powerful jaws.

5 Based on the information provided in the graph, what would be the most effective revision to the underlined word?

A. NO CHANGE
B. incredible
C. overrated
D. unmatched

Based on the informational graphic, we can see that although the bite force of the hippopotamus is formidable, there are other animals with stronger bite forces (alligators and crocodiles), so choices A and D are incorrect. *Overrated* (choice C) is also not an appropriate choice, considering that hippos have one of the top four bite forces in the animal kingdom according to the graph. As hippos possess an incredible bite force, **the correct answer is B**.

Be prepared to encounter a variety of informational graphics on test day. These can take the form of tables, charts, graphs, or illustrations, and the information itself in the graphic can take a variety of quantitative forms. You'll be tasked with analyzing and interpreting the data provided and determining how it relates to the passage and topic.

EFFECTIVE LANGUAGE USE QUESTIONS

Questions that fall into the Effective Language Use category are designed to analyze how effectively authors make key language choices to achieve a variety of important rhetorical goals, which include the following:

- **Syntax:** ensures that text in each passage is coherent and arranged properly, and it delivers a logical flow of thoughts and ideas

- **Precision:** ensures that information in each passage is clear, focused, and to the point

- **Concision:** ensures that each passage is free from repetition and distracting wordiness

- **Style and Tone:** ensures that each passage maintains a consistent voice, mood, and effect

Let's take a closer look at each of the core areas of Effective Language Use.

SYNTAX

Syntax refers to the appropriate arrangement of words to create well-constructed sentences in a piece of writing. It is one of those "unseen girders" that provides essential structural support to every phrase, sentence, and paragraph. Without proper syntax, your writing would descend into a chaotic, unintelligible mess, leaving your readers confused, bewildered, and lost.

On the SAT® Writing and Language Test, you'll be tasked with analyzing and making key decisions regarding an author's use of syntax for the passages you'll encounter. Syntax questions often require you to analyze connections between related sentences; determine how sentences can be combined to enhance cohesion, emphasis, and flow; and make revisions to improve flow and cohesion.

Let's take a look at a sample question involving syntax:

> Sir Isaac Newton is widely regarded as the father of modern classical **6** physics. Sir Isaac Newton is also recognized as one of the most influential scientific theorists in world history. Newton's formulations on the laws of motion and universal gravitation revolutionized scientific theory and understanding. His contributions to science and mathematics still help shape our understanding of the universe, nearly three centuries after his death.

6 Which of the following answer choices most effectively combines these two sentences?

- **A.** physics, Sir Isaac Newton
- **B.** physics Sir Isaac Newton,
- **C.** physics and Mr. Newton
- **D.** physics and

The correct answer is D. The first two sentences of this paragraph contain the same subject (Sir Isaac Newton) and can be effectively combined with the coordinating conjunction *and*: *Sir Isaac Newton is widely regarded as the father of modern classical physics and is also recognized as one of the most influential scientific theorists in world history.* Combining the sentences using only a comma creates a comma splice, and combining the sentences with no punctuation between them creates a run-on sentence, so we can eliminate choices A and B. The subject does not need to be repeated twice in the same sentence, so we can eliminate choice C.

> **ALERT:** On test day, your goal is *not* to revise the author's perspective or point of view to align it with yours. Remembering this when taking the test will help you save time and avoid some tricky answer choice traps that simply revise the author's intended meaning.

PRECISION

Language precision is often something you quickly recognize when you encounter it in a piece of writing. When we read something that's direct, precise, and on target, it's often easy to follow, memorable, and a joy to read. Conversely, most of us would appreciate the opportunity to avoid a piece of writing that's vague, meandering, and generally imprecise—which generally makes for a confusing and frustrating reading experience.

Furthermore, the author of a piece of writing that lacks precision runs the risk of losing his or her authority regarding the topic—even if he or she is an expert in the subject—and may lose the audience altogether.

Precision questions on the SAT® Writing and Language Test often ask you to make decisions regarding the use of words or phrases in order to appropriately convey an author's intended meaning. Here's a sample Precision question, similar to those you may encounter on test day:

> Alfred Hitchcock is a famous twentieth-century English movie director. His catalog of scary and thrilling films have garnered him the **7** <u>unavoidable</u> title of "The Master of Suspense." Among his more memorable works are *The Birds* and *Psycho*. During his lifetime, Hitchcock earned two Golden Globe Awards, an Academy Award for Best Picture, and he even achieved knighthood in 1979.

7 A. NO CHANGE
   B. unofficial
   C. overused
   D. irreversible

In this question, we're being asked to make a decision regarding precise word choice. As written (choice A), the underlined word *unavoidable* adds a confusing element to the sentence, as this title is not something that cannot be avoided. There's no reason to think that the title is overused or irreversible, so choices C and D are incorrect. The most logical word choice to describe this title, which was not granted by any official office or governing body, is *unofficial*. **The correct answer is B.**

CONCISION

Strong writing reflects a thorough understanding of word economy—making cogent, concise, and effective points in as few words as possible. Unnecessary or repetitive words, phrases, and sentences can turn a lean and mean piece of well-structured writing into a bloated, rambling, and confusing mess.

On the SAT® exam, you'll likely be tested on your ability to recognize and fix issues of verbosity and word redundancy in the passages provided. These types of questions are typically focused at the sentence level; you'll be tasked with identifying and eradicating wordiness to improve the flow of sentences and, as a result, improve the passages as a whole. However, you typically don't need to analyze the entire passage to handle these types of questions.

 If a question involves the option to delete text, this is often a signal that there may be issues involving redundancy or wordiness to address.

Let's tackle a sample concision question:

[1] The bearded dragon—actually a lizard—is widely considered to be the fastest reptile in the animal kingdom. [2] Bearded dragons have been measured to attain speeds equivalent to 25 miles per hour. [3] No other reptile is faster, on average, than this swift creature. [4] The beard of this lizard, which is the fleshy underside of its throat, is not used while running, but rather as a courtship tool and a warning to potential rivals. **8**

---

8 Which of the sentences should be deleted in order to eliminate redundancy and maximize concision?

- **A.** Sentence 1
- **B.** Sentence 2
- **C.** Sentence 3
- **D.** Sentence 4

While reading this paragraph, did you note any information repeated multiple times? Sentence 1 tells us that the bearded dragon "is widely considered to be the fastest reptile in the animal kingdom." Therefore, we don't need to be retold in sentence 3 that "No other reptile is faster, on average, than this swift creature." Sentence 3 can be eliminated without losing any information, so **the correct answer is C.**

Style and Tone

When a writer is plotting out a piece of writing, he or she has to think about the audience, which will help guide the appropriate style and tone. When you read a piece of writing, you should be able to determine how the writer feels about the topic and how the writer wants to make his or her readers feel. Writers employ elements of style and tone to create their intended effects.

A writer shouldn't be using the same formal style and tone in a professional letter or technical academic journal article as he or she would in a casual email or friendly letter. The following is a list of common formal and informal writing categories with which you should generally be familiar.

Formal	Informal
Technical journal	Blog post
Academic paper	Entertainment magazine article
Newspaper article	Fictional story
Scientific study	Novel
Professional correspondence	Personal essay
Educational textbook	Post on social media site
Professional presentation	Friendly e-mail or tweet

The passages you will encounter won't necessarily announce the kinds of writing they are, but you'll be able to tell if they require formal or informal language based on how they're written. On test day, you'll be tasked with recognizing the intended style and tone of a passage, and ensuring that it remains appropriately consistent throughout. The following are the sorts of logical inconsistencies that you'll need to be able to recognize and fix on the SAT® Writing and Language Test:

- Does a writer shift between an active or passive voice in the passage?

- Does the writer use—or misuse—a specific stylistic flourish to create a certain effect on the audience?

- Does a writer seem to be in favor of a particular topic, and then suddenly seem to take a negative stance without rhyme or reason?

- Does a writer establish a cheerful mood, and then suddenly things get dark for no logical reason?

Let's tackle a sample style and tone question:

> DataGraphics, Inc. recently reported its fiscal year revenue results. The company, a key producer of electronics components for mobile phones and computers, missed its annual revenue goal by 16%. "We're extremely **9** bummed out by these results, and rest assured that we're making the necessary internal changes to ensure that next year's results are better," the CEO responded to stockholders. Despite her claim, the CEO was fired and replaced within the following week.

9 **A.**   NO CHANGE
    B.   excited
    C.   disappointed
    D.   in a funk

This question requires that you recognize the formal style and tone of this paragraph, which is reporting the economic results of a specific business, DataGraphics, Inc. As written (choice A), the underlined phrase seems awkward. *Bummed out* is a phrase more appropriate for an informal piece of writing, like an e-mail or text message between friends. A statement by a corporate CEO to stockholders would be more formal and reflect the seriousness of missing the annual revenue goal. Choice D is also too informal and thus incorrect. Choice B is incorrect because it reflects the opposite sentiment than what the CEO would want to project. Choice C is the most appropriate answer choice given the style and tone of the paragraph. **The correct answer is C.**

Additional Writing and Language Skills Tested on the SAT® Exam

Remember that each type of Expression of Ideas question on the SAT® Writing and Language Test will assess your skill in the following areas:

- **Words in Context** questions gauge your mastery of effective and appropriate word choice, based on context.

- **Command of Evidence** questions test your ability to grasp how effectively a piece of writing conveys information to enhance meaning, sharpen claims, and provide support.

- **Analysis in History/Social Studies and in Science** questions measure your ability to critically read and analyze passages based on these important topic areas.

ATTACKING PASSAGES AND EXPRESSION OF IDEAS QUESTIONS FOR A PERFECT SCORE

Now you have a better sense of the main types of Expression of Ideas questions that you'll encounter on the SAT® Writing and Language Test. We know you're gunning for a perfect score—and we know that practice makes perfect—so let's tackle some practice questions in the context and format that you'll encounter on test day—in a complete passage. We'll also cover proven strategies and techniques for effectively attacking the sorts of passages and questions you'll encounter in this test section. Let's get started!

The following passage includes five questions that are designed to test your skills with Expression of Ideas questions.

Edward Hopper: An American Life

Some know the art before the artist, and for American realist painter and printmaker Edward Hopper, that's often the case. Many people instantly recognize *Nighthawks*, the **1** famous and instantly recognizable 1942 oil painting of a quasi-desolate, street-side coffee shop that's widely considered a classic example of the American Realism art movement, but fewer people can easily name the artist, or recognize the name Edward Hopper if they run across it. That said, Hopper's prolific artistic catalog—reflecting his vision of modern American life—places him soundly at the vanguard of this bold twentieth- century art movement. **2**

Edward Hopper was born in upstate New York in the late nineteenth century, 1882 to be exact, to a comfortable Baptist family of Dutch descent—the son of a dry goods merchant. Hopper was a fine student, and showed a predilection for artistic endeavors from an early age. He began drawing as a young boy, encouraged and supported by his parents, and by the time Hopper was a teenager, he was painting—using oils, charcoals, and watercolors to depict that natural world that enveloped his childhood existence. He showed an early interest in nautical subject matter and found great inspiration in the ships and sailing vessels that occupied the northern Hudson River that flowed near his family home.

After graduation, Hopper decided not to pursue his initial career choice of naval architect, instead opting to follow his artistic passion. On the insistence of his parents, Hopper received an education in commercial art in New York City, in an effort to have a means of stable and ③ <u>uncertain</u> income. New York City has been a home to a wide variety of artists and creative individuals over the years. It was here that he found the early artistic influences that would help shape his burgeoning artistic sensibilities, including his art teacher Robert Henri, who encouraged his students to let their art reflect their real interests in the world. Hopper's early years after art school reflected an intense inner struggle to find his artistic purpose and voice, as well as a struggle between creative and commercial demands. It wasn't until his trip to Massachusetts in 1912 to find fresh inspiration and paint the natural world, and his first painting sale (entitled *Sailing*) at the Armory Show in 1913, did things turn around for Edward Hopper, and a clear path forward emerged. ④

Edward Hopper's artistic output and notoriety slowly grew, and after getting married in 1924, his artistic voice and sensibilities quickly flourished and matured with the help of his wife, who devoted herself to supporting Edward's career. Hopper found and embraced his spare yet bold painting style and his uncanny ability to capture the quiet beauty and bittersweet desperation of rural and urban American life, from the cold Manhattan streets to the natural splendor of the New England landscapes that surrounded him. Hopper died in 1967 in his New York City studio, less than a year before his wife Josephine died. ⑤

① **A.** NO CHANGE
   B. famous or instantly recognizable
   C. infamous
   D. famous

② Which of the following sentences would make an effective transition between paragraphs 1 and 2?

   A. Edward Hopper married Josephine Nivison, an artist whom he initially met during art school.
   B. Let's review the origin and key events of the famous Armory art show, where Hopper sold his first painting.

   C. How did Edward Hopper spend the final years of his important life?
   D. Let's take a closer look at the life of this fascinating individual.

③ **A.** NO CHANGE
   B. fluctuating
   C. steady
   D. influential

4 Which of the following sentences in paragraph 3 can be deleted without affecting the theme of the passage?

A. After graduation, Hopper decided not to pursue his initial career choice of naval architect, instead opting to follow his artistic passion.

B. On the insistence of his parents, Hopper received an education in commercial art in New York City, in an effort to have a means of uncertain income.

C. New York City has been a home to a wide variety of artists and creative individuals over the years.

D. Hopper's early years after art school reflected an intense inner struggle to find his artistic purpose and voice, as well as a struggle between creative and commercial demands.

5 Which of the following would make an effective concluding sentence to the passage?

A. His contributions to the art world and his influence on successive generations of new artists is undeniable.

B. Who is your favorite artist, and why have you chosen this person?

C. Edward Hopper spent the majority of his prolific adult years divided between homes in Manhattan and Cape Cod.

D. Let's explore some of Edward Hopper's professional commercial work.

Now let's take a closer look at how you can effectively tackle this passage and its questions.

ATTACKING WRITING AND LANGUAGE PASSAGES

Yes, you're keenly aware that the clock is ticking on test day and that you only have 35 minutes to read and analyze the Writing and Language passages and answer 44 multiple-choice questions on this section of the exam.

However, you're an elite student and can move quickly and efficiently on any given academic task—especially one that can help you achieve your goal of earning a perfect score. So, consider mastering the following quick yet helpful strategies for attacking SAT® passages as time well spent on your quest for a perfect score.

Step 1: Analyze the passage type.

After you read each passage, take quick but careful note of what type of passage it is and what the main ideas are. Was it informational? Was it a persuasive piece? Does it present opposing sides of a controversial issue? Did it cover a significant event in history or a seminal figure? This process will help you identify—and remember—the main purpose of the passage, which will help you save time in the long run as you attack the questions.

The passage we're working with here is an informational biographical snapshot of Edward Hopper, an influential twentieth-century artist.

Step 2: Note general passage construction and organization.

This step is especially useful for attacking Expression of Ideas questions, which include issues of organization. Quickly note the general construction of the piece—this will really help you make determinations about proper placement and movement of new words, phrases, sentences, and paragraphs if the need arises in the questions that follow.

Paragraph 1 provides a general overview of the life of Hopper. Paragraph 2 covers his early years. Paragraph 3 covers his post-graduate years and struggle to find hid artistic voice. Paragraph 4 covers his later years, success, and his death.

Step 3: Note any glaring rhetorical issues.

Does something strange jump out at you while reading a passage? Is there information that's clearly missing, strangely worded, or glaringly out of place? If so, consider making a brief mental or written note about it. The passages you'll encounter on test day are carefully designed with meticulous attention to detail, so you can be sure that any glaring errors are intentional—and that you'll be tasked with fixing them on test day. Did anything stand out for you while reading "Edward Hopper: An American Life"? If so, consider making a quick note of it.

Again, *don't* spend a great deal of time on these steps—you don't even have to write them down if you feel it throws off your test-taking pace. However, it might be to your benefit to quickly go through these steps when attacking each reading passage, regardless of what it's about, so you'll be well prepared to handle any type of question that you may face.

On your quest for a perfect test score, make sure you're *always* reading critically when tackling passages on the SAT® Writing and Language Test.

ATTACKING EXPRESSION OF IDEAS QUESTIONS

If you carefully break down and analyze the passages you encounter on the SAT® exam, you'll be well prepared to attack any type of Expression of Ideas question you'll encounter on test day. We'll show you how using the Expression of Ideas questions associated with the passage "Edward Hopper: An American Life."

1 **A.** NO CHANGE
   B. famous or instantly recognizable
   C. infamous
   D. famous

Attacking the question: This is a concision question, and like every question you'll encounter on the SAT® Writing and Language Test, you should first identify what's being asked of you before attempting to answer it. A good strategy for starting is to quickly scan the answer choices. Here, you'll see a series of variations of the underlined phrase in the passage, which should immediately signal you that you're being asked to make a word choice decision and that something *may* be wrong with the sentence as written. Now we know what we're dealing with!

Perhaps while you first read the passage, you encountered the issue underlined here and quickly discovered the correct way to fix it. If so, that's great—mark it and move on. If not, take a methodical approach. Go back to the underlined portion and reread it. Does the issue and answer reveal itself now? If so, you know what to do—mark it and move on. If not, keep reading.

Scan the answer choices and look for clues. There seems to be some variation in how the words *famous* and *instantly recognizable* appear—or do not appear. That's a possible clue that this is at the heart of the question. Reread the underlined portion of the passage, and you may discover that this is a question of redundancy. Using both *famous* and *instantly recognizable* is clearly redundant because they essentially mean the same thing. Which answer choice fixes this issue? This question is at the heart of a key strategy for attacking Writing and Language Test questions—the correct answer will always be the choice that best improves the passage. Make all of your decisions with this in mind.

In this case, **the correct answer is D**. A quick way to test it is to plug in the correct answer and see if it works. Choice D eliminates the redundancy without affecting the author's intended meaning—thereby improving the passage. As written, choice A contains the original redundancy problem. Choices B and C confuse or alter the meaning of the sentence and do not fix the redundancy.

A key point worth noting for this and other questions you may encounter on test day is this: Don't try to select answer choices out of context! Some answer choices may *seem* to be the most appropriate or best choices when scanning the list of options, but you won't be able to confidently choose the correct answers unless you're fully aware of how it works within the context of the passage. On the SAT®, context is key!

---

2 Which of the following sentences would make an effective transition between paragraphs 1 and 2?

    A. Edward Hopper married Josephine Nivison, an artist whom he initially met during art school.

    B. Let's review the origin and key events of the famous Armory art show, where Hopper sold his first painting.

    C. How did Edward Hopper spend the final years of his important life?

    D. Let's take a closer look at the life of this fascinating individual.

Attacking the question: This is a transition question, and it is asking you to determine which sentence among the answer choices would make the most effective transition between paragraphs 1 and 2. Questions involving adding transition sentences between paragraphs are common on this section of the exam. Let's get to the heart of what's being asked here and attack the question.

The question focuses on a transition sentence between paragraphs 1 and 2. When you see the term *transition sentence* in a question, it may help to think of a bridge. Remember earlier in the chapter when we suggested making a few quick notes on the structure and organization of the reading passages you'll encounter? Those notes will really come in handy when attacking organization questions. We've already noted that paragraph 1 provides a general overview of the life of Edward Hopper, and paragraph 2 covers his early years. Scan the answer choices. Would any of them serve as an effective bridge between these two concepts?

We can quickly eliminate choice A, which contains information that is better suited for paragraph 4. Choices B and C also contain information that is best suited for later in the passage. **The correct answer is D.** We can check by plugging it into the passage and seeing that it works quite well.

 A. NO CHANGE
B. fluctuating
C. steady
D. influential

Attacking the question: This is a classic word choice precision question; the varied selection of words among the answer choices should immediately signal you that you're dealing with a word choice question. Again, for these and other types of questions on the Writing and Language Test, context is key. Let's examine the sentence that contains the underline in question. What's the main idea of the sentence? It highlights Hopper's parents' urging that Edward receive an education in commercial art for a stable income. Which word among the answer choices supports the notion of a stable income? **The correct answer is C.** A *steady* income supports this notion. An *uncertain* income (choice A), *fluctuating* income (choice B), or *influential* income (choice D) don't fit within the passage.

4 Which of the following sentences in paragraph 3 can be deleted without affecting the theme of the passage?

A. After graduation, Hopper decided not to pursue his initial career choice of naval architect, instead opting to follow his artistic passion.
B. On the insistence of his parents, Hopper received an education in commercial art in New York City, in an effort to have a means of steady income.
C. New York City has been a home to a wide variety of artists and creative individuals over the years.
D. Hopper's early years after art school reflected an intense inner struggle to find his artistic purpose and voice, as well as a struggle between creative and commercial demands.

Attacking the question: This strategy question is trying to gauge your ability to recognize what information in a passage is critical and what is superfluous. We've already established that this passage is an informational biographical snapshot of Edward Hopper, an influential twentieth-century artist. We've also established that paragraph 3 covers his post-graduate years and struggle to find his artistic voice, so we can quickly hone in on the correct answer. Do you see how this strategy can prove valuable? Which of these answer choices does *not* fit in with these established themes, or is the *least* best fit? **The correct answer is C.** This information about New York City in general, while possibly interesting, does not support or directly relate to the central theme, Hopper's life, while the other answer choices do.

5 Which of the following would make an effective concluding sentence to the passage?

A. His contributions to the art world and his influence on successive generations of new artists is undeniable.

B. Who is your favorite artist, and why have you chosen this person?

C. Edward Hopper spent the majority of his prolific adult years divided between homes in Manhattan and Cape Cod.

D. Let's explore some of Edward Hopper's professional commercial work.

Attacking the question: Here's a classic strategy question that's asking you to make a decision on the best way to conclude the passage. A great first step for tackling this question is to quickly ask yourself, "What makes an effective essay conclusion?" A strong essay conclusion is often a poignant and memorable wrap-up of the main themes and ideas that lie at the core of the written piece.

Referring back to our notes, this passage is an informational biographical snapshot of Edward Hopper, an influential twentieth-century artist. The concluding paragraph covers his later years, success, and his death. Do any of the answer choices capture the spirit of these central ideas? **The correct answer is A.** This sentence refers to Edward Hopper's legacy on the art world after a long and successful career, which effectively ties back to the main idea of the passage. Choice B is a question posed to readers, which is not the most appropriate conclusion. Choice C is a supportive detail, which is not appropriate for a concluding sentence. Choice D is a lead-in sentence for additional information, which is not an effective way to end a passage.

Bring Your Best Test-Taking Tools!

We can't say this enough: The tools in your test-taking arsenal that have served you well thus far in your academic career will be among your *best* tools when taking the SAT® exam. The *key* here is to practice before test day, to make sure you're comfortable using your test-taking skills within the format and timing of the official exam.

Some skills are transferable for any test—some aren't. We recommend you work on combining your existing skills with the strategies provided in this book, and with careful practice, you'll have an effective mix of tools in your corner on test day!

Now that you have a thorough understanding of how Expression of Ideas questions are tested on the SAT® Writing and Language Test, the types of questions you'll likely encounter on test day, and effective strategies for attacking both the passages and the various question types, your best approach between now and test day is to get as much practice and review as possible, so you can get comfortable with the timing and format of the exam, build a comfortable test-taking pace, get accustomed with using the right strategies for each question type, and get closer to your goal of a perfect SAT® score!

EXPRESSION OF IDEAS PRACTICE

Complete the following problems. Answers and explanations follow on page 289.

Citizens United vs. Federal Election Commission: In Focus

In 2010, history bore witness to a court case whose outcome had a significant and lasting effect on how America's "political machine" operates and is funded, and has fueled a divisive rift among individuals regarding the ethical parameters of campaign finance contributions and how campaign spending is regulated. Let's take a closer look at this landmark freedom of speech case, which was adjudicated by the United States Supreme Court, including the key viewpoints of those who fiercely support and oppose the resultant decision. **1**

[1] The core decision point in *Citizens United vs. Federal Election Commission* was whether or not Citizens United, a conservative not-for-profit group, could air and purchase advertising on television for a short film that was critical of Hillary Clinton during the 2008 presidential election. [2] It was the position of the Federal Election Commission that this was a violation of an existing federal law whose purpose was to restrict certain entities, such as unions and corporations, from funding certain electioneering communications—in essence, **2** enhancing the amount of influence union and corporate money can have on advertisements and political tools designed to influence the hearts and minds of voters. [3] Let's take a close look at the dispute at the heart of the case. **3**

The Supreme Court ultimately ruled that independent political expenditures could not be restricted, as it would violate the constitutionally protected right to free speech that all citizens and entities enjoy. As a result of the ruling in *Citizens United vs. Federal Election Commission*, unions, corporations, and other similar entities now had the right to spend unlimited sums of money on communications and advertising tools designed to support an individual candidate or political party. **4**

[1] Critics of the *Citizens United vs. Federal Election Commission* decision have argued that this ruling essentially allows corporate and political entities with large pools of money to have an **5** unfettered ability to influence political campaigns and elections—and provide targeted political support—through persuasive advertising and other means of influential communication. [2] They claim that although this case doesn't allow unlimited direct campaign contributions to candidates,

the ruling does provide wealthy entities and the individuals who are at their helms plenty of avenues to indirectly and unfairly influence politics—and their own agendas. **[3]** For example, several billion dollars are spent during the average modern presidential election cycle. **[4]** Those who support the decision of the U.S. Supreme Court claim that it is within their constitutional rights and freedoms—particularly the right to free speech—to publicly voice their opinions on political races and their candidates as they see fit. **[5]** They also claim that since this case does not affect direct financial contributions to campaigns, then there is no corruption or unfair influence of the political process at play here. **[6]** Regarding this case, one thing is certain, and that is that vigorous debate and strong opinions on both sides of the issue exist. **[7]** **6** Only time, and the passage of time, will tell if public opinion on *Citizens United vs. Federal Election Commission* shifts or holds—and if the ruling by the U.S. Supreme Court stands firm. **7**

Public Opinion Survey on *Citizens United vs. Federal Election Commission* Decision

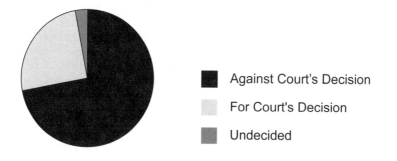

Against Court's Decision

For Court's Decision

Undecided

1 The author wishes to open paragraph 1 with a sentence that will set the theme and tone of the passage. Which of the following would most effectively accomplish this?

A. Does your school have a mock trial or debate club that lets you practice and build your rhetorical skills?

B. The history of the United States is filled with many significant court battles that have taken place within the country's judicial system.

C. It can be argued that *Brown v. The Board of Education* was among the most influential and historic court cases in the history of the United States.

D. What is the most difficult decision that you have had to make in your life?

2 **A.** NO CHANGE
   B. highlighting
   C. limiting
   D. evading

3 To make paragraph 2 most logical, sentence 3 should be

   A. placed where it is now.
   B. placed before sentence 1.
   C. placed after sentence 1.
   D. moved to the following paragraph.

4 Which of the following sentences would make an effective transition between paragraphs 2 and 3?

   A. Are you eager to vote in a political campaign?
   B. Do people vote with their hearts or their minds?
   C. What court cases do you consider influential?
   D. But what did the court think about the issue?

5 **A.** NO CHANGE
   B. encumbered
   C. litigious
   D. voluminous

6 **A.** NO CHANGE
   B. Only time or the passage of time, will tell
   C. Only time will tell
   D. Will tell only time or the passage of time

7 For the sake of unity and coherence, which of the following sentences does not belong in paragraph 4?

   A. Sentence 1
   B. Sentence 2
   C. Sentence 3
   D. Sentence 4

8 The author wants to add the following information to the essay:

The Supreme Court vote was split 5-4 on the ruling in *Citizens United vs. Federal Election Commission.*

Into which paragraph would it be the most effective to insert this sentence?

   A. Paragraph 1
   B. Paragraph 2
   C. Paragraph 3
   D. Paragraph 4

9 Which choice most effectively establishes the main topic of the passage?

   A. *Citizens United vs. Federal Election Commission* is an important but controversial case that affects how money is spent during political campaigns.
   B. *Citizens United vs. Federal Election Commission* is a recent but insignificant case that affects how people vote for Supreme Court Justices.

C. *Citizens United vs. Federal Election Commission* is an historic but disputed case that affects how politicians can spend their campaign funds.

D. *Citizens United vs. Federal Election Commission* is a disastrous but relevant case that affects how corporations make direct contributions to political candidates.

10 You decide to report the survey results in the pie chart in an online article. Which of the following would be the most appropriate article title?

A. Public Opinion Mostly Supports Supreme Court Decision

B. Public Opinion Largely Against Supreme Court Decision

C. Public Opinion Undecided Regarding Supreme Court Decision

D. Most People are Disinterested in Supreme Court Decision

Answer Key and Explanations

1. B	**3.** B	**5.** A	**7.** C	**9.** A
2. C	**4.** D	**6.** C	**8.** B	**10.** B

1. **The correct answer is B.** This question asks you to make a decision about including additional supporting information in the passage. In particular, you're being tasked with adding an introductory sentence; introductory sentences should serve to grab the reader's attention and help set the theme and tone of the passage. The passage discusses a significant court battle, and choice B effectively introduces the piece of writing: The history of the United States is filled with many significant court battles that have taken place within the country's judicial system. Choice A poses a tangential question to readers; the passage is not about mock trials or rhetorical skills. Choice C discusses a famous case that's not covered in the passage. Choice D is too broad of a question to make an effective and targeted opening to this passage.

2. **The correct answer is C.** This question is designed to gauge your ability to recognize appropriate word choice based on the context of the sentence in which it appears. In this sentence, the underlined word describes how the Federal Election Commission viewed the move by Citizens United, in regards to the amount of influence union and corporate money can have on advertisements and political tools designed to influence the hearts and minds of voters. According to the sentence, the Federal Election Commission thought that this was a violation of an existing federal law whose purpose was to *restrict* certain entities. Therefore, we can infer that this existing federal law was designed to *limit* union and corporate influence, so choice C is the best choice here. Choices A and B would have the opposite effect on the intended meaning of the sentence. Choice D would not make sense given the context of the passage.

3. **The correct answer is B.** This question tasks readers with the appropriate organization of information within a passage. Let's take a closer look at the sentence in focus. This sentence effectively introduces what the paragraph is about—a closer look at the heart of the dispute in *Citizens United vs. Federal Election Commission.* So, the sentence would make a good introductory topic sentence, which is most effective at the beginning of the paragraph (choice B). The other answer choices are incorrect because a topic sentence such as this is awkward and out of place when following the information it introduces.

4. **The correct answer is D.** This question is tasking you with determining how best to effectively transition between paragraphs and ideas within the passage. Here, we are searching for an effective transition sentence between paragraphs 2 and 3. The best approach is to capture the core ideas of each of these paragraphs, and figure out which sentence best serves as a bridge between the ideas. Paragraph 2 discusses the core dispute at the heart of *Citizens United vs. Federal Election Commission*. Paragraph 3 discusses the U.S. Supreme Court's ruling on the case. Which sentence best serves to bridge these two core notions? Choice D is the most effective transition, moving from the ideas in paragraph 2 to focus on what the court thought about the issue, which is the focus of paragraph 3. Choices A, B, and C move to tangential or superfluous topics, and are inappropriate choices.

5. **The correct answer is A.** Here, you're being asked to determine appropriate word choice given its context within a sentence in the passage. Let's take a closer look at the sentence. We are told earlier in the passage that the "Supreme Court ultimately ruled that independent political expenditures could not be restricted." Which word amongst the answer choices means that their ability to influence political campaigns and elections, and provide targeted political support through persuasive advertising and other means of influential communication, is unrestricted? Choice A, *unfettered*, is the correct answer. Choice B would have the opposite intended meaning. Choices C and D don't make sense given the context of the passage.

6. **The correct answer is C.** This question is designed to gauge your ability to identify superfluous or inappropriate text within a piece of writing, in an effort to enhance the overall economy of the piece. Let's take a closer look at the sentence in question, and the underlined portion in particular. If you read the sentence as written (choice A) and something seemed a bit awkward, your instincts are sharp—the phrase "only time will tell" does not require the redundant "and the passage of time" in the sentence. Choice C fixes this redundancy: *Only time will tell if public opinion on Citizens United vs. Federal Election Commission shifts or holds—and if the ruling by the U.S. Supreme Court stands firm.* Choices B and D fail to fix the redundancy and introduce additional confusion into the sentence.

7. **The correct answer is C.** This question is asking you to make a strategic contextual decision regarding information in the passage—specifically, determining what information doesn't belong in a paragraph. After reading the paragraph, try and determine what its core topic is. This paragraph covers the primary claims of the critics and supporters of *Citi-*

zens United vs. Federal Election Commission. Scan the sentences in the paragraph—do any of them seem out of place? Choice C provides general information about how much money is typically spent during the average modern presidential election cycle, and does not belong in the paragraph. The other answer choices are more closely aligned with the purpose and topic of the paragraph.

8. **The correct answer is B.** This question is designed to measure your ability to add supportive text to the appropriate place within a piece of writing. The sentence being added provides supplementary information to the U.S. Supreme Court's decision regarding *Citizens United vs. Federal Election Commission*. Which paragraph within the passage covers this? Paragraph 2 (choice B) discusses the court's decision regarding the case, and is the correct place for this sentence.

9. **The correct answer is A.** This question requires you to recognize and identify the central theme of the passage. After reading each passage it might be a good idea to keep your thoughts regarding its main idea in mind, which could prove useful for answering a wide range of questions. Choice A best captures the main idea of this passage: *Citizens United vs. Federal Election Commission* is an important but controversial case that effects how money is spent during political campaigns. The information provided in the passage serves to support this theme. Choice B is incorrect; the passage isn't arguing that the case is insignificant and the case does not pertain to how people vote for Supreme Court Justices. Choice C is incorrect as well, as *Citizens United vs. Federal Election Commission* does not pertain to how politicians can spend their campaign funds. Choice D is also incorrect; the passage does not take the position that this case was disastrous, and the case does not pertain to how corporations make direct contributions to political candidates.

10. **The correct answer is B.** This question asks you to interpret the results of the graphic associated with the passage, which is a survey regarding public opinion on the court's decision on *Citizens United vs. Federal Election Commission*, and determine an appropriate article title reporting its results. An article title would serve to effectively summarize the survey results. A proper interpretation of the pie chart would indicate that the majority of survey respondents are largely against the U.S. Supreme Court's decision, so choice B is correct. The other answer choices reflect a misinterpretation of the pie chart and survey results.

SUMMING IT UP

- The SAT® Writing and Language Test is one of two tests that comprise the Evidence-Based Reading and Writing section. It is a 35-minute test, and you'll answer 44 questions that will task you with making qualitative editorial decisions designed to improve the writing passages included in the test.

- The purpose of this test is to gauge your abilities to read critically, recognize errors and weaknesses in writing, and make substantive fixes to improve written work.

- **Expression of Ideas questions** assess your ability to recognize and address key structural issues that impact the overall effectiveness of a piece of writing, including organization, development, and effective language use.

- **Organization questions** are designed to assess how well you can make decisions about effective grouping, distribution, and arrangement of ideas at the word, phrase, sentence, and paragraph levels. These will include the following question types:

  - When answering Expression of Ideas questions, make sure you're fully aware of what you're being asked and that you're taking into account the entire context of the passage.

  - **Logical Sequence questions** will test your ability to recognize if information provided in the passage—either a word, phrase, sentence, or paragraph—is in the correct and most effective order, and if it isn't, you'll be tasked with fixing it.

  - **Introductions, Conclusions, and Transitions questions** will test your ability to recognize the proper use and placement of information to introduce, conclude, and connect ideas within a passage.

- **Development questions** will task you with identifying, revising, adding, and deleting key elements of the passages provided so that each piece of writing achieves its intended purpose. These will include the following question types:

  - **Proposition questions** address the main topic elements of each passage, including topic sentences, thesis statements, and core claims made by an author.

  - **Support questions** address the supportive elements of each passage, which include supportive information and details that bolster a writer's central ideas or claims made in a piece of writing.

  - **Focus questions** ask about the relevant elements of each passage, which requires you to make judgments regarding whether or not information presented supports, detracts, or is irrelevant to an author's purpose and central claims.

  - **Quantitative Information questions** ask about supplemental quantitative elements for a given passage. These graphical elements can take the form of graphs, charts, tables, illustrations, etc., and you'll need to determine their purpose, accuracy, and level of effectiveness in relation to the passages.

- **Effective Language Use questions** are designed to analyze how effectively authors make key language choices to achieve a variety of important rhetorical goals, which includes the following:
  - **Syntax:** Ensuring that text in each passage is coherent and arranged properly, and delivers a logical flow of thoughts and ideas.
  - **Precision:** Ensuring that information in each passage is clear, focused, and to the point.
  - **Concision:** Ensuring that each passage is free from repetition and distracting wordiness.
  - **Style and Tone:** Ensuring that each passage maintains a consistent voice, mood, and effect.

- **Words in Context questions** will gauge your mastery of effective and appropriate word choice, based on context within the passages provided. You will need to be able to use available context clues to make decisions that impact tone, style, and syntax, with the goal of improving a given piece of writing.

- **Command of Evidence questions** are designed to test your ability to grasp how effectively a piece of writing conveys ideas and information, and to make critical improvements to enhance meaning, sharpen a claim or argument, and provide appropriate details and support.

- **Analysis in History/Social Studies and in Science questions** measure your ability to critically read, comprehend, and analyze passages based on these important topic areas—and to make key decisions on how best to improve them.

- When tackling SAT® Writing and Language Test questions, first analyze the passage type, then note general essay construction and organization, and then note any glaring issues.

- Remember these tips to help you reach your goal of a perfect SAT® Writing and Language Test score:
  - Always read critically and bring your best editing eye on test day; when you read each passage make note of anything that seems off, including redundant words and phrases, and text that seems completely off-topic or just barely related to the central ideas of the passage.
  - Pay attention to the precise location of details you are reviewing in a passage, which are typically provided in the question stems. This will provide you with crucial contextual cues for answering questions.
  - Every decision you make on this section of the SAT® exam should improve the quality and effectiveness of the passages.

CHAPTER 10: STANDARD ENGLISH CONVENTIONS QUESTIONS

OVERVIEW

- Standard English Conventions: An Overview
- Sentence Structure Questions
- Conventions of Punctuation Questions
- Conventions of Usage Questions
- Attacking Standard English Convention Questions for a Perfect Score
- Standard English Conventions Practice
- Summing It Up

The previous chapter covered one type of question you'll encounter on the SAT® Writing and Language Test: Expression of Ideas. This chapter covers the other type: Standard English Conventions. Together, they comprise the SAT® Writing and Language Test, which, alongside the Reading Test, comprise the Evidence-Based Reading and Writing component of the SAT®. We know that's a lot to remember, but don't forget—being informed *before* test day arrives gives you an advantage over your test-taking peers. When it comes to the SAT® exam, knowledge is power—especially if your goal is a perfect score.

NOTE: Standard English Conventions and Expression of Ideas questions *do not* appear separately on the exam—these question types are blended together in the writing passages you'll encounter on test day.

This chapter provides *everything* you need to get prepared for Standard English Conventions questions on test day. We'll start with a comprehensive overview of the major content areas tested; move to in-depth coverage and review of the topics that are tested in each area; provide the most effective advice, tips, and strategies for test day success; and finish up with helpful test-like practice. This chapter is designed to get you fully informed and test ready, build your skills and confidence, and bring your ultimate goal well within reach: a perfect score on the SAT® exam.

STANDARD ENGLISH CONVENTIONS: AN OVERVIEW

Standard English Conventions are the core rules and practices that lie at the heart of writing and language. They are the collectively agreed upon guidelines for connecting words, constructing phrases and sentences, creating written works of every imaginable genre and type, and conveying thoughts that effectively communicate your ideas to others. It's not difficult to see why this is such an important area—and one worth testing on a test as important as the SAT® exam!

NOTE: The SAT® Writing and Language Test is a 35-minute exam that's comprised of 44 multiple-choice questions. You'll need to work intelligently and at an appropriate test-taking pace in order to achieve test day success. Make the most of the tools in this book to effectively prepare and develop a test-taking pace that works best for you!

Standard English Conventions questions on the SAT® exam fall into three main categories: Sentence Structure, Conventions of Punctuation, and Conventions of Usage.

As discussed in the previous chapter, you'll encounter issues related to each of these core topic categories in a series of carefully constructed passages on the SAT® Writing and Language Test. Each writing passage will contain a set of targeted multiple-choice questions designed to measure your abilities in these subject areas.

Some of these questions will refer to underlined portions of text within the passages; others will ask you to consider *adding*, *eliminating*, or *revising* text within the passage to align the writing with the core tenets of standard English writing—always with the goal of improving each passage and making it a more appropriate and effective piece of written communication.

We'll now take an in-depth look at the topics that comprise each of these core categories, along with expert advice and strategies for tackling the types of questions you can expect to encounter on test day.

SENTENCE STRUCTURE

Sentence Structure questions focus on identifying and fixing issues involving sentence construction and sentence formation. You can expect to encounter questions involving parallel structure; modifier placement; sentence boundaries including grammatically incomplete and ineffective sentences; inappropriate pronoun shifts; and inappropriate shifts in voice, mood, and verb tense. It may sound intimidating but, really, these questions simply will assess your ability to tackle concepts you've covered throughout your life—both in English/language arts classes and in the writing you do in your personal life—including letters, e-mails, texts, notes, and more. We all know the difference between a well-constructed sentence and a rambling, incoherent one and can tell which is more effective.

Let's take a look at a sample Sentence Structure question that you might encounter on test day:

> Sasha had a busy Friday yesterday. She had to deliver an important science presentation to her classmates, which counted for 30 percent of her final course grade. She woke up after a restless night of sleep, brush her teeth, and ate breakfast before she raced out the door. She needed to get to school early to prepare.

1 **A.** NO CHANGE
   B. brushing her teeth
   C. brushed her teeth
   D. brush some teeth

This is a common Parallel Structure question. Sentences with correct parallel structure have all of their parts moving cohesively and in the same tense and direction. You may have noticed something awkward while reading the underlined portion of the sentence. The verb *brush* is written in the present tense, while the other action words in the sentence (*woke* and *ate*) are in the past tense, reflecting the fact that these activities occurred yesterday. That's a problem, and on the SAT® exam, it's your job to find and fix such sentence structure issues. Since the paragraph established early on that these events occurred yesterday, we can determine that the past tense is correct for the action that occurs. If you know the past tense of *brush*, select the answer choice and move on. If you need some more time, scan the answer choices and plug each into the sentence if needed. **The correct answer is C.** The past tense of *brush* is *brushed*. If you need to make sure, plug it into the sentence and check:

She woke up after a restless night of sleep, <u>brushed her teeth</u>, and ate breakfast before she raced out the door.

That's correct, and you can move on with confidence!

Bottom line: Following the rules of good sentence construction and formation helps ensure that your thoughts and ideas are properly communicated to others. The makers of the SAT® exam recognize how important of a skill this is, and the test is designed to make sure your skills in this area are well honed.

The questions that you can expect to encounter on the SAT® exam will measure your ability to understand the relationships between and among clauses, the placement of modifiers, and shifts in construction—and fix these issues when you find them in the passages provided. You'll also have to spot and fix fragments, run-ons, and incorrect sentence shifts—in pronouns, mood, voice, and more.

CLAUSES

Just as you can't have a sentence without a subject and verb that express a complete thought, you can't have a sentence without clauses.

We'll let you in on a little secret: a subject and verb that express a complete thought is a clause. It's an independent clause because it can stand on its own.

> **Independent clause:** *The lion roars.*

A clause that cannot stand on its own, even though it has its own subject and verb, is a dependent, or subordinate, clause.

> **Subordinate clause:** *as the antelope flees*

A subordinate clause needs to be paired with an independent clause to be part of a complete sentence, like this:

> *The lion roars as the antelope flees.*

There are four different sentence structures that you'll commonly encounter. Notice that each one always includes at least one independent clause.

A simple sentence has only one independent clause:

- *The snake slithers.*
- *The hippo grunts.*

A compound sentence has two independent clauses that are typically joined in one of two ways:

1. With a **conjunction** (for example *if, and,* and *but*) to connect the clauses:

   The snake slithers and the hippo grunts.

2. With a **semicolon:**

   The snake slithers; the hippo grunts.

A complex sentence has *one* independent clause and at least one subordinate clause:

   The snake slithers away when the hippo grunts.

Notice that, with the addition of the conjunction *when*, the once-independent clause *the hippo grunts* is now acting as a dependent clause modifying the independent clause, *The snake slithers.*

A compound-complex sentence has *at least two* independent clauses and *at least one* subordinate clause:

- *The snake slithers away when the hippo grunts, and the monkey watches from its tree.*

- *The snake slithers away when the hippo grunts; the monkey watches from its tree.*

 Be on the lookout for comma splices on test day. A semicolon is the only punctuation that can join clauses without a conjunction. Using only a comma is known as a comma splice—and it is wrong.

CONJUNCTIONS

You may have noticed the important role that conjunctions play in various sentence structures. They are the words that connect clauses and phrases in sentences and help writers clearly and effectively communicate sentences with multiple thoughts and ideas.

When a conjunction joins independent clauses of equal importance, it is known as a coordinating conjunction.

For example:

   The appetizer was delicious, but the main course was inedible.

In this compound sentence, *but* is the coordinating conjunction. If you divide the sentence before and after the coordinating conjunction, you will still have two independent clauses of equal importance.

For example:

- *The appetizer was delicious.*
- *The main course was inedible.*

If a conjunction joins a subordinate clause to an independent clause, it is known as a subordinating conjunction.

> *The vacation that I didn't want to take was actually amazing.*

In this sentence, the subordinate clause is *that I didn't want to take*, which is not a complete sentence on its own. The subordinating conjunction is *that*.

Here are some other common coordinating and subordinating conjunctions that you can expect to encounter on the SAT® exam:

Coordinating Conjunctions		
and	for	or
but	nor	so
	yet	

Subordinating Conjunctions		
after	since	whereas
although	that	wherever
as	though	whether
because	unless	which
before	until	while
even though	when	who
if	whenever	why

Fragments and Run-ons

Two of the most common sentence structure errors are fragments and run-ons—be on the lookout for these on test day, and make sure you know how to fix them.

A fragment is a piece of a sentence, and is not complete on its own.

For example:

Jogging on the track.

Who was jogging on the track? We'll never know until we fix this sentence fragment. This sentence needs a subject, as follows:

The amateur sprinter is jogging on the track.

Mystery solved! The subject-verb pair *The amateur sprinter is* rescued this sentence from the confusing fragment heap.

 ALERT: Sometimes, writers intentionally break the rules and use fragments and run-on sentences creatively to achieve a particular effect, typically referred to as creative license. However, as far as the SAT® Writing and Language Test is concerned, fragments and run-on sentences are *always* wrong and need to be fixed.

Run-on sentences are the opposite of fragments, but they are just as incorrect. They occur when two independent clauses are incorrectly joined. There are two types of run-on sentences:

Comma splice: *The amateur sprinter is jogging on the track, he loves chilly autumn mornings.*

Fused sentence: *The amateur sprinter is jogging on the track he loves chilly autumn mornings.*

A run-on sentence can be corrected in one of four ways:

1. Separate the independent clauses into sentences:

   The amateur sprinter is jogging on the track. He loves chilly autumn mornings.

2. Use a comma and a coordinating conjunction:

   The amateur sprinter is jogging on the track because he loves chilly autumn mornings.

3. Use a semicolon:

   The amateur sprinter is jogging on the track; he loves chilly autumn mornings.

4. Subordinate one of the sentences:

   The amateur sprinter, who loves chilly autumn mornings, is jogging on the track.

Now it's a clearly expressed thought!

MODIFIERS

Modifiers such as adjectives, adverbs, descriptive phrases, and clauses need to be placed correctly in sentences. Otherwise, you can end up with some *very* bewildering thoughts.

Two common modifier issues that you can expect to encounter on the SAT® exam are misplaced modifiers and dangling modifiers. Let's examine them more closely.

A misplaced modifier creates confusion because it's not placed next to the word it's supposed to modify.

For example:

> *Lawrence walked across the floor because he didn't want to disturb his brother napping in the room below his carefully.*

In this sentence, the modifier *carefully* is not where it should be. In fact, its placement makes it seem as though *his brother* was napping carefully. How do you nap carefully? You have to be conscious and careful about where information is placed in sentences.

The adverb *carefully* would be put to better use modifying *walked*:

> *Lawrence walked carefully across the floor because he didn't want to disturb his brother napping in the room below his.*

Excellent! In this sentence, the modifier *carefully* is no longer misplaced.

Dangling modifiers are often more confusing than misplaced ones. The object they are meant to modify is nowhere in the sentence. Take a look at this sentence:

> *Anxious about the presentation, the sales reports scatter across the floor.*

The modifier in this sentence is *Anxious about the presentation*. But there's a problem: we don't know exactly *who* was anxious about the presentation. This sentence's lack of a subject leaves the modifier dangling without anything to modify. A subject needs to be added to give the modifier something to do, as follows:

> *Anxious about the presentation, Luis watched the sales reports scatter across the floor.*

The addition of the subject *Luis* gives the phrase *anxious about the presentation* something to modify.

 Make sure you choose the right subject for the modifier to modify. Read the passage very carefully so you can make the best selection.

Parallel Structure

Sentences with correct parallel structure have all of their parts moving cohesively and in the same tense and direction. You can't place a word or phrase that's going backward into the past alongside one that's moving into the future, for example. Parallel structure crumbles when groups of words combine different types of phrases, clauses, and parts of speech.

For example:

> Next Monday morning, I will pay my phone bill, finish my term paper, and went to the post office.

This sentence begins by describing things that are going to happen in the future—*Next Monday morning*, to be precise. Everything is smooth until that final phrase: *went to the post office*. It's written in the past tense, which violates the parallel structure of a sentence that is otherwise written in the future tense. Let's take a look at a revised version of the sentence:

> Next Monday morning, I will pay my phone bill, finish my term paper, and go to the post office.

This version corrects the parallel structure by putting the phrase *went to the post office* into the future tense (*go to the post office*), where it belongs.

Keep in mind, a sentence does not need to be written entirely in the same tense to be correct. It just needs to be structured correctly.

For example, the sentence *I ate a burrito yesterday, and I am going to eat a sandwich tonight* does not violate the rules of good parallel structure.

Correlative Conjunctions

You need to be mindful of parallel structure when dealing with correlative conjunctions. These are conjunctions that work in pairs: *either . . . or, neither . . . nor*, and *not only . . . but also*. Mixing correlative conjunctions is another way to violate parallel structure.

For example:

> Neither the dress or the hat will be appropriate for the event.

Oops! *Neither* indicates a negative and *or* indicates a positive. So, what does this sentence mean? Are the dress and hand appropriate attire for the event or aren't they? We'll know only if the parallel structure is repaired:

> Either the dress or the hat will be appropriate for the event.

Here, we know that at least one piece of clothing is appropriate for the event.

CONVENTIONS OF PUNCTUATION

You're undoubtedly aware of the importance of good punctuation in writing. Without it, a piece of writing can devolve into a confusing mess.

Conventions of Punctuation questions focus on recognizing and adhering to the rules and standards of appropriate punctuation. These questions will test your ability to tackle a wide array of familiar punctuation issues—including the rules of within-sentence and end-of-sentence punctuation, plural and possessive forms of pronouns and nouns, proper use of nonrestrictive and parenthetical items, items in simple and complex lists, and unnecessary or superfluous punctuation.

Let's take a look at a sample Conventions of Punctuation question that you might encounter on test day:

> Valerie had to travel from Baltimore to Chicago for an important work conference this morning. Her plane landed safely, and she arrived at the airport on time. After retrieving her baggage, she needed to find a taxi that can take her to her hotel room. She went up to the information desk and asked the clerk, **2** "Where can I catch a taxi to my hotel!" The clerk gave her clear and careful directions to the nearest taxi stand.

2 **A.** NO CHANGE
   B. "Where can I catch a taxi to my hotel."
   C. "Where can I catch a taxi to my hotel"
   D. "Where can I catch a taxi to my hotel?"

This is a common Conventions of Punctuation question involving end-of-sentence punctuation. You'll need to know which type of ending punctuation is appropriate for a wide variety of sentences on test day. Let's review the underlined quote in the paragraph. If you know what type of punctuation is needed here, that's great—select the answer choice and move on. If you need some more time, let's keep going. The appearance of the question word *where* gives us a valuable context clue—it tells us that we're dealing with a question. Now we know that we'll need a question mark to properly punctuate this sentence. Scan the answer choices, and find the correctly punctuated version. **The correct answer is D.** If you need to make sure, plug it into the sentence and check:

> She went up to the information desk and asked the clerk, "Where can I catch a taxi to my hotel?"

You have found your correct answer.

You can expect to encounter a wide array of punctuation issues within the writing passages. It will be your job to identify and fix them appropriately. This section covers the most-tested punctuation concepts; master them before test day and make the most of the practice later in this chapter to help you reach your perfect score goal!

END-OF-SENTENCE PUNCTUATION

Every sentence must eventually come to an end, which means that the one form of punctuation you will *always* see in every complete sentence is end-of-sentence punctuation.

These are probably the very first punctuation marks you learned about:

- **The period (.):** good for ending most declarative sentences
- **The exclamation point (!):** used for ending exclamations, which indicate extreme excitement
- **The question mark (?):** absolutely necessary for ending questions

Make sure you know the right punctuation for the situation. A question can be asked excitedly, but it still needs to end with a question mark, not an exclamation point.

End-of-sentence marks are usually pretty straightforward. You probably already know that you shouldn't end a question with a period or an exclamation with a question mark.

These marks become slightly trickier when quotation marks are added to the punctuation mix. End-of-sentence punctuation usually belongs *inside* the quotation marks:

> Van asked, "What time is our meeting today?"

Exceptions to the rules do occur, so be careful on test day, for example, when the quotation marks indicate a title, and placing end-of-sentence punctuation within the marks might give the false impression that the mark is part of the title. Here is an example:

> Have you read the new novel "A New Tomorrow"?

COMMAS

Let's continue with one of the most common forms of punctuation—and one that's commonly misused. Some writers overuse commas, and using them without rhyme or reason can make your sentences awkward or confusing.

Here's an example of a sentence with way too many commas:

> After, Jacob finished the final, exam he breathed, a huge sigh of relief stretched, his arms and smiled.

It's quite a mouthful, and it's a bit difficult to figure out what's happening. Let's take a look at the corrected version:

> After Jacob finished the final exam, he breathed a huge sigh of relief, stretched his arms, and smiled.

This version is much easier to follow!

While there is the odd situation in which the use of a comma is up to the writer, there are almost always very definite rules for comma use. Let's look at some of the most important ones.

Introductory or Transitional Words and Phrases

Commas should be used to offset introductory words or phrases from the words that follow.

Here are some examples:

- *Surprisingly, the new laptop was much cheaper than Jamie expected.*
- *Barry showed up late for the big client meeting on Thursday. Unfortunately, his boss was not pleased.*

Compound Sentences

Compound sentences consist of two independent clauses, which means that both parts of the sentence would be complete sentences on their own. Each independent clause in a compound sentence with a conjunction needs a comma to separate it.

For example:

> Gheeta had vegetable fajitas for lunch in the school cafeteria, but Laird doesn't like vegetables.

Gheeta had vegetable fajitas for lunch in the school cafeteria is the first independent clause. *Laird doesn't like vegetables* is the second independent clause. The conjunction is *but,* and a comma is used to separate those clauses correctly.

Nonrestrictive Phrases

A nonrestrictive phrase is not essential to the meaning of the sentence. It should be separated with one comma if it comes at the beginning or end of the sentence and two commas if it is placed in the middle.

Read this sentence:

> My new suede boots, which I received as a birthday present, are much too narrow.

This sentence would still make sense without the phrase *which I received as a birthday present*. It would read as *My new suede boots are much too narrow*, which is a perfectly fine sentence. This means the phrase is nonrestrictive and should be enclosed in commas, like it is in the previous example. However, if that phrase were restrictive—or essential to the meaning of the sentence—no commas would be needed.

For example:

> The new suede boots I received as a birthday present are much too narrow.

Series

Each item in a simple series or list should be separated by a comma.

For example:

> I purchased a new backpack, wallet, and cell phone case at the mall yesterday.

In this sentence, a comma also precedes the conjunction *and* (also known as a serial or Oxford comma), although this is not a hard and fast rule. Some writers prefer not to use that extra comma. So, the following sentence is also technically correct:

> I purchased a new backpack, wallet and cell phone case at the mall yesterday.

 The decision to place a comma before the conjunction in a series of items is up to the writer. Passages on the SAT® exam use the comma before the conjunction, but you will not be expected to answer questions about such situations without concrete rules.

For more complex lists of items, semicolons are often used, as in the following example:

> Each morning, I brush my hair; feed my little brother, sister, and parrot; and pack a lunch, notebook, and pens in my book bag.

When multiple verbs refer to multiple items in a series within a single sentence, you can see how semicolons can come in handy to keep things organized.

Appositives

An appositive is a word or phrase that describes or identifies a noun. An appositive phrase contains a noun or pronoun and often one or more modifiers, and appears directly before or after the noun it describes. In general, appositives need to be separated with commas.

For example:

My new kitten Enzo, a cute grey Persian, keeps curling up on my lap.

In this sentence, the appositive is *a cute grey Persian*, and commas are used to separate it correctly.

 Note that if we change the sentence a bit to read, "*My new kitten Enzo keeps curling up on my lap,*" the proper noun *Enzo* acts as an appositive to the word *kitten*. It is restrictive and does not require a comma.

Quotations

When quoting a complete phrase that someone said, quotation marks are needed, and one or more commas are required to separate it from the rest of the sentence.

See how the commas are used in these examples:

- *Victor declared, "That movie was the best one I've seen all summer."*
- *"That movie was the best one I've seen all summer," Victor declared.*
- *"That movie," Victor declared, "was the best one I've seen all summer."*

Note that if that quotation includes end-of-sentence punctuation, a comma is not needed at the end of it.

For example:

- *"That movie was the best one I've seen all summer!," Victor declared.* (**Incorrect!**)
- *"That movie was the best one I've seen all summer!" Victor declared.* (**Correct!**)

APOSTROPHES AND POSSESSION

Apostrophes are most often used to indicate that a word is a contraction or to show possession in a sentence.

The correct use of apostrophes in contractions mostly depends on placing the apostrophe in the right place within a word:

- *Ca'nt* (**Incorrect!**)
- *Can't* (**Correct!**)

You'll also need to recognize when a word that looks like a contraction is not a contraction:

- *it's* (a contraction of *it is*)
- *its* (the possessive form of *it*)

Using apostrophes in possessive words is a little trickier. For the most part, the apostrophe will be placed before the letter -*s*.

For example:

- *Derrick's wallet*
- *the ferret's cage*

However, if the possessive word is plural and ends with an *s*, the apostrophe belongs after the -*s*.

For example:

- *the glasses' lenses*
- *the trains' engines*

This rule is different when a specifically named person is doing the possessing. For people whose names end in *s*, an apostrophe and an extra *s* is required.

For example:

- *James's car*
- *Lars's new wristwatch*

When more than one noun is doing the possessing, only the last noun in the pair or list needs an apostrophe.

For example:

- *Darcy and Cindy's sleepover party*
- *the grocer and butcher's shared entrance*

When more than one noun is doing the possessing of different things, both nouns in the pair or list need an apostrophe:

- *Darcy's and Cindy's timecards*
- *the grocer's and the butcher's stores*

COLONS

Colons are typically used to introduce a list or series of examples:

> *Jeremy bought everything he needed for his upcoming backpacking trip: a canteen, hiking boots, a sleeping bag, and a tent.*

Colons are also used to offset and emphasize an example:

> *My favorite song gives listeners a powerful message: Love conquers all.*

They can also be placed after a salutation in a letter:

> *To Whom It May Concern:*

And can be used to separate a title from a subtitle in a piece of work like a book or movie:

> *Alien Hunter: The Sequel*

However, colons should *not* be used to separate objects and verbs, or prepositions and objects:

- **Incorrect:** *This new novel is: boring.*
- **Incorrect:** *My favorite pizza is topped with: pepperoni, mushrooms, olives, and pineapple.*

SEMICOLONS

Semicolons can be used in place of conjunctions in compound sentences, joining the independent clauses just as *and, or, but,* or *because* would.

For example:

> *I was nervous about the algebra exam all night; I had no reason to worry.*

As previously mentioned, semicolons are also used in complex lists that contain items with commas, to keep all those commas from becoming confusing.

For example:

> *This birthday dinner contains only the best ingredients: potatoes and scallions, which I bought at the farmer's market; cilantro, which I grew in a pot in the kitchen; and pork chops, which I got from the best butcher in town.*

 Don't forget that colons and semicolons are not interchangeable. Each punctuation mark has its own function.

Dashes

Much like commas, dashes tend to get overused and misused. A big problem with dashes is that they're almost never absolutely necessary according to the rules of mechanics, so a lot of writers just aren't sure what to do with them. You're about to become one of the lucky few who know when to use them!

Like the colon, a dash can be used to offset and emphasize a single example:

> *My best friend in the entire world is loyal, fun, and brave—my dog, Oliver.*

Dashes are also useful for indicating a pause or interruption in dialogue, and two dashes can be used to separate an example or examples in the middle of a sentence:

> *The book contained everything I liked—action, intrigue, and romance—and I couldn't put it down.*

Parentheses

Sometimes, a few extra details are needed to make a sentence as informative as it can be—but those details aren't always easy to cram into the natural flow of the sentence. In such cases, parentheses are in order. Parentheses are often used to enclose additional examples that tend to be a little less relevant to a sentence than the ones you'd place between dashes.

For example:

> *My neighbor, Mrs. Glendolin (who used to babysit me when I was an infant), recently moved to Boca Raton, Florida.*

 DO NOT skip over portions of Writing and Language passages just because they're not numbered. Sentences that don't correspond to questions directly may contain valuable context clues and can still help you select correct answers.

Unnecessary Punctuation

Making sure that a piece of writing is clear of unnecessary/incorrect punctuation is important for ensuring that it is free from confusing errors and effectively conveys its intended meaning. Just as missing punctuation can lead to awkwardness and confusion, unnecessary punctuation can have the same effect. Let's look at an example:

> *Once, the wolf reached the peak of the high, cliff it howled at, the slowly, setting sun.*

Don't be concerned if you had trouble reading this sentence. Did the wolf just howl once? What exactly is "the peak of the high"? The meaning and flow of this sentence is clearly being disrupted by its inappropriate punctuation. Its abundance of unnecessary commas makes it confusing, and obscures its intended meaning. Commas are among the most overused—and misused—types of internal punctuation, and on test day you should always be on the lookout for unnecessary commas and other forms of punctuation. Let's look at a corrected version of our example:

> Once the wolf reached the peak of the high cliff, it howled at the slowly setting sun.

This version is *much* easier to follow and understand.

CONVENTIONS OF USAGE QUESTIONS

Following the rules of sound grammar and usage is essential—in school, in life beyond the classroom, and on the SAT® exam. Conventions of Usage questions on the SAT® exam will test your ability to tackle some extremely important writing and language concepts, such as properly using possessives and determiners, subject-verb agreement, logical comparisons, recognizing conventional English language expressions and their appropriate use, proper pronoun use, and correctly identifying and using frequently confused words.

Let's take a look at a sample Conventions of Usage question that you might encounter on test day:

> The photographer hides behind a bush and watches a group of wild gazelles cross the desert plain. The animals move cautiously in a tight pack. The smallest gazelle **3** jump over a boulder and lands on the other side. The gold rising sun lights the peaceful scene perfectly.

---

3 **A.** NO CHANGE
 B. jumps over
 C. jumped over
 D. jumping over

This is a common subject-verb agreement question. Sentences with correct agreement have their subjects and verbs aligned in both form and tense. Let's take a look at the underlined portion of the sentence. A quick scan of the answer choices shows us that a variety of forms of the verb *to jump* are on display. This signals us that it's our job to determine the correct verb form needed here in order to correctly answer the question. We first need to determine *who* or *what* is performing the action in order to determine the appropriate verb form for the sentence. Here, the *smallest gazelle*, a singular subject, is presently moving over a boulder, so the present tense of the singular form of the verb *to jump* is needed.

If you know the correct verb form needed here, select the answer choice and move on. If you need some more help, let's move forward. Scan the sentence and see if we can find any more helpful clues. If you're looking carefully, you'll notice that another verb, *lands*, is also in this sentence. It isn't underlined, so we can safely assume that it's in the correct form. Scan the answer choices, and see if you can find the correct singular present verb form for *to jump*. **The correct answer is B.** If you need to make sure, plug it into the sentence and check:

> *The smallest gazelle jumps over a boulder and lands on the other side.*

These questions can appear in a variety of formats on test day; some will be obvious, and others will be more subtle. This section covers the most essential usage concepts—the ones that you'll need to know and use on test day. Use the practice and review in this chapter to sharpen your skills and get test ready. You'll need to be at the top of your game if you're aiming for a perfect score!

While incorrect punctuation won't necessarily make a sentence sound wrong, poor grammar almost certainly will. Thinking about how sentences sound can help you select the best answers to usage questions.

Nouns

The subject of any sentence is most often a noun: the person, place, or thing performing the action that the sentence describes. Some Conventions of Usage questions on the SAT® exam will likely involve subjects of sentences, often in terms of how they agree with verbs or pronouns.

Before we discuss how nouns interact with other words, let's look at some specific noun forms.

Plural Nouns

The nice thing about nouns is that they have only two general forms: singular and plural.

- The singular form is the most basic: *goose, bird, otter, lampshade, mango,* and *mushroom*—these are all nouns in their most basic singular form.

- Making a singular noun plural is often as simple as adding the letter *s* to the end (for example: *cat* becomes *cats*). Plural nouns get tricky only when they are irregular—hard-and-fast rules for creating irregular plural nouns are often tough to apply to a language as complicated as English. We can't simply say that you're always safe adding *-es* to the end of all nouns that end in *-o* to make them plural. For example, the plural of *avocado* is *avocados*.

While you're not expected to memorize every single irregular verb for the SAT® exam, it's a good idea to familiarize yourself with some of the most common, which appear in the following table.

Common Irregular Plural Nouns

Noun ends with-	Creating the plural form	Examples
-f	change *f* to *v* and add *–es*	**singular:** calf **plural:** calves
		singular: elf **plural:** elves
		singular: half **plural:** halves
		singular: leaf **plural:** leaves
		singular: shelf **plural:** shelves
		singular: thief **plural:** thieves
		singular: wolf **plural:** wolves
-fe	change *f* to *v* and add *–s*	**singular:** knife **plural:** knives
		singular: life **plural:** lives
		singular: wife **plural:** wives
-is	change to *–es*	**singular:** axis **plural:** axes
		singular: analysis **plural:** analyses
		singular: parenthesis **plural:** parentheses

Noun ends with-	Creating the plural form	Examples
-o	add –es	**singular:** echo **plural:** echoes **singular:** hero **plural:** heroes **singular:** potato **plural:** potatoes **singular:** tomato **plural:** tomatoes
-ous	change to -ice	**singular:** louse **plural:** lice **singular:** mouse **plural:** mice
-s	add -es	**singular:** class **plural:** classes **singular:** boss **plural:** bosses
-us	change to -i	**singular:** alumnus **plural:** alumni **singular:** fungus **plural:** fungi

There are a few other variations of irregular plural nouns that do not involve changing the last letter or two of the singular form. Fortunately, most of these should be very familiar to you.

Nouns that require -ee- to be changed to -oo- for their plural form:

singular: foot	**plural:** feet
singular: goose	**plural:** geese
singular: tooth	**plural:** teeth

Nouns that require the addition or substitution of -en for their plural form:

singular: child	**plural:** children
singular: man	**plural:** men
singular: ox	**plural:** oxen
singular: woman	**plural:** women

Finally, there are the nouns that require no change whatsoever to become plural:

singular: deer	**plural:** deer
singular: fish	**plural:** fish
singular: offspring	**plural:** offspring
singular: series	**plural:** series
singular: sheep	**plural:** sheep
singular: species	**plural:** species

Collective Nouns

Collective nouns are interesting because they have some of the flavor of plural nouns since they seem to describe more than one thing.

For example:

- *A bunch of tourists in a **group***
- *A group of sailors in a **squadron***
- *Several birds in a **flock***

However, while the individual nouns in these collections are plural (*tourists, sailors, birds*), the collections of them can be either singular or plural. Whether to treat a collective noun as singular or plural depends on the context of the sentence. If the sentence refers to the whole group as a single entity, you need to use a singular verb.

For example:

> *The board of directors has called a special meeting.*

Also, when a group noun is used with a singular determiner, like *this, that,* or *each*, use a singular verb.

For example:

> *Each band has to sign in before entering the concert hall.*

When a sentence stresses the individuals of a group, you need to use a plural verb.

For example:

> *My English Literature class are divided in their opinions of the essay.*

While correct, the above sentence sounds a bit awkward. Many writers will solve this issue by adding *members* or *members of* to a sentence that includes a collective noun, thus making a plural verb the obvious choice:

My English Literature class members are divided in their opinions of the essay.

Familiarize yourself with some common collective nouns.

army	audience	band	board	class
committee	company	corporation	council	department
faculty	family	firm	flock	group
herd	jury	majority	navy	public
school	senate	society	team	unit

AGREEMENT

When words in a sentence agree, things tend to go smoothly. When they don't, there can be trouble. You can ensure that the elements in sentences don't clash by recognizing when they are—and aren't—in agreement.

Subjects and verbs need to agree in terms of number. The same is true of pronouns and antecedents, which also need to agree in terms of gender.

Subject-Verb Agreement

Every complete sentence has a subject and a verb.

- The subject is the noun doing the action.
- The verb is the action that the subject is doing.

Simple, right? Actually, it can be—a sentence with just a subject and a verb can be really simple.

For example:

> The dolphin flips.

That sentence has only three words, but it's still a complete sentence because it has a subject and a verb. Just as important, the subject and verb agree: the singular subject *dolphin* agrees with the singular verb *flips*. (That's right, the verb is singular even though it ends with the letter -*s*.)

Determining whether or not subjects and verbs are in agreement can get a little more complicated in sentences with compound subjects.

For example:

> The dolphin and the sea lion flip.

Neither *dolphin* nor *sea lion* ends with an *s*, so they may not look plural, but they work together as a compound subject when joined with a conjunction (*and*). This means that they require a plural verb and, as you may have guessed, the plural verb does not end in an extra -*s*.

However, if the conjunction were *or* or *nor*, a singular verb would be required.

For example:

> *Neither the dolphin nor the sea lion flips.*

Once again, the compound subject and verb are in agreement.

> Subject-verb agreement can get confusing when there is a word or phrase between the subject and verb. Make sure you have identified the entire subject and verb correctly before figuring out whether or not they agree.

Pronoun/Antecedent Agreement

Pronouns and antecedents also need to play nice. A pronoun replaces a specific noun. Its antecedent is the noun the pronoun replaces. Since it would sound clumsy to say *Sara mows Sara's lawn*, most writers would replace the second *Sara* with a pronoun:

> *Sara mows her lawn.*

This is much better, right? In this sentence, *Sara* is the antecedent and the pronoun is *her*, a female pronoun. Both are in agreement in this sentence. It is also singular, which is appropriate since Sara is only one woman.

Now, if the sentence read *Sara mows his lawn*, and we know that Sara is a woman, it would lack pronoun-antecedent agreement in terms of gender (unless, of course, if Sara was mowing some guy's lawn). If it read *Sara mows their lawn* it would sound as if Sara was mowing a lawn owned by two or more people other than herself.

However, *their* would be necessary in a sentence with a compound antecedent. For example, maybe Sara co-owns her lawn with a friend named Ginnie. Then the sentence could read *Sara and Ginnie mow their lawn*. Compound antecedents are a bit more complicated when the conjunction is *or* or *nor* instead of *and*. In such cases, you will select your pronoun based on which antecedent it is nearest.

For example:

- *Neither my friend nor my sons brought their coolers to the baseball game.*
- *Neither my sons nor my friend brought his cooler to the baseball game.*

Both of these sentences are written correctly. Since the plural antecedent *sons* is closer to the pronoun in sentence 1, the plural pronoun *their* is required. Since the singular antecedent *friend* is closer to the pronoun in sentence 2, the singular pronoun *his* is required.

Now, if your antecedent is a collective noun, selecting the right pronoun depends on what the collective noun is doing and how it is doing it. If every member of the collective noun is doing the exact same thing as a single unit, the singular pronoun is needed.

For example:

The marketing team delivered its presentation effectively.

In this example, everyone on the team is working on the same presentation, and the singular pronoun *its* is used correctly. However, if all of the members of that collective noun are doing their own things, a plural pronoun is in order.

For example:

The marketing team delivered their individual presentations effectively.

This example describes how the members of the team handled their individual presentations, and it uses the plural pronoun *their* correctly.

SELECTING PRONOUNS

On your quest for a perfect score, selecting appropriate pronouns given the context of the sentences they will appear in is another challenge you should be prepared to face on the Language and Writing Test.

Perspective will be a factor when figuring out the best way to use pronouns on test day. Let's look at a few essential rules:

- A **first-person pronoun** (*I, me, we, us*) is necessary when a writer is referring to herself or himself.

- A **second-person pronoun** (*you*) is needed when the writer is addressing the reader.

- A **third-person pronoun** (*she, he, her, him, they, them*) is needed when the pronoun refers to a third person who is neither writing nor reading the passage.

Choosing the right pronoun can be tricky in sentences that pair them with nouns. Which of the following examples is correct?

- *Gus and I went to the movies.*

- *Gus and me went to the movies.*

In such cases, try removing the noun and saying the sentence with just the pronoun (*I went to the movies? Me went to the movies?*). Chances are that the wrong pronoun will now seem more obvious.

Relative Pronouns

Relative clauses are like adjectives: they exist to describe. Restrictive relative clauses cannot stand on their own. You can recognize a relative clause from the presence of a relative pronoun.

The relative pronouns *who, whom, whose,* and *that* all refer to people; the relative pronouns *that* and *which* refer to things.

The relative clauses in the following sentences are underlined:

- *Mr. Marshall, who used to live next door to me, is the head manager at my new job.*
- *The person to whom you want to speak is not at home.*
- *Florida, which is where I went on vacation last year, is located at the bottom of the United States.*

Reflexive Pronouns

When a subject needs a pronoun to refer to itself, a reflexive pronoun fits the bill. In fact, *itself* is a reflexive pronoun, as is any pronoun that ends with *self* or *selves.*

- There are five **singular reflexive pronouns:** *myself, yourself, himself, herself, itself.*
- There are three **plural reflexive pronouns:** (*ourselves, yourselves, themselves*).

Interrogative Pronouns

To interrogate is to question, and interrogative pronouns are used to ask questions.

- There are five main **interrogative pronouns**: *whose, who,* and *whom* refer to people exclusively; *what* refers to things exclusively; and *which* can refer to people or things.

Who vs. Whom

A common confusion regarding interrogative pronouns is when to use *who* and when to use *whom.*

Who is used as the **subject** of a question (example: *Who called at 3 a.m. last night?*).

Whom is used as the **object** of a question (example: *To whom am I speaking?*).

The addition of the suffix -*ever* also creates six less common interrogative pronouns: *whatever, whichever, whoever, whomever, whosever,* and *whomsoever.*

Possessive Pronouns

Apostrophes are used when indicating that a noun *possesses* something. More often than not, you can just add an apostrophe and an *-s* onto the end of a word to make it possessive.

For example:

- *That violin is **Gilbert's**.*
- *There is a toothbrush in **Jess's** sink.*

The extra *-s* is not necessary with a possessive noun that already ends in *-s* but is not someone's name.

For example:

- *The **lions'** cubs played in the grass.*
- *Those **plates'** designs are really beautiful.*

Pronouns, however, usually have their very own forms to show possession. Since pronouns such as *his, her, its, their, my, mine, yours, their,* and *theirs* already show possession, they don't need an apostrophe or an extra *-s*.

For example:

- *The phone is **mine**.*
- *Their dog is coming to the park with **us**.*
- ***Her** uncle is volunteering at the zoo tomorrow.*

The only pronouns that do need that apostrophe and extra *-s* are *anybody, anyone, everybody, everyone, no one,* and *nobody*.

For example:

- ***Anybody's** guess is as good as mine.*
- ***Everybody's** time should be spent helping others.*

Remember that *it's* is *not* the possessive form of *it*; it is a contraction of *it is*.

Verb Tense

Verbs are words that refer to action, and their tense indicates when that action happened. Did the action already happen? If so, then the verb is in the past tense. Are you still waiting for the action to happen? If so, then the verb is in the future tense.

Past, present, and future are the most basic points in time. However, there are quite a few more than three verb tenses. Let's take a quick look at possible verb tenses:

- **Simple present tense** indicates an action happening now: *I am here.*

- **Present progressive tense** indicates an action happening now that will continue into the future: *I am dancing.*

- **Present perfect progressive tense** indicates an unfinished action: *I have been working all day.*

- **Present perfect simple tense** indicates an action that occurred in the past but continues to be relevant: *I have never eaten lentils.*

- **Past perfect simple tense** indicates an action that occurred in the past but is now complete: *When Sherri woke up yesterday morning, she realized that she had missed her dental appointment.*

- **Past simple tense** indicates an action that happened already: *I watched the movie.*

- **Past progressive tense** pairs a past tense verb with a continuous verb ending in *-ing*: *I was laughing.*

- **Past perfect progressive tense** reflects on an ongoing action from the past: *By the 1990s, hip-hop had been a popular form of music for several years.*

- **Future simple tense** indicates an action that will happen later: *I will be at work by 9:00 a.m.*

- **Future progressive tense** indicates an action that will happen later and continue: *I will be volunteering all day on Sunday.*

- **Future perfect simple tense** indicates the completion of an action that will happen later: *I will have finished vacuuming the bedroom by noon today.*

- **Future perfect progressive tense** indicates an incomplete action that will happen later: *I will have been cleaning for four hours by the time my parents arrive.*

Adjectives and Adverbs

As we've already established, the only completely essential elements of a sentence are its subject and verb.

For example:

The penguin waddles.

Once again, this is a complete sentence. But is it a particularly *interesting* sentence? Writing a sentence with nothing but a subject and a verb is like making soup with nothing but water and tomatoes. Where are the other flavors, the words that give a sentence some unique and memorable character?

In a sentence, adjectives (words that describe nouns) and adverbs (words that describe verbs) add some extra sentence flavor. Think of them as the spices of a sentence.

Let's add some spice to our previous example:

The curious penguin waddles humorously.

Now there's a sentence that paints a more vivid picture! The adjective *curious* shows that the penguin might be waddling over to something it wants to investigate further. The adverb *humorously* shows us that the penguin must be a funny site to see. It's certainly a more engaging sentence now.

Let's take a look at the different forms of adjectives and adverbs you should know before taking the SAT® exam.

Comparative and Superlative Adjectives

Big! Bigger! Biggest! Adjectives and adverbs change form when they are used to make a comparison.

The comparative form is used when comparing two things.

comparative adjectives:

This piano is <u>larger</u> than the last one.

Jen feels <u>more relaxed</u> than she did before she napped.

comparative adverbs:

Today's lecture seemed to go by <u>more quickly</u> than last week's lecture did.

Flo is taking her test preparation <u>more seriously</u> than she ever had before.

The superlative form is used when comparing three or more things.

superlative adjectives:

Perry is the <u>weirdest</u> fish I own.

Alshad is the <u>tallest</u> student in my class.

superlative adverbs:

Out of everyone in the company, Candice works the <u>fastest</u>.

This is the <u>slowest</u> I have ever jogged.

As you may have noticed, simply adding -*er* to the end of comparative adjectives and -*est* to the end of superlative adjectives is not always enough. Once again, there are a number of exceptions you need to understand to use comparative and superlative adjectives correctly.

Case	Adjective	Comparative	Superlative
One- and two-syllable adjectives ending in -*e* do not need an extra -*e*	close huge polite	closer huger politer	closest hugest politest
One-syllable adjectives ending in a consonant need to have that consonant doubled	big sad thin	bigger sadder thinner	biggest saddest thinnest
One- and two-syllable adjectives ending in -*y* need to change that -*y* to an -*i*	dry heavy tiny	drier heavier tinier	driest heaviest tiniest
Certain adjectives with two or more syllables remain the same but need the addition of *more* for comparatives and *most* for superlatives	beautiful complete important	more beautiful more complete more important	most beautiful most complete most important
Irregular adjectives require their own special alterations in the comparative and superlative forms	bad far good little many	worse farther better less more	worst farthest best least most

For comparative adverbs, adding *more* is usually enough, and superlative adverbs usually only need *most*.

For example:

- *I laughed <u>more softly</u> than Morgan did.*
- *The car runs <u>most smoothly</u> on paved roads.*

As you may have guessed, there are exceptions to this rule, but don't worry—there aren't as many exceptions for adverbs as there are for adjectives. Basically, any adverb that does not end in -*ly* should be treated the same way you would treat it if it were being used to modify a noun instead of a verb.

Adverb	Comparative	Superlative
bad	worse	worst
far	farther	farthest
fast	faster	fastest
good	better	best
hard	harder	hardest
little	less	least
long	longer	longest
loud	louder	loudest
many	more	most
quick	quicker	quickest
soon	sooner	soonest

One thing you need to make sure of when taking the exam is that comparatives and superlatives are actually being used to make a comparison.

You may have seen an advertisement that boasts, *Our product is better!* Well, your product is better than what? Obviously, the implication is that the product is better than other similar products, but the comparison is not correct and complete if that information is not stated directly, as follows:

Our product is better than other similar products!

This may not be the catchiest slogan in the world, but it is a complete comparison. Remember that incomplete comparisons are incorrect when you're reading SAT® Writing and Language Test passages.

CONVENTIONAL EXPRESSIONS

For some students, conventional expressions or idioms can be confusing because they use words to mean something other than their literal meanings.

For example, if you were to *pull the wool over someone's eyes*, you probably would not *literally* grab a wool scarf and pull it over that person's eyes. However, you may *deceive* them, which is the idiomatic meaning of *pull the wool over someone's eyes*. See what we mean? Idioms can be tricky.

Idiom questions on the Writing and Language Test often require you to identify mistakes in their wording. So, even if you don't know what the idiom *bite off more than you can chew* means, you may still have heard it before, and you should be able to recognize that *bite off more than you can see* is not a correctly composed idiom (you may also deduce that biting with your eyes is both difficult and uncomfortable).

Here are some other common idioms that you may encounter:

Idiom	Meaning
Actions speak louder than words.	What one does is more important than what one says.
Back to the drawing board	Time to start all over again!
Barking up the wrong tree	Making the wrong choice
Beat around the bush	Avoid the topic
Bite off more than you can chew	Take on too large of a task
Costs an arm and a leg	Very expensive
Cry over spilled milk	Complain about something that cannot be changed
Feel under the weather	Feel ill
Has a lot on the ball	Is very competent
Hit the sack	Go to bed
Kill two birds with one stone	Accomplish two tasks with a single action
Let sleeping dogs lie	Do not provoke a potentially unpleasant situation
Let the cat out of the bag	Reveal a secret
Piece of cake	Easy
Take with a grain of salt	Not take something too seriously
The whole nine yards	Everything

A good way to become familiar with a wide variety of idioms is to read a lot in your daily life. Writers love to use idioms, and the more you see them, the more comfortable you'll be in facing them on test day!

PREPOSITIONAL PHRASES

Prepositions indicate time and direction, and are pretty straightforward. Prepositional phrases, however, are a bit less straightforward. In fact, they're very similar to idioms in that they cannot be explained with simple rules—you just have to get familiar with them and decide what works best.

As the old lesson goes, a preposition is anywhere a mouse can go: *over, under, sideways, down, in, out, at, from, above, to, inside, outside, before, after, forward, toward*, etc.

A prepositional phrase combines a preposition with one or more words. For example, *at home* is a common prepositional phrase. Technically, there is nothing grammatically wrong with saying *in home* (*I didn't go to the park last weekend; I was in home*); however, it simply isn't common to say *I was in home*, and you'll need to be aware of the most commonly used prepositional phrases on test day.

Here are a few common prepositions you should remember:

among friends	in the grass	at work	in your mind
at home	in the room	at the beach	on the lawn
at the office	in the tree	in my heart	on the road
at play	in the window	in the doorway	on the roof
at school	in the yard	in the family	over the top

FREQUENTLY CONFUSED WORDS

The English language contains many frequently confused words—words that may look or sound alike but have completely different meanings, so using them interchangeably in your writing can have serious negative consequences. You may encounter these tricky word pairs on test day, and should be able to correctly identify the correct word required in a sentence given the context.

Here are a few common frequently confused words that you should be aware of—and on the lookout for—on test day:

accept	to receive something
except	the exclusion of something
advice	a recommendation to follow
advise	to recommend something
affect	to influence (*verb*), or an emotional response (*noun*)
effect	a result (*noun*) or to cause (*verb*)
allude	to make an indirect reference to
elude	to successfully avoid
altogether	thoroughly
all together	everyone or everything in a single place
accent	a pronunciation common to a region
ascent	the act of rising or climbing
assent	consent or agreement
brake	a device for stopping a vehicle
break	to destroy into pieces
capital	a major city
capitol	a government building
coarse	feeling rough
course	a path or an academic class series
complement	something that completes another thing
compliment	praise or flattery
conscience	a sense of morality
conscious	awake or aware
dessert	final course in a meal, typically sweet
desert	a dry and sandy area
desert	to abandon
die	to lose life; one of a pair of dice
dye	to change or add color to
hear	to sense sound using an ear
here	in this particular place
hole	an opening
whole	a complete and entire thing
its	the possessive form of *it*
it's	a contraction for *it is*

lead	a type of metal substance, or to guide
led	past tense of *to lead*
loose	not tightly fastened
lose	to misplace
metal	a type of hard substance
medal	a flat designed disk, often given in recognition of an accomplishment
mettle	courage or spirit
miner	a worker in a mine
minor	an underage person (*noun*), or less important (*adj.*)
peace	free from war
piece	part of a whole
pedal	the foot lever of a vehicle used to generate power
petal	part of a flower
peddle	to sell
personal	intimate, or owned by a person
personnel	employees or staff
plain	simple and unadorned
plane	to shave wood (*verb*), or an aircraft (*noun*)
precede	to come before
proceed	to continue
presence	attendance
presents	gifts
principal	foremost (*adj.*); head figure of a school (*noun*)
principle	a moral conviction or basic truth
reign	to rule
rein	a strap to control an animal (*noun*), or to guide or control (*verb*)
right	correct, or opposite of left
rite	ritual or ceremony
write	to put words on paper
road	a path
rode	the past tense of *to ride*
sight	scene or picture
site	place or location
cite	to document or quote (*verb*)
stationary	standing still
stationery	a type of writing paper

than	besides
then	at that time or next
their	possessive form of *they*
there	in a specific place
they're	contraction for *they are*
through	finished, or into and out of
threw	past tense of *to throw*
thorough	complete
to	toward
too	also or very (used to show emphasis)
two	number following one
weak	not strong
week	seven consecutive days
weather	climate conditions
whether	if
where	in which place
were	past tense of *to be*
which	one of a group
witch	female sorcerer
whose	possessive for *of who*
who's	contraction for *who is*
your	possessive for *of you*
you're	contraction for *you are*

LOGICAL COMPARISONS

People make comparisons all the time—both in their daily lives as well as in writing. The key to making logical comparisons is to make sure that the things being compared are similarly balanced and equivalent. But what happens if we make an illogical comparison? Illogical comparisons occur when dissimilar or illogical things are compared, leading to an awkward or confusing result—as in the following example:

> Both Jerome and Patricia have new dogs. Jerome and Patricia took their new dogs to the veterinarian, and had them weighed. According to the vet's scale, Jerome's dog is heavier than Patricia.

According to the last sentence of this paragraph, *Jerome's dog* and *Patricia* were weighed on the vet's scale. That certainly doesn't sound right, does it? A review of the earlier portion of the paragraph confirms this—Jerome's dog and Patricia's dog were weighed on the vet's scale. We have an illogical comparison to fix. Let's take a look at a corrected version:

> Both Jerome and Patricia have new dogs. Jerome and Patricia took their new dogs to the veterinarian, and had them weighed. According to the vet's scale, Jerome's dog is heavier than Patricia's dog.

Much better—the problem is solved, the illogical comparison is fixed, and all is well. Be on the lookout for illogical comparisons on the exam and be prepared to fix them.

ATTACKING STANDARD ENGLISH CONVENTIONS QUESTIONS FOR A PERFECT SCORE

Now you should have a better sense of the main topics and types of Standard English Conventions questions that you'll likely encounter on the SAT® Writing and Language Test. As we've said before, thorough practice and review are your best strategies for achieving your perfect score goal.

Let's take the next step on your journey toward a perfect SAT® score with practice questions in the context of a complete passage. We'll also cover proven strategies for effectively attacking questions in the answer explanations that follow.

We'll revisit our passage on "Edward Hopper: An American Life" from the previous chapter, but with Standard English Conventions questions that you may encounter on test day. Best of luck!

Edward Hopper: An American Life

Some know the art before the artist, and for American realist painter and printmaker Edward Hopper, that's often the case. Many people instantly recognize *Nighthawks*, the famous 1942 oil painting of a quasi-desolate, street-side coffee shop that's widely considered a classic example of the American Realism art movement, but less people can easily name the artist, **1** or recognized the name Edward Hopper if they run across it. That said, Hopper's prolific artistic catalog—reflecting his vision of modern American life—places him soundly at the vanguard of this bold twentieth-century art movement. Let's take a closer look at the life of this fascinating individual.

Edward Hopper was born in upstate New York in the late nineteenth century, 1882 to be exact, to a comfortable Baptist family of Dutch descent—the son of a dry goods merchant. Hopper was a fine student, and showed a predilection for artistic endeavors from an early age. He began drawing as a young boy, encouraged and supported by his parents, and by the time Hopper was a teenager he was painting— **2** using, oils charcoals and watercolors to depict the natural world that enveloped his childhood existence. He showed an early interest in nautical subject matter, and found great inspiration in the ships and sailing vessels that occupied the northern Hudson River that flowed near his family home. Hoping to capture the majesty of nature, **3** the paintings often featured beautiful natural settings.

After graduation, Hopper decided not to pursue his initial career choice of naval architect, instead opting to follow his artistic passion. On the insistence of his parents, Hopper received an education in commercial art in New York City, in an effort to have a means of stable and steady income. It was here that he found the early artistic influences that would help shape his burgeoning artistic sensibilities, including his art teacher Robert Henri, who encouraged his students to let their art reflect their real interests in the world. **4** Hoppers early years, after art school reflected an intense inner struggle to find both his artistic purpose and voice, as well as a struggle between creative and commercial demands. It wasn't until his trip to Massachusetts in 1912 to find fresh inspiration and paint the natural world, and his first painting sale (entitled *Sailing*) at the Armory Show in 1913, did things turn around for Edward Hopper, and a clear path forward emerged.

Edward Hopper's artistic output and notoriety slowly grew, and after getting married in 1924 his artistic voice and sensibilities quickly flourished and matured with the help of his wife, who devoted **5** themselves to supporting Edward's career. Hopper found and embraced his spare yet bold painting style, and his uncanny ability to capture the quiet beauty and bittersweet desperation of rural and urban American life, from the cold Manhattan streets to the natural splendor of the New England landscapes that surrounded him. Hopper died in 1967 in his New York City studio, less than a year before his wife Josephine died. His contributions to the art world and his influence on successive generations of new artists are undeniable.

1 A. NO CHANGE
B. or recognizing the name
C. or recognize the name
D. or recognizes the name

2 A. NO CHANGE
B. using, oils charcoals, and watercolors
C. using oils charcoals and watercolors,
D. using oils, charcoals, and watercolors

3   **A.**   NO CHANGE

      B.   Hopper often featured beautiful natural settings in his paintings.

      C.   the paintings often captured beautiful natural settings in Hopper's world.

      D.   the paintings rarely featured beautiful natural settings.

4   **A.**   NO CHANGE

      B.   Hoppers early years

      C.   Hopper's, early years

      D.   Hopper's early years

5   **A.**   NO CHANGE

      B.   himself

      C.   herself

      D.   itself

ATTACKING EXPRESSION OF IDEAS QUESTIONS

Let's carefully break down and analyze the Standard English Conventions questions associated with the passage "Edward Hopper: An American Life." The strategies used to tackle these questions can help you tackle the Expression of Ideas questions you'll encounter on test day.

1   **A.**   NO CHANGE

      B.   or recognizing the name

      C.   or recognize the name

      D.   or recognizes the name

Attacking the question: This question is asking you to determine the appropriate verb tense given the context of the sentence. If you're unsure of what type of question you're dealing with, you can often find a clue among the answer choices. In this question, the tense of the verb *to recognize* is varying, which signals what type of question this is.

Now that we know what type of question this is, the next step is to review the sentence in which the underline appears in. As written (choice A), the sentence has an issue with parallel structure—the verb *name*, referring to the people who can "easily name the artist" is in the present tense while the verb *recognized*, referring to the same people, is in the past tense. Now, we need to determine what the correct tense for this sentence is. Since the sentence refers to what people *can* do, not what they *have already done*, the present tense is correct for this sentence, so **the correct answer is C**. Choices B and D both contain incorrect verb forms of *to recognize*.

If you have time, it's always helpful to plug your answer into the sentence to check if it works:

> Many people instantly recognize *Nighthawks*, the famous 1942 oil painting of a quasi-desolate, street-side coffee shop that's widely considered a classic example of the American Realism art movement, but less people can easily name the artist, or *recognize* the name Edward Hopper if they run across it.

Yes, that works, so you can be confident you found the correct answer!

---

2 **A.** NO CHANGE
 B. using, oils charcoals, and watercolors
 C. using oils charcoals and watercolors,
 D. using oils, charcoals, and watercolors

Attacking the question: This is a question involving a simple list of items in a sentence. If you quickly recognized the issue while reading the passage, that's great. Quickly answer the question when you encounter it and move on. Remember, the key to developing and maintaining an effective test-taking pace is to save time on the questions that are easier for you so you can have sufficient time to tackle the more challenging questions.

If you need a bit more time to determine the correct answer, let's keep going. Remember, scanning the answer choices can help you to determine what the question is about. We can see that there are variations in comma placement throughout the answer choices, so we have a clue that commas are the theme here. Remember what we said in this chapter about simple lists of items in sentences—they are separated by commas. As written (choice A), the lack of commas between items creates confusion in the sentence. Choices B and C also fail to correctly separate all of the list items. Let's take a look at choice D. Each of the items in the list of paint supplies—*oils, charcoals, and watercolors*—is correctly separated by a comma. **The correct answer is D** because it adds some much needed "comma clarity" to the sentence.

---

3 **A.** NO CHANGE
 B. Hopper often featured beautiful natural settings in his paintings.
 C. the paintings often captured beautiful natural settings in Hopper's world.
 D. the paintings rarely featured beautiful natural settings.

Attacking the question: While reading this passage, you may have noticed that this sentence as written (choice A) sounded a bit awkward. Were the paintings hoping to capture the majesty of nature? That certainly sounds odd, and it is because it's the result of a dangling modifier. Remember, a dangling modifier creates confusion in a sentence because it's modifying an object that is not in the sentence.

To correct the sentence, we need a little context. *Who* was hoping to capture the majesty of nature? Based on the available context clues, we can determine that this sentence is referring to Edward Hopper—the subject of the passage. Now that we know who the modifier refers to, we need to determine which answer choice fixes the dangling modifier issue. Choice C doesn't mention Hopper until the end of the sentence, and choice D doesn't mention Hopper at all, so we can determine that they're both incorrect. **The correct answer is B** because it fixes the issue by bringing Hopper into the sentence. We can check to make sure it's correct by inserting it into the sentence:

*Hoping to capture the majesty of nature, Hopper often featured beautiful
natural settings in his paintings.*

This version of the sentence makes it clear who's hoping to capture the majesty of nature,
and is the correct answer.

---

4 **A.**   NO CHANGE
    B.   Hoppers early years
    C.   Hopper's, early years
    D.   Hopper's early years

Attacking the question: This question involves the correct way to indicate possession,
and the appropriate use of within-sentence punctuation. In this sentence, the *early years*
that we are referring to belong to Hopper, so we need to use the correct possessive form
of this noun. Remember, apostrophes are used when indicating that a noun *possesses*
something. More often than not, you can just add an apostrophe and an -s onto the end
of a word to make it possessive.

We can quickly eliminate choices A and B, as they are both missing the required apostrophe. Choices C and D both contain the correct possessive form—*Hopper's*—but one
of them contains a comma and one doesn't. Now our job is to determine if the comma
in question is needed or not. The comma awkwardly divides the possessor (*Hopper's*)
and the item in possession (*early years*), and shouldn't be used here. Therefore, **the
correct answer is D**. Let's do a quick check to confirm:

*Hopper's early years after art school reflected an intense inner struggle
to find both his artistic purpose and voice, as well as a struggle between
creative and commercial demands.*

The sentence works well, and now we're sure we're correct and can move on. Don't
forget—commas are among the most overused and misused types of punctuation, and
you need to remain vigilant against their incorrect use!

---

5 **A.**   NO CHANGE
    B.   himself
    C.   herself
    D.   itself

Attacking the question: Let's place this sentence and the answer choices under our
careful analytical lens. The underlined word in the sentence is a *pronoun*, and the answer
choices are all *pronouns* too—so we can quickly determine that we need to put on our
"proper pronoun cap" in order to tackle this question.

The first step in determining proper pronoun usage is to figure out the *antecedent*—the
noun or nouns that it is replacing. In this sentence, the underlined pronoun refers to
whoever devoted time "to supporting Edward's career." If we go further back into the
sentence, we read that it was *his wife* who supported him. Which pronoun among the

answer choices should replace Edward Hopper's wife? The singular pronoun *herself* should be used to replace the singular noun, *wife*, so **the correct answer is C.**

Building Your SAT® Study Plan

Use the practice and review in this chapter to help guide your study plans between now and test day.

If a review concept or topic is challenging for you to master, or if you find yourself struggling with a specific type of question during practice, consider devoting more time to studying it than others that are easier for you.

You can also try using a ranking system for test topics (i.e., *easy*, *medium*, and *hard*), and divide your study time accordingly to ensure that harder topics get more attention.

Using a carefully constructed SAT® study plan will help you earn your best possible scores and achieve test day success!

STANDARD ENGLISH CONVENTIONS PRACTICE

Now it's time to put your Standard English Conventions skills to the test! Read and carefully analyze the following full-length passage. The 10 questions that follow it are designed to test your understanding of the passage, as well as your ability to recognize and use appropriate English language Answers and explanations follow on page 339.

Should America Keep the Electoral College?

The process of voting for and electing presidents and vice presidents in the United States has come under scrutiny in recent years. Since the country's beginnings, the United States **1** will be using a system known as the *electoral college* to elect its two key leaders. The electoral college is based on a specific subset of representative state electors who are selected to elect candidates to office. Some claim that this system has worked well for every presidential election in American history and **2** she says that there's no need to fix what isn't broken. Others claim that this system is overly complicated and unfair, and that electing presidents should be based on a *popular vote* system— where each person gets one vote and all votes are equal. Let's take a closer look at this debate, and both sides of the issue.

The electoral college system currently in place uses a group of 538 electors to choose its **3** leaders these electors reflect the following congressional contingent: 435 members of the U.S. House of

Representatives, 100 members of the U.S. Senate, and 3 electors who represent the District of Columbia. In order to win the presidential election, a candidate needs to earn a minimum of 270 electoral votes. When a candidate wins the *popular vote* (the majority of the citizen's individual votes) in a state, they earn the state's pot of *electoral votes*. Because these electoral votes are apportioned differently per state based on the number of citizens each state has, the number of electors per state varies widely.

Let's look at an example. Jen is from California and Rick is from Wyoming. California has 55 electoral votes and Wyoming only has 3 electoral votes. Based on the electoral college, some would argue that **4** Jen's vote has more power than Rick does. States with more people have more voting power than less populous states, and based on the rules of electing presidents and vice presidents in the United States, candidates can win elections by winning a majority of the electoral votes and still lose the popular vote—they can effectively become president without having a majority of people vote for them. Some folks think this is unfair, and for many this lies at the heart of the debate.

Some individuals feel that that the electoral college system needs to be abandoned, and that the process of electing presidents and vice presidents should be simplified so that each **5** citizen's vote has the same voting power. They want the presidential election to be rooted in winning the popular vote; in sum, each citizen—regardless of which state he or she lives in and how many people live in that state—has one vote, and the candidate who earns the majority of popular votes wins the election. Proponents of adopting the popular vote **6** system, argue, that not only does this simplify the election process, it makes for a more fair and democratic election system, one in which all votes are equal. Some who support maintaining the electoral college system point to the wisdom of the founding fathers of the United States, who decided at the nation's inception that the wisdom of a small group of elected officials will ultimately make better choices than the larger collective whole. They also claim that it **7** help promote and protect the varied interests of different states whose needs and concerns are not equal across the country, but instead are based on such factors as **8** geography history demographics climate and economy.

The debate about whether or not the American presidential election, a seminal event that occurs every four years, should be based on the electoral college or a popular vote system continues to rage on, and it seems to gather momentum whenever a new election cycle begins. 9 Only time will talk about whether or not our current system changes. What's your opinion regarding this 10 issue. Perhaps the question regarding which system to use should be put to a vote—but deciding which type of voting system this should be based on might not be so easy to determine.

1 **A.** NO CHANGE
    B. once used
    C. has been using
    D. has never used

2 **A.** NO CHANGE
    B. he says
    C. it says
    D. they say

3 **A.** NO CHANGE
    B. leaders; these
    C. leaders, these
    D. leaders these,

4 **A.** NO CHANGE
    B. Jen has more power than Rick's vote does.
    C. Jen has more power than Rick does.
    D. Jen's vote has more power than Rick's vote does.

5 **A.** NO CHANGE
    B. citizens' vote
    C. citizen vote
    D. citizen vote's

6 **A.** NO CHANGE
    B. system, argue
    C. system argue
    D. system—argue,

7 **A.** NO CHANGE
    B. help promoted
    C. helping promote
    D. helps promote

8 **A.** NO CHANGE
    B. geography history, demographics climate, and economy
    C. geography, history, demographics, climate, and economy
    D. geography; history, demographics; climate, and economy

9 **A.** NO CHANGE
    B. Only time will discuss
    C. Only time will think about
    D. Only time will tell

10 **A.** NO CHANGE
    B. issue? Perhaps
    C. issue Perhaps
    D. issue! Perhaps

ANSWER KEY AND EXPLANATIONS

1. C	3. B	5. A	7. D	9. D
2. D	4. D	6. C	8. C	10. B

1. **The correct answer is C.** This question is testing your ability to recognize the appropriate verb phrase tense given its context within a sentence. As written (choice A), the verb phrase *will be using* is in the future tense, indicating that this is something that we will be using sometime in the future. However, according to this sentence this is something that has been in use "since the country's beginnings," so the future tense is incorrect here. Choice B (*once used*) is in the past tense and leads us to believe that the electoral college is no longer in use, which is also incorrect. Choice D is incorrect because it stands in direct opposition to the information provided in the passage regarding the use of the Electoral College system in the United States. Choice B is the correct answer here—the Electoral College system has been and is presently in use, and will likely be so for the foreseeable future, so this is the correct tense for the sentence.

2. **The correct answer is D.** This question involves determining correct pronoun use. In order to determine the correct pronoun for the underlined portion of the sentence, we need to determine the antecedent it is replacing. In this example, *some*, referring to some people who "claim that this system has worked well for every presidential election in American history," is the antecedent. Therefore, we need a plural pronoun and verb form to make this sentence correct. Choices A, B, and C contain singular pronoun and verb forms and are incorrect. Choice D deploys the correct plural forms, *they say*, and is the correct answer.

3. **The correct answer is B.** As written (choice A), this sentence is a run-on and needs some attention in order to fix it. There are two distinct independent clauses here: "The electoral college system currently in place uses a group of 538 electors to choose its leaders" and "these electors reflect the following congressional contingent: 435 members of the U.S. House of Representatives, 100 members of the U.S. Senate, and 3 electors who represent the District of Columbia." As discussed in the chapter, semicolons are effectively utilized to separate closely related independent clauses in a sentence. Choice B correctly uses a semicolon and is the correct answer. Choice C and D incorrectly use commas; they are incorrect to separate independent clauses in a sentence.

4. **The correct answer is D.** This is an illogical comparison question; this type of question is often subtle and requires a careful analytical eye while reading the passages. As written, the sentence is making an illogically comparison between *Jen's vote* and *Rick himself*, so is incorrect. Based on the context of the paragraph and sentence, we can determine that the sentence actually wants to compare the power of *Jen's vote* and *Rick's vote*. Choice D fixes this problem, and we can check by plugging it into the sentence: *Based on the Electoral College, some would argue that Jen's vote has more power than Rick's vote does.* This makes things much clearer. Choices B and C fail to repair the confusion between the people involved in the comparison and their respective voting power, and are both incorrect.

5. **The correct answer is A.** This question is designed to test your knowledge of possessive nouns. Remember that creating the possessive form of most simple singular nouns entails adding an apostrophe and letter *s* to the end of the person, place, or thing that maintains possession. In this sentence, each *citizen* is the possessor and his or her vote is the item in possession. The sentence is correct as written (choice A), and *citizen's vote* is the correct possessive form. Choice B uses the possessive plural form of citizen (*citizens'*), which is incorrect here since we are referring to the vote of each citizen individually. Choice C is incorrect because it fails to utilize any possessive noun form. Choice D is incorrect because it mistakenly uses the possessive form of *vote*.

6. **The correct answer is C.** This question is testing your ability to recognize necessary vs. unnecessary punctuation in a sentence. Unnecessary punctuation can add a real element of awkwardness and confusion to a sentence, which is the case in how it's written in the passage (choice A). As mentioned in the chapter, commas are among the most overused and misused types of punctuation. Here, the commas add unnecessary pauses around the verb *argue*. Choice B also contains an unnecessary comma, and is also incorrect. Choice D inserts an em-dash, typically used to create an even longer pause within a sentence or to highlight relevant text; here, it's unnecessary and incorrect. Choice C correctly removes the commas and creates a more cohesive sentence with an improved flow: *Proponents of adopting the popular vote system argue that not only does this simplify the election process, it makes for a more fair and democratic election system, one in which all votes are equal.*

7. **The correct answer is D.** This question is testing your ability to utilize appropriate subject-verb agreement. As written (choice A), there is a lack of agreement between the singular subject *it* and the plural *help*. Choice D is correct; it fixes the error by using the appropriate singular present form *helps* in the sentence. Choice B fails to fix the incorrect plural *help* and instead incorrectly deploys the past tense *promoted*. Choice C also fails to utilize the correct form of *helps* and instead uses the present continuous form *helping* without the requisite *is* (*is helping*), and is also incorrect.

8. **The correct answer is C.** This question is testing your ability to correctly separate items in a simple list with the appropriate punctuation within a sentence. The sentence as written (choice A), which fails to separate the list items with any punctuation, is a run-on and is incorrect. Choice C correctly fixes the problem—the items in a simple list within a sentence should be separated by commas. Choice B fails to separate all the list items by commas correctly. Choice D intersperses semicolons with commas, and is incorrect. Semicolons are used to separate items in more complex series of lists.

9. **The correct answer is D.** This question focuses on your ability to recognize conventional English language expressions and their appropriate use. The sentence is incorrect as written; it incorrectly interprets a conventional expression, thereby creating confusion within the sentence. Choices B and C also utilize incorrect versions of the expression. Choice D correctly utilizes the proper conventional expression: Only time will tell whether or not our current system changes.

10. **The correct answer is B.** This question is testing your ability to utilize proper end-of-sentence punctuation given the context of the sentence in which it appears. What type of sentence are we facing here? The appearance of the word *What's* at the beginning signals us that we're dealing with a question, so a question mark is the correct punctuation to use here. Choice B correctly adds a punctuation mark to the end of the sentence: *What's your opinion regarding this issue?* Choice A incorrectly uses a period. Choice C neglects to use any punctuation and is incorrect. Choice D incorrectly utilizes an exclamation point, which is used to indicate an exclamation or a feeling of shock or surprise, not at the end of a question.

SUMMING IT UP

- **Standard English Conventions questions** assess your knowledge of the guidelines of English language and grammar: connecting words, constructing phrases and sentences, creating written works of every imaginable genre and type, and conveying thoughts that effectively communicate ideas to others.

- **Sentence Structure questions** focus on identifying and fixing issues involving sentence construction and sentence formation. You can expect to encounter questions involving parallel structure, modifier placement; sentence boundaries, including grammatically incomplete and ineffective sentences; inappropriate pronoun shifts; and inappropriate shifts in voice, mood, and verb tense.

- **Independent clauses** contain a subject and a verb and make sense on their own.

- **Subordinate clauses** contain a subject-verb pair but must be linked to an independent clause to be correct.

- **Fragments** are partial sentences that lack either a subject or a verb. They are grammatically incorrect.

- **Run-on sentences** are grammatically incorrect compound or complex sentences that fail to link their parts with the necessary conjunction or punctuation.

- **Modifiers** are words and phrases that describe. **Misplaced modifiers** are not placed next to the words they are supposed to modify. They are grammatically incorrect. **Dangling modifiers** have no object to modify.

- **Parallel structure** occurs when all groups of words in a sentence are written in the same tense and form. When such words are not in the same tense or form, the sentence is grammatically incorrect. Failing to pair correlative conjunctions correctly also violates parallel structure.

- **Conventions of Punctuation questions** focus on recognizing and adhering to the rules and standards of appropriate punctuation. You can expect to encounter a wide array of punctuation issues: within sentence punctuation including dashes, colons, and semicolons; plural and possessive forms of nouns and pronouns; end-of-sentence punctuation including periods, exclamation points, and question marks; the correct use and display of parenthetical, tangential, and nonrestrictive items in a sentence; correctly displaying items in a series, utilizing commas and semicolons for simple and complex lists; and addressing unnecessary and superfluous punctuation.

- **End-of-sentence punctuation** includes the period, the exclamation mark, and the question mark. When a sentence ends with quotation marks used to indicate dialogue, the end-of-sentence punctuation is placed *within* the quotation marks. If the quotation marks indicate a title and placing end-of-sentence punctuation within the marks might give the false impression that the mark is part of the title, the end-of-sentence punctuation is placed *after* the closing quotation marks.

- **Commas** are used to separate introductory words and phrases, clauses in compound sentences, nonrestrictive phrases, items in series, appositives, and quotations.

- **Apostrophes** are used to separate letters in contractions and indicate possession. When indicating possession, an apostrophe is usually followed by the letter -*s*. However, no extra -*s* is necessary if the possessing word ends in -*s* and is not someone's name.

- **Colons** are used to introduce a list of items or offset an example.

- **Dashes** are used to offset examples and indicate a pause or interruption in dialogue.

- **Parentheses** often enclose tangential or bonus information that cannot be fit into a sentence naturally.

- **Conventions of Usage questions** focus on identifying and adhering to standard writing and language practices. You should be prepared to tackle questions involving possessives and possessive determiners including contractions and adverbs, issues involving subject-verb agreement, appropriate pronoun use for clarity, appropriate and logical comparisons of like vs. unlike terms, recognizing standard conventional English language expressions and their appropriate use, and correctly identifying and using frequently confused words.

- **Plural nouns** do not always end with -*s*; there are several variations among plural nouns depending on the words' letters. **Collective nouns** can be both singular and plural.

- **Subjects and verbs** are in agreement when they are in the same form. They both need to be either singular or plural and not a combination of both forms.

- **Pronouns and antecedents**—the words for which the pronouns stand in—need to be in agreement. They need to agree in terms of number, gender, and person.

- **Relative pronouns** signal relative clauses, which are used to describe nouns; **reflexive pronouns** refer back to their subjects; **interrogative pronouns** are used when asking a question; **possessive pronouns** show ownership.

- **Verb tense** indicates when the action the verb describes takes place.

- **Comparative adjectives and adverbs** are used when comparing two things. They usually end in -*er*. **Superlative adjectives and adverbs** are used when comparing three or more things. They usually end in -*est*.

- **Idioms** use words to mean something other than their literal meanings.

- **Prepositional phrases** combine a preposition with other words to indicate direction and time. Their particular word often depends on common usage.

- **Illogical comparisons** occur when dissimilar or illogical things are compared, leading to an awkward or confusing result.

CHAPTER 11:
THE SAT® ESSAY

OVERVIEW

- The SAT® Essay: An Overview
- How the SAT® Essay Is Scored
- Inside the Prompt
- Preparing Your SAT® Essay
- Managing Your Time
- Avoiding Common Mistakes
- Getting a Perfect Score
- An SAT® Essay Walk-Through
- Summing It Up

The next stop in your journey toward a perfect performance on the SAT® exam is the Essay portion, though it won't actually count toward that score of 1600. The SAT® Essay is a separate entity from the multiple-choice section of the exam.

NOTE: If you have a particular college in mind, be sure to find out whether it requires you to take the SAT® Essay before deciding whether or not to take this portion of the exam.

You may have heard some details about how the SAT® Essay is formatted and scored throughout your school career. Well, be prepared to forget about much of what you may have learned, because the SAT® Essay was redesigned quite drastically in March 2016. Don't worry, though. This chapter will give you all the most up-to-date information on what you'll encounter on the Essay, how it is scored, and of course, how you can achieve your highest score.

Learning how to get a perfect score on the SAT® Essay will involve a thorough explanation of how to prepare for the test, a detailed looked at the essay itself, and crucial advice on the best ways to manage your time and sidestep common mistakes. Throughout this chapter, you'll also get to put what you've learned to the test by writing your own essay in response to three high-level practice prompts. There's a lot to digest in this chapter, so take your time and take comfort in the knowledge that you're in the hands of the test-prep experts who want nothing more than to guide you to your perfect score!

THE SAT® ESSAY: AN OVERVIEW

Whether or not you already knew a few things about the version of the Essay administered before March 2016, you'll need to know some basics about what's on the test. Here's a quick and neat rundown on the SAT® Essay:

- The SAT® Essay is an optional portion of the exam. Unless the school you want to attend requires you to take the SAT® Essay, you may decide not to take it without affecting your overall score, so that perfect 1600 is still achievable.

- The SAT® Essay is administered after the multiple-choice sections.

- The prompt on which you will base your essay is a reading passage of approximately 650-750 words in length.

- You will be expected to include evidence from the passage in your essay.

- You will have 50 minutes to read the prompt and compose your essay. You will receive three individual scores for your essay. Each score covers its own category: reading, analysis, and writing.

NOTE: The three scores you'll receive for your SAT® Essay are combined neither with each other nor with any other score you receive on the exam.

Now that you know the basics, we'll go a lot further in depth about each point. First of all, it is important to be aware that the SAT® Essay is optional. Some schools or educational institutions may require their students to take the essay, but most students will have the choice of whether or not take this portion of the SAT® exam. The obvious question you may be asking now is, "Why in the world would I want to make this challenging and high-stakes test even more involved than it already is?" That's a fair question, and we actually have some good answers for you. As you know, your SAT® score is often important to the college, university, or other higher education school you plan to attend. Some of these institutions expect to see how you performed on the SAT® Essay, so there's not much of a choice involved.

However, even if your desired school doesn't require you to take the essay, you actually may still want to do it. Taking the test and studying your score will give you insight into your strengths and weaknesses as a writer, and you will be doing a lot of writing throughout your college career. What you learn from taking the SAT® Essay may actually be of great use as you continue your schooling. You'll learn how to analyze an argument, how to write engagingly and informatively, and how to analyze what you've read. You will also learn where your weaknesses may be, so that you know which skills you'll need to sharpen to tackle all of that writing you'll do in college.

As we've stated, you will have 50 minutes to take the essay. Don't expect to be writing your essay for those entire 50 minutes, though. The prompt you need to read before writing your essay is pretty lengthy—between 650 and 750 words long. You will need to leave yourself ample time to read that prompt carefully, analyze the author's information and point of view, take notes, and pull pieces of evidence from the prompt to support your analysis. You might think 50 minutes may not sound like much time to accomplish all that *and* write a strong essay, but you shouldn't fret about time. Later in this chapter, you'll learn more about organizing and managing your work to make the most of those 50 minutes.

Past versions of the SAT® Essay required test takers to respond to an argument with their *own* positions, but the new version asks you to analyze an argumentative passage. So instead of giving your own point of view in your essay, you will think deeply about the *author's* point of view. You'll consider the following questions:

- What is the topic being discussed?
- What is the author's stance on that topic?
- How does the author present her or his argument?
- What does the author do to persuade the reader that his or her position is the correct one?

Answering those questions will *not* require you to draw on your own knowledge, experiences, or beliefs. Everything you need to answer them will be in the prompt passage. The most important details will serve as valuable evidence to support the findings you present in your essay.

NOTE: There is only one prompt on the SAT® Essay. The essay prompt is the directions that tell you exactly what you need to do in your essay after reading that 650- to 750-word passage you have to analyze. While the prompt passage will be different every time you take the SAT® Essay, the essay prompt itself will basically always be the same. You'll learn exactly how that prompt is worded later in this chapter.

HOW THE SAT® ESSAY IS SCORED

As mentioned earlier in this chapter, your SAT® Essay will receive three different scores:

1. Your **Reading score** rates your comprehension of the prompt based on the accuracy and thoroughness of the details in your essay.

2. Your **Analysis score** rates how well you examined and explained how the author constructed the argument in the prompt and how persuasive that argument is.

3. Your **Writing score** rates how well you constructed, worded, and organized your essay.

Two scorers will read your essay, and each of them will give you a reading, analysis, and writing score. That means you'll get two scores for each of those categories at first, but those two scores will be combined to come up with your final score in each category. However, your scores for each category will not be combined with each other. You get one score each for reading, analysis, and writing, not a single score for the essay as a whole. This will be really helpful if you're taking the essay to improve your college-level writing skills. By examining these individual scores, you may learn that you're very strong when it comes to crafting your writing, but you could use some work when it comes to analyzing a text composed by someone else.

The scorers will rate your essay using a scale of 1 to 4. After the two scorers' scores are added up, you will see that your score for each category will be on a scale of 2 to 8: 8 is a perfect score and 2 is a much less perfect one.

So if, for example, the scorers combined scores for your essay were 5 for reading, 4 for analysis, and 7 for writing, the score you'll receive will look like this:

5/4/7

SAT® Essay scorers do not just pull these numbers out of their hats. They follow a strict rubric to come up with your three scores. The scoring guidelines within the rubric are summarized below:

Score 4 (Advanced)

Reading	The response shows a comprehensive understanding of the source text, including the author's key claims, use of details and evidence, and the relationship between the two; is error-free regarding fact or interpretation within the text; and demonstrates a complete understanding of the source text, skillfully using evidence from the text (i.e., direct quotations, paraphrases, or both).
Analysis	The response offers an "insightful" and in-depth evaluation of the author's use of evidence and stylistic or persuasive features in building an argument and consistently uses relevant supporting details that address the task.
Writing	The response includes all of the features of a strong essay, including a precise central claim, body paragraphs, and a strong conclusion; it incorporates a variety of sentence structures and is virtually free of all convention errors.

Score 3 (Proficient)

Reading	The response shows an appropriate understanding of the source text, including the author's key claims and use of details in developing an argument.
Analysis	The response offers an effective evaluation of the author's use of evidence and stylistic or persuasive features in building an argument; it uses appropriate supporting details and evidence that are relevant and focused on the task.
Writing	The response includes all of the features of an effective essay, including a precise central claim, body paragraphs, and a strong conclusion; it incorporates a variety of sentence structures and is relatively free of common grammatical errors.

Score 2 (Partial)

Reading	The response shows some understanding of the source text, including the author's key claims; it uses limited textual evidence and incorporates unimportant details.
Analysis	The response offers a limited evaluation of the author's use of evidence and stylistic or persuasive features in building an argument; its supporting details are lacking and/or irrelevant to the writing task.
Writing	The response does not provide a precise central claim nor an effective introduction, body paragraphs, and conclusion; it incorporates little variety of sentence structures and contains numerous errors in grammar and conventions.

Score 1 (Inadequate)

Reading	The response demonstrates little or no understanding of the source text or the author's use of key claims.
Analysis	The response offers no clear evaluation of the author's use of evidence and stylistic or persuasive features in building an argument; supporting details and evidence are non-existent or irrelevant to the writing task.
Writing	The response lacks any form of cohesion or structure; it incorporates little variety in sentence structure and includes significant errors in convention that make it difficult to read.

To check out the official SAT® Essay rubric, visit *https://collegereadiness.collegeboard.org/sat/scores understanding-scores/essay*.

INSIDE THE PROMPT

You've already learned some valuable information about the SAT® Essay prompt in this chapter, but we're not through discussing this crucial element of the essay yet. First it will be helpful to take a close look at how the prompt will appear. The prompt has three components: the passage introduction, the prompt passage, and the actual essay prompt.

Before the prompt passage, there will be a short introduction to set you on the right path. It will basically always look like this:

As you read the passage below, consider how (the author) uses

- evidence, such as facts or examples, to support claims.
- reasoning to develop ideas and to connect claims and evidence.
- stylistic or persuasive elements, such as word choice or appeals to emotion, to add power to the ideas expressed.

Now it's time for the prompt passage. As we already told you, that passage will be a 650- to 750-word-long argumentative passage. This means the author is not just describing or explaining a topic. She or he is taking a position on a topic and arguing to persuade the reader that her or his position is the correct one. The passage may be about a subject you know nothing about, but the SAT® Essay will not require you to have any special knowledge about that topic. As was the case with the passages on the SAT® Reading Test, all of the information you'll need to know on the SAT® Essay will be contained in the prompt passage.

NOTE: The prompt passage on the SAT® Essay is about the same length as one of the longer passages on the SAT® Reading Test.

After reading the prompt passage, you will read the actual essay prompt, which will explain exactly what you need to accomplish with your essay. The prompt will basically always look like this:

Write an essay in which you explain how (the author) builds an argument to persuade her/his audience that (author's claim). In your essay, analyze how (the author) uses one or more of the features listed above (or features of your own choice) to strengthen the logic and persuasiveness of her/his argument. Be sure that your analysis focuses on the most relevant features of the passage.

Your essay should not explain whether you agree with (the author's) claims, but rather explain how the author builds an argument to persuade her/his audience.

While it is important to identify the topic and the author's position on that topic, merely picking out details will not help you get the best score possible on the SAT® Essay. You will have to analyze and understand why the author is taking the position she or he takes and how well she or he convinces the reader that this position is correct. You'll accomplish this by analyzing the author's evidence, reasoning, and stylistic or persuasive elements.

Sometimes, Less Is More

You aren't required to analyze all three elements—the author's evidence, reasoning, *and* stylistic or persuasive element—in your essay. You might decide to focus on just one or two of these elements. You can still get a top score with a thorough and well-supported analysis of one or two of the elements. Remember that time is also a factor of the test, and you do not want to waste too many of your 50 minutes trying to cover all three elements in depth.

Evidence	The facts, statistics, quotations, results, and other data the author supplies to support her or his argument.	**Questions to ask yourself about Evidence:** • What kinds of evidence does the author use? • Does the author rely too much on a certain type of evidence? • Does the author support every claim with some form of evidence? • Does the evidence come from reliable sources (experts, university websites, textbooks, etc.) or unreliable sources (blogs, Wikipedia, people who have no background in the topic, etc.)? • Are certain uses of evidence stronger than others?
Reasoning	The logic behind the author's argument.	**Questions to ask yourself about Reasoning:** • How much does the passage rely on reasoning? • How up front is the author about his or her reasoning? Does the author describe thought processes and state conclusions explicitly or more implicitly? • Does the author use evidence to support claims logically and clearly? • Do the claims and evidence the author uses ever weaken her or his argument?

Stylistic or Persuasive Elements	The rhetorical tactics the author uses to make the argument.	**Questions to ask yourself about Stylistic or Persuasive Elements:** • Does the author make any direct or implied appeals to the reader, such as appeals to the reader's sense of justice, prejudices, or opinions about his or her own intelligence? • Does the author attempt to stir the reader's emotions either explicitly or implicitly: is she or he trying to make the reader feel joyful, outraged, saddened, righteous, etc.? • How does the author use words to stir the reader's emotions? • Does the author use description to shape a particular mood, atmosphere, or tone—and if so, what is that mood, atmosphere, or tone?

Those questions you might ask yourself in the final column are not just valuable for comprehending the prompt; they can also be very helpful in writing your essay, because you'll be answering some of them in depth in your essay.

Here is another key point you must keep in mind throughout this process: Be prepared for a prompt passage to contain an argument with which you do not personally agree. You may feel the urge to editorialize on the argument or slip your own opinions into your essay. Remember that your essay will be analytical, not personal, and it is not the place to voice whether or not you agree or disagree with the argument. Your only job is to analyze the effectiveness of that argument. Including your personal opinions in your essay can lower your score since it might deprive your analytical score.

A Full-Length Sample Prompt

Now it's time to read a full-length, high-level sample prompt. Remember, you would have to read, analyze, take notes, write your essay, and check your essay for errors in 50 minutes.

As you read the passage below, consider how Maria Montessori uses

- evidence, such as facts or examples, to support claims.
- reasoning to develop ideas and to connect claims and evidence.
- stylistic or persuasive elements, such as word choice or appeals to emotion, to add power to the ideas expressed.

The following passage is excerpted from *The Montessori Method* **by Maria Montessori.**

To prepare teachers in the method of the experimental sciences is not an easy matter. When we shall have instructed them in anthropometry and psychometry in the most minute manner possible, we shall have only created machines, whose usefulness will be most doubtful. Indeed, if it is after this fashion that we are to initiate our teachers into experiment, we shall remain forever in the field of theory. The teachers of the old school, prepared according to the principles of metaphysical philosophy, understood the ideas of certain men regarded as authorities, and moved the muscles of speech in talking of them, and the muscles of the eye in reading their theories. Our scientific teachers, instead, are familiar with certain instruments and know how to move the muscles of the hand and arm in order to use these instruments; besides this, they have an intellectual preparation which consists of a series of typical tests, which they have, in a barren and mechanical way, learned how to apply.

The difference is not substantial, for profound differences cannot exist in exterior technique alone, but lie rather within the inner man. Not with all our initiation into scientific experiment have we prepared *new masters*, for, after all, we have left them standing without the door of real experimental science; we have not admitted them to the noblest and most profound phase of such study,—to that experience which makes real scientists.

And, indeed, what is a scientist? Not, certainly, he who knows how to manipulate all the instruments in the physical laboratory, or who in the laboratory of the chemist handles the various reactives with deftness and security, or who in biology knows how to make ready the specimens for the microscope. Indeed, it is often the case that an assistant has a greater dexterity in experimental technique than the master scientist himself. We give the name scientist to the type of man who has felt experiment to be a means guiding him to search out the deep truth of life, to lift a veil from its fascinating secrets, and who, in this pursuit, has felt arising within him a love for the mysteries of nature, so passionate as to annihilate the thought of himself. The scientist is not the clever manipulator of instruments, he is the worshipper of nature and he bears the external symbols of his passion as does the follower of some religious order. To this body of real scientists belong those who, forgetting, like the Trappists of the Middle Ages, the world about them, live only in the laboratory, careless often in matters of food and dress because they no longer think of themselves; those who, through years of unwearied use of the microscope, become blind; those who in their scientific ardour inoculate themselves with tuberculosis germs; those who handle the excrement of cholera patients in their eagerness to learn the vehicle through which the diseases are transmitted; and those who, knowing that a certain chemical preparation may be an explosive, still persist in testing their theories at the risk of their lives. This is the spirit of the men of science, to whom nature freely reveals her secrets, crowning their labours with the glory of discovery.

There exists, then, the "spirit" of the scientist, a thing far above his mere "mechanical skill," and the scientist is at the height of his achievement when the spirit has triumphed over the mechanism. When he has reached this point, science will receive from him not only new revelations of nature, but philosophic syntheses of pure thought.

It is my belief that the thing which we should cultivate in our teachers is more the *spirit* than the mechanical skill of the scientist; that is, the *direction* of the *preparation* should be toward the spirit rather than toward the mechanism. For example, when we considered the scientific preparation of teachers to be simply the acquiring of the technique of science, we did not attempt to make these elementary teachers perfect anthropologists, expert experimental psychologists, or masters of infant hygiene; we wished only to *direct them* toward the field of experimental science, teaching them to manage the various instruments with a certain degree of skill. So now, we wish to *direct* the teacher, trying to awaken in him, in connection with his own particular field, the school, that scientific *spirit* which opens the door for him to broader and bigger possibilities.

> Write an essay in which you explain how Maria Montessori builds an argument to persuade her audience that her method for preparing teachers to teach the experimental sciences is the best method. In your essay, analyze how Montessori uses one or more of the features listed above (or features of your own choice) to strengthen the logic and persuasiveness of her argument. Be sure that your analysis focuses on the most relevant features of the passage.
>
> Your essay should not explain whether you agree with Montessori's claims, but rather explain how the author builds an argument to persuade her audience.

PREPARING FOR YOUR SAT® ESSAY

If you've gotten far enough in your schooling career to take the SAT® exam, you've probably already written a fair share of essays. While you may not have ever written the kind of analytical essay you will write on the SAT® exam, you won't exactly be reinventing the essay here. That means that much of what you've learned about essay writing applies to your SAT® Essay.

You may even have a method of your own that already works best for you. In that case, feel free to stick with it if you've found that your method has earned you strong grades on your essays in the past. If you don't have a set method already, then this section could really be helpful, because we're about to review some smart ways to prepare your essay before you even start writing it. Here it goes.

Take Good Notes

Relying on your memory too much can cost you valuable minutes on the SAT® Essay. To keep yourself from constantly having to jump back to the prompt passage to find the relevant ideas, details, and evidence to which you will refer in your essay, take good notes while reading it.

> Good notes are short and clear. They may not be clear to anyone but you, but if you understand your notes, that's all that matters.

As you read the prompt passage, remain aware of the author's most important ideas and the way she or he supports those ideas. Maybe the author made a particularly interesting point she supported with a thought-provoking quotation, or perhaps he made a weak point he failed to support at all. If such an idea or piece of supporting evidence seems like it will be important to your analysis, make a note of it. It could be a simple phrase such as, "fails to support criticism of government" or it might even just refer to a relevant line in the prompt passage, such as "see first line paragraph 2 for strong point about technology."

Your notes won't just keep you from having to memorize every detail in the prompt passage; they can also help you accomplish the following:

- Formulate and clarify your analysis.

- Form the basis of the more polished sentences you will actually use in your essay.

- Help you decide which information is most relevant to your essay and which information can be left out.

The Introductory Paragraph

No matter what your topic is or how you approach it, every essay needs an introduction. You never just throw your readers into the deep end of the pool by discussing details and evidence without letting them know what you are discussing and how you plan to discuss it. Those are the kinds of key details that belong in your introductory paragraph.

Remember that great writing does not just hinge on the accuracy and thoroughness of your details and analysis. It should also be engaging to read. It should grab your readers' attentions and make them want to keep reading. Here are some tips for getting your essay off to a strong and engaging start.

- Do not begin your essay with a blunt description of your purpose. "I will now explain why an argumentative essay is well reasoned" is not a very interesting introduction. Hold back your purpose for a sentence to draw your readers in more effectively. Just don't wait too long to get to your purpose, because that could lose your readers' attention, too.

- Try posing a question to your readers that you will then answer as you get deeper into your analysis. For example, you may begin an analysis of a prompt passage about an argumentative essay with questions such as:

    ◦ "What makes an argumentative essay effective?"

    ◦ "Have you ever read an argument that completely lacked logic and coherence?"

- Be creative, but make sure your question suits the tone and point of your analysis.

- Establish your tone from the very beginning. Are you planning to employ a somewhat humorous tone to engage your readers or a more serious one intended to reach a more academic audience?

 Just as a strong introduction will really grab and engage your readers, a weak one will lose them. A weak introduction can also lose you points in Writing, so writing a strong one is a good start to getting that perfect 8/8/8 score.

The Body

After your introduction, you will get into your analysis. Although you are not exactly writing an argumentative essay, you will still be making a point, which is whether the prompt passage is an effective or ineffective argument. Making your own point effectively involves these steps:

- Addressing every task in the prompt.

- Analyzing the prompt passage thoughtfully.

- Supporting your analysis with evidence from the prompt passage.

The body is the section of your essay that will be most influential in gaining you points in Reading and Analysis.

The Conclusion

Just as you would not want to begin an essay in a way that leaves readers bewildered and lacking a firm idea of what you are discussing, you do not want to leave them hanging either. Every strong essay has a strong conclusion. This is another part of the essay that could cause you to gain or lose Writing points, so be sure to include these steps:

- Finish with a clear statement that wraps up the central idea of your essay.
- Write an interesting final sentence that does not merely restate your conclusion in a blunt manner but instead leaves your readers with some food for thought.

ALERT: Overly blunt explanations of your conclusions are amateurish and can cost you Writing points. For example, "In conclusion, the passage was not a very good argument," is a clumsy and weak way to end your essay.

Before you begin writing your essay, it will be helpful to jot down a quick outline of it, noting what you will cover in your introduction, body, and conclusion.

Here's an example of an outline for an essay responding to the prompt about Maria Montessori's argument:

Intro: establish that writer's point about preparing teachers for experimental sciences is persuasive

Paragraph 1: author is an authority with a strong grasp of history

Paragraph 2: she uses evidence and examples to support her argument

Paragraph 3: author's academic tone makes her argument believable

Conclusion: wrap up how author's knowledge, evidence, and tone make argument effective

Editing

Writing your essay is the main part of this section of the SAT® exam, but placing that final period on your essay is not the end of the task. Now it's time to read over your work and make sure it is as effective as possible and free of errors. This process is called editing, and you should leave yourself 5 to 10 minutes to edit your essay at the end of the test. That is not a ton of time, so you'll have to make the most of those minutes because leaving sloppy errors in your essay can cost you points in Writing. Keep these goals in mind when editing your essay:

- Make sure your essay follows the essay format. It will need serious work if it does not have an introduction, body, or conclusion.

- Correct any errors in language, grammar, spelling, mechanics, and syntax. These kinds of errors may cost you more than Writing points. No matter how strong your ideas are, careless language errors can make it hard for the scorers to understand your ideas, which could also cost you points in Reading and Analysis.

- Make sure you've used strong and varied vocabulary. If you notice that you repeat the same words or phrases more than a couple of times, you should vary them to avoid losing Writing points.

- Make sure your sentence structures are varied, too. If every sentence is a simple sentence or a compound sentence, your essay will become tedious to read and lose you Writing points.

- Make sure your tone is consistent. For example, do not craft an essay that is mostly informative in tone and then slip a silly joke into the middle of it. Violations of tone can cost you Writing points.

MANAGING YOUR TIME

You're probably starting to get the idea that you'll be spending your 50 minutes doing a lot more than writing your essay. So, you don't want to get too hung up on reading the prompt passage, taking notes, or outlining your essay, because that might cost you some of those precious minutes. We're now going to discuss hints for keeping you from getting hung up like that by managing your time effectively.

Allot yourself 10 minutes to read the prompt and take notes, since you will be doing both at the same time. You may want to give the prompt a quick active read before going back and reading it closely. If so, hold off on taking notes until that close read because taking notes will slow down the active reading.

Take a look back at Chapter 3 of this book to review reading actively and closely. This will help you with both the SAT® Reading Test and the SAT® Essay.

Next, you will outline your essay. This will prevent you from constantly worrying about what you're going to discuss next, which would really waste time. Save time by jotting down the main ideas of your introduction, body paragraphs, and conclusion. Five minutes should be plenty of time to sketch out your outline.

Now it's time to start writing your essay. If you took strong notes while reading closely, and you've composed a clear and strong outline, you can mostly focus on stringing together the ideas in your notes and outline in a way that is clear, engaging, and grammatically correct. You should still leave yourself plenty of time to write your essay, though. About 25 to 30 minutes should be enough.

Finally, it's editing time. If you've taken effective notes, made a good outline, and paid attention to your use of language while writing, editing should not be a major task. However, it is normal to make some sloppy errors here and there. Hopefully, correcting those sloppy errors will be all you'll have to do while editing, so 5 to 10 minutes should suffice.

Here's a summary of an ideal time management system:

Total test time: 50 minutes
Reading the prompt while taking notes: 10 minutes
Outlining your introduction, body, and conclusion: 5 minutes
Writing your essay: 25–30 minutes
Editing your essay: 5–10 minutes

AVOIDING COMMON MISTAKES

Here's one more thing to think about while editing your SAT® Essay: Some students tend to make the same mistakes over and over. These are easy pitfalls to tumble into when writing essays because they may not necessarily seem like major errors, but they are things you will want to avoid. Familiarizing yourself with the most common mistakes is the best way to sidestep them.

Here's a basic rundown of the most common mistakes students make on the SAT® Essay.

Blank Space

You will have a certain amount of page space to fill when writing your essay, and ending up with a lot of blank space is a hint that your essay is not long or thorough enough. Be sure to use most of the page space available to you without resorting to filler tactics, such as repeating ideas and information needlessly or loading your writing with pointless adjectives and adverbs to boost your word count.

 ALERT: Filler tactics will never fool the essay scorers, so never resort to using them.

Misused Words and Phrases

Did you ever hear someone use the word "literally" when they actually meant its opposite, "figuratively"? This is the kind of mistake people make all the time because they do not fully understand the meaning of the words they use. Avoid using any word or figurative phrase if you are not completely sure of its meaning. Misusing words and phrases cannot just alter the meaning of your writing; it can also make you look a bit silly.

Too Many Ideas

No one is expecting you to write a book. It is not necessary for you to address every single idea that pops into your head while writing your essay. You simply won't have time to do that. Quality is more important in your essay than quantity is, so prune out any ideas that might distract you from explaining your best ideas as thoroughly as you need to.

Forgetting Your Evidence

The prompt passage will be a weak argument if the author forgets to include supporting evidence. The same thing is true of your essay. Do not forget to support every one of your claims with some form of supporting evidence that comes from the passage. Your evidence can be direct quotes or paraphrases of the passage author's ideas, but evidence needs to be in your essay no matter what form it takes.

Wordiness

Scorers will best understand your essay if it is clear and concise. Wordiness is when your sentences are so cluttered with ideas and descriptions that they cease to make sense. Avoid wordiness with clear and concise sentences.

Correcting an Error and Making a New One

Sometimes, fixing one error can create another one. Maybe you decided to delete an irrelevant piece of information but forgot to also delete another reference to that information later in your essay. Make sure that adding or deleting information does not create new mistakes.

Panicking

Take it easy. Relax. Take a deep breath. For most schools, the SAT® Essay is the least important part of the exam, so it won't do you any good to worry about it excessively. We're not saying the SAT® Essay isn't important, but panicking is never necessary, and it certainly won't help you write a strong essay. If you find yourself panicking, maybe an attitude adjustment is all you need. Get enthusiastic about what you're writing. Get into the idea of celebrating the effectiveness of the passage prompt or exposing its faulty arguments with great writing and convincing evidence. Basically, have a little fun with your writing.

> **TIP**
> You're less likely to panic when you're enjoying your work, and that enjoyment will come through, making your essay more engaging for the scorers and winning you Writing points.

GETTING A PERFECT SCORE

We have reviewed the essay writing essentials necessary for all students to write effective essays. Of course, you're not like all students. You're a high achiever who wants to do more than write an effective essay; you want to get a perfect score. Getting that perfect score is the next thing we're going to address in this chapter.

As they say, practice makes perfect, and practicing essay writing is really the best path to that perfect score. With its high-level practice prompts, this chapter is a great way to start practicing. However, you may want to get in some extra practice.

Remember that the SAT® Essay mainly tests your ability to do three things: read, analyze, and write. Try reading a movie review in a newspaper or online. After all, movie reviews are essentially argumentative essays. Read it carefully, analyze it, and write an essay detailing your analysis. Then try evaluating your own work according to the SAT® Essay rubric with brutal honesty. Find your strengths and weaknesses.

In all your writing, pay strict attention to those essential elements of the perfect SAT® Essay. Ask yourself the tough questions:

- Are my main idea and supporting details clear?
- Is my writing clear, concise, and grammatically correct?
- Is my evidence strong and consistent?
- Is my structure clear?
- Is my tone consistent?
- Is my vocabulary varied and at a high level?

After analyzing a relatively simple argumentative essay, such as a movie review, try moving on to a more complex piece of argumentative writing, such as a political editorial or even an article in a science journal.

TIP Evaluating your own work can be hard. If you think you're being too easy on yourself, try allowing someone else to evaluate and score your work using the rubric with strict honesty.

At first, leave yourself more than 50 minutes to prepare, write, and edit your practice essay. As you craft more practice essays, try to get your time closer to the 50-minute timeframe you'll have to work within on the SAT® Essay.

You should also become familiar with some of the most common persuasive techniques to figure out which ones the author of the prompt passage uses. Accurately referring to these techniques by name might even score you a few points on the SAT® Essay. These persuasive techniques include the following:

- **Logos:** the appeal to the reader's logic or reason
- **Inductive reasoning:** conclusions based on clearly stated evidence
- **Deductive reasoning:** conclusions based on generalizations
- **Ethos:** the appeal to the reader's sense of character, ethics, or morality
- **Pathos:** the appeal to the reader's emotions

You should also become familiar with the logical mistakes, or fallacies, authors often make when composing argumentative essays. Here's a list of the most common persuasive errors, or logical fallacies:

- **Ad populum:** A simplistic appeal to the reader's emotions that intends to take advantage of the reader's assumed prejudices while failing to provide logical support. (Example: Illegal immigrants are taking your jobs!)
- **Begging the question:** A conclusion that assumes the claim proves the conclusion. (Example: Dangerous dogs should be banned.)
- **Circular argument:** A conclusion that just restates the claim (Example: Eloise is an excellent writer because her writing is always excellent.)
- **Either/or:** An either/or construction that oversimplifies an argument (Example: Either we vote for that candidate, or the country will collapse into ruin.)
- **Hasty generalization:** A conclusion drawn with insufficient evidence (Example: Julie isn't in school today, so she's probably been in a horrible accident.)
- **Post hoc ergo hoc:** A confusion of sequence and cause and effect (Example: After Manuel got off the bus, he slipped, so getting off buses causes people to slip.)

- **Slippery slope:** The suggestion that if one thing happens, other things will naturally happen without strong evidence to support this chain of events (Example: If I don't get up on time, I'll miss my bus, then I won't get to school on time, then I won't graduate, and then I'll never find a decent job.)

Be sure you know the names and definitions of all logical fallacies. Referring to specific logical fallacies in your essay could help you earn extra points, but mistaking one fallacy for another could cost you points.

AN SAT® ESSAY WALK-THROUGH

Now that you know what makes a high-level SAT® Essay, you're going to examine a sample essay to find out how it earns a top score. You'll begin by reading a prompt, but instead of answering this one yourself, you'll see another test taker's essay, which we'll walk you through by explaining what this test taker did right. To best mirror the way SAT® Essays are scored, we'll examine how this sample essay measures up in terms of those three key factors in the scoring rubric: Reading, Analysis, and Writing.

Since our essay exemplar is a high-scoring one, let's just quickly review what makes an essay a high scorer according to our summarized rubric:

Score 4 (Advanced)	
Reading	The response shows a comprehensive understanding of the source text, including the author's key claims, use of details and evidence, and the relationship between the two; is error-free regarding fact or interpretation within the text; and demonstrates a complete understanding of the source text, skillfully using evidence from the text (i.e., direct quotations, paraphrases, or both).
Analysis	The response offers an "insightful" and in-depth evaluation of the author's use of evidence and stylistic or persuasive features in building an argument and consistently uses relevant supporting details that address the task.
Writing	The response includes all of the features of a strong essay, including a precise central claim, body paragraphs, and a strong conclusion; it incorporates a variety of sentence structures and is virtually free of all convention errors.

Score 3 (Proficient)

Reading	The response shows an appropriate understanding of the source text, including the author's key claims and use of details in developing an argument.
Analysis	The response offers an effective evaluation of the author's use of evidence and stylistic or persuasive features in building an argument; it uses appropriate supporting details and evidence that are relevant and focused on the task.
Writing	The response includes all of the features of an effective essay, including a precise central claim, body paragraphs, and a strong conclusion; it incorporates a variety of sentence structures and is relatively free of common grammatical errors.

Score 2 (Partial)

Reading	The response shows some understanding of the source text, including the author's key claims; it uses limited textual evidence and incorporates unimportant details.
Analysis	The response offers a limited evaluation of the author's use of evidence and stylistic or persuasive features in building an argument; its supporting details are lacking and/or irrelevant to the writing task.
Writing	The response does not provide a precise central claim nor an effective introduction, body paragraphs, and conclusion; it incorporates little variety of sentence structures and contains numerous errors in grammar and conventions.

Score 1 (Inadequate)

Reading	The response demonstrates little or no understanding of the source text or the author's use of key claims.
Analysis	The response offers no clear evaluation of the author's use of evidence and stylistic or persuasive features in building an argument; supporting details and evidence are non-existent or irrelevant to the writing task.
Writing	The response lacks any form of cohesion or structure; it incorporates little variety in sentence structure and includes significant errors in convention that make it difficult to read.

You'll begin by reading the prompt, which is followed by the sample essay. After you digest the essay, we'll break down its strengths with a careful walkthrough. Keep in mind that, while the sample essay that follows is a top scorer, it is not the only way to respond to the prompt effectively. There is no single way to write the best essay. There are many possibilities.

Let's get started.

As you read the passage below, consider how Arthur Brisbane uses

- evidence, such as facts or examples, to support claims.

- reasoning to develop ideas and to connect claims and evidence.

- stylistic or persuasive elements, such as word choice or appeals to emotion, to add power to the ideas expressed.

"We Long for Immortal Imperfection—We Can't Have It," by Arthur Brisbane

All our longings for immortality, all our plans for immortal life are based on the hope that Divine Providence will condescend to let us live in another world as we live here.

Each of us wants to be himself in the future life, and to see his friends as he knew them.

We want to preserve individuality forever and ever, when the stars shall have faded away and the days of matter ended.

But what is individuality except imperfection? You are different from Smith, Smith is different from Jones. But it is simply a difference of imperfect construction. One is more foolish than another, one is more irresponsibly moved to laughter or anger— that constitutes his personality.

Remove our imperfections and we should all be alike—smooth off all agglomerations of matter on all sides and everything would be spherical.

What would be the use of keeping so many of us if we were all perfect, and therefore all alike? One talks through his nose, one has a deep voice. But shall kind Providence provide two sets of wings for nose talkers and chest talkers? Why not make the two into one good talker and save one pair of wings?

Why not, in fact, keep just one perfect sample, and let all the rest placidly drift back to nothingness? Or, better, why not take all the goodness that there is in all the men and women that ever were and melt it all down into one cosmic human being? ——

The rain drops, the mist and the sprays of Niagara all go back to the ocean in time. Possibly we all go back at the end to the sea of divine wisdom, whence we were sent forth to do, well or badly, our little work down here:

Future punishment? We think not.

One drop of water revives the wounded hero—another helps to give wet feet and consumption to a little child. It all depends on circumstances.

Both drops go back to the ocean. There is no rule that sends the good drop to heaven and the other to boil forever and ever in a sulphur pit. ——

Troubles beset us when we think of a future state and our reason quarrels always with our longings. We all want—in heaven—to meet Voltaire with his very thin legs. But we cannot believe that those skinny shanks are to be immortal. We shall miss the snuff and the grease on Sam Johnson's collar. If an angel comes up neat and smiling and says "Permit me to introduce myself —I am the great lexicographer," we shall say "Tell that to some other angel. The great Samuel was dirty and wheezy, and I liked him that way."

And children. The idea of children in heaven flying about with their little fluffy wings is fascinating. But would eternal childhood be fair to them? If a babe dies while teething, shall it remain forever toothless? How shall its mother know it if it is allowed to grow up?

Listen to Heine—that marvellous genius of the Jewish race:

"Yes, yes! You talk of reunion in a transfigured shape. What would that be to me? I knew him in his old brown surtout, and so I would see him again. Thus he sat at table, the salt cellar and pepper caster on either hand. And if the pepper was on the right and the salt on the left hand he shifted them over. I knew him in a brown surtout, and so I would see him again."

Thus he spoke of his dead father. Thus many of us think and speak of those that are gone. How foolish to hope for the preservation of what is imperfect!

How important to have FAITH, and to feel that reality will surpass anticipation, and that whatever IS will be the best thing for us and satisfy us utterly.

Write an essay in which you explain how Arthur Brisbane builds an argument to persuade his audience that perfection on Earth is necessary to be welcomed into the afterlife. In your essay, analyze how Brisbane uses one or more of the features listed above (or features of your own choice) to strengthen the logic and persuasiveness of his argument. Be sure that your analysis focuses on the most relevant features of the passage.

Your essay should not explain whether you agree with Brisbane's claims, but rather explain how the author builds an argument to persuade his audience.

Here is an example of the highest standard—an essay with a perfect score.

Student Sample 8/8/8

The concept of an afterlife is prevalent in most cultures throughout history, as is the notion that attaining perfection is the key to being accepted into that glorious afterlife. However, writer Arthur Brisbane argues that the striving for perfection might seriously hinder our experiences here on Earth. By focusing on worlds that may or may not exist beyond this one, we might actually be diluting our own individualities in the living realm. Although his writing is lively and even amusing, flaws in his argument and the topic itself become apparent when one cuts through that humorous surface.

Brisbane employs images and conceptions of the afterlife as a way into his argument, painting a suitably heavenly picture of an eternal world in which every person would get "to see his friends as he knew them" in life for all eternity. He goes on to discuss somewhat superficial aspects of our individualities, such as the way we look and talk, and how one might believe that modifying them toward some common standard of "perfection" might be considered tickets to the afterlife. He counters this assumption by suggesting that such matters might be meaningless and how we all might have a path to the afterlife regardless of our personal traits just as "the sprays of Niagara all back to the ocean in time."

The somewhat humorous tone of Brisbane's focus on superficial aspects of the human heighten when he launches into a discussion of the fantastical things some people expect to find in the afterlife. He imagines people who assume they'll hobnob with major historical figures such as Voltaire and Sam Johnson. He imagines children transforming into angels who fly around on "little fluffy wings." His mocking tone is a means to encourage us readers to share his opinions, a technique that implies we too would deserve mockery if we disagreed with him.

Brisbane's mocking argument is, indeed, amusing, but it also suffers from a key problem. He uses humor to deflect the fact that there is very little evidence to support such emphatic statements as "We think not" in response to the question of whether or not there will be some "future punishment" for failing to attain perfection on Earth. Instead, he offers that impossible-to-prove theory about all souls traveling to the afterlife as all drops of Niagara's waters return to the ocean. He does manage to include one piece of extended evidence when he quotes Heine, a "marvelous genius of the Jewish race" by Brisbane's own estimation. That very introduction smacks of begging the question, as Brisbane seems to expect us to accept Heine's words as examples of "marvelous genius" since that is how Brisbane introduces Heine. Furthermore, the "marvelous genius" theories in this quotation are impossible to prove with or without knowing what gives Heine the authority to speak with such authority.

Perhaps that is the essential problem of Brisbane's argument overall: he is arguing something that is impossible to prove. Since the existence of an afterlife is impossible to prove, Brisbane's positions about it cannot be proven either. As it stands, his argument ultimately feels like an attempt to present himself as an authoritative voice who can declare "We think not" with confidence regarding a topic that no earthly person is capable of proving with confidence.

Now that you have read this high-level sample, we can begin our walk-through, which will involve a brief overview of its outline before examining how each paragraph measures up in terms of Reading, Writing, and Analysis.

Before you reread the essay, it is important to keep its structure in mind. Notice how carefully outlined it is. It begins with a clear introduction, carries on with three paragraphs each with its own particular subtopic, and finishes with a strong and provocative conclusion.

Introduction

> The concept of an afterlife is prevalent in most cultures throughout history, as is the notion that attaining perfection is the key to being accepted into that glorious afterlife. However, writer Arthur Brisbane argues that the striving for perfection might seriously hinder our experiences here on Earth. By focusing on worlds that may or may not exist beyond this one, we might actually be diluting our own individualities in the living realm. Although his writing is lively and even amusing, flaws in his argument and the topic itself become apparent when one cuts through that humorous surface.

Reading: Introductions are generally too brief to really give an adequate idea of how well the essay writer comprehended the passage, and this one is no different. However, there are no errors here. It is clear that the essay writer understood Brisbane's main argument ("Arthur Brisbane argues that the striving for perfection might seriously hinder our experiences here on Earth").

Analysis: The introductory paragraph is not where writers do their deepest analyses, so it is also difficult to evaluate analysis as it pertains to this first paragraph. Nevertheless, the essay writer does a fine job of setting up the main thrust of the analysis that will follow ("Although his writing is lively and even amusing, flaws in his argument and the topic itself become apparent").

Writing: This is where our high-level essay writer really gets to shine in the introduction. The writing is consistently excellent. There is a strong opening statement that introduces the topic without giving away too much about Brisbane's argument or the essay writer's own analysis of that argument, and that provides an engaging hook to the essay. The opening sentence flows naturally into a brief and accurate description of Brisbane's argument before flowing into a teasing summation of the essay writer's analysis. Words are spelled correctly. Grammar is impeccable. The vocabulary is varied and high-level enough to catch the attention of the scorers.

Body Paragraph 1

Brisbane employs images and conceptions of the afterlife as a way into his argument, painting a suitably heavenly picture of an eternal world in which every person would get "to see his friends as he knew them" in life for all eternity. He goes on to discuss somewhat superficial aspects of our individualities, such as the way we look and talk, and how one might believe that modifying them toward some common standard of "perfection" might be considered tickets to the afterlife. He counters this assumption by suggesting that such matters might be meaningless and how we all might have a path to the afterlife regardless of our personal traits just as "the sprays of Niagara all back to the ocean in time."

Reading: The first paragraph in the essay's body focuses on how Brisbane makes his point by using colorful images. The essay writer has interpreted the ways Brisbane uses these images accurately, demonstrating a careful reading of the prompt. Direct and accurate quotations of the prompt passage also reveal strong reading comprehension.

Analysis: This is not quite relevant yet, as the essay writer has not really begun to analyze Brisbane's argument. This paragraph mainly just explains Brisbane's argument and how he makes it. Nevertheless, the essay writer's accurate interpretation of Brisbane's points and images does reveal the beginnings of a careful and accurate analysis. The essay writer has correctly interpreted that Brisbane tends to focus on the superficial. Nevertheless, the essay writer's analytical powers will be more apparent in the paragraphs that follow.

Writing: Once again, the essay writer proves considerable compositional strengths with fine use of sentence structure and vocabulary. There are no errors.

Body Paragraph 2

The somewhat humorous tone of Brisbane's focus on superficial aspects of the human heighten when he launches into a discussion of the fantastical things some people expect to find in the afterlife. He imagines people who assume they'll hobnob with major historical figures such as Voltaire and Sam Johnson. He imagines children transforming into angels who fly around on "little fluffy wings." His mocking tone is a means to encourage us readers to share his opinions, a technique that implies we too would deserve mockery if we disagreed with him.

Reading: The essay writer's strong reading comprehension continues to be apparent with additional accurately rendered examples and quotations from the passage. The essay writer appears to grasp Brisbane's point completely while understanding how Brisbane uses his images to convey that point.

Analysis: This paragraph builds on ideas in the previous paragraph naturally, providing more examples of Brisbane's focus on superficiality while also finally identifying his tone as "humorous" and "mocking." There is also a deeper analysis of that tone as the essay writer explains the effect that humorous and mocking tone is intended to have on readers.

Writing: The essay writer's own serious tone is a strong contrast to Brisbane's more humorous, mocking tone, making the essay writer appear rather authoritative in contrast to Brisbane. The essay writer also subtly provokes the reader into sharing his or her own analysis by drawing the reader in with the cagily selected phrase "to encourage *us* readers." Grammar, wording, vocabulary, and structure continue to be strong.

Body Paragraph 3

Brisbane's mocking argument is, indeed, amusing, but it also suffers from a key problem. He uses humor to deflect the fact that there is very little evidence to support such emphatic statements as "We think not" in response to the question of whether or not there will be some "future punishment" for failing to attain perfection on Earth. Instead, he offers that impossible-to-prove theory about all souls traveling to the afterlife as all drops of Niagara's waters return to the ocean. He does manage to include one piece of extended evidence when he quotes Heine, a "marvelous genius of the Jewish race" by Brisbane's own estimation. That very introduction smacks of begging the question, as Brisbane seems to expect us to accept Heine's words as examples of "marvelous genius" since that is how Brisbane introduces Heine. Furthermore, the "marvelous genius" theories in this quotation are impossible to prove with or without knowing what gives Heine the authority to speak with such authority.

Reading: Accurate quotations and references to the prompt passage continue to show off the essay writer's reading comprehension skills.

Analysis: This is the paragraph that best flaunts the essay writer's analytical skills. The essay writer notes the effect of Brisbane's tone, but shows that it is not enough to base an argument on humor. The essay writer reveals Brisbane's failure to support emphatic, seemingly definitive statements, his use of the logical fallacy of "begging the question," and the failure of his evidence to prove his main argument convincingly.

Writing: Writing continues to be both well-constructed and careful. The phrase "by Brisbane's own estimation" cleverly reveals how an idea Brisbane attempts to present as fact is actually just an opinion. The ironic use of the phrase "marvelous genius" in the final sentence is used to mocking effect without violating the overall serious and authoritative tone of the essay.

Conclusion

Perhaps that is the essential problem of Brisbane's argument overall: he is arguing something that is impossible to prove. Since the existence of an afterlife is impossible to prove, Brisbane's positions about it cannot be proven either. As it stands, his argument ultimately feels like an attempt to present himself as an authoritative voice who can declare "We think not" with confidence regarding a topic that no earthly person is capable of proving with confidence.

Reading: This element is least relevant in the concluding paragraph since it is most important for the essay writer to show that he or she comprehended the passage prompt in the essay's body. Nevertheless, the concluding paragraph does not reveal any last-minute comprehension errors, so it does not undermine the high level of comprehension displayed in the rest of the essay.

Analysis: The essay writer's analytical powers are still going strong in this final paragraph as she or he summarizes the essential flaw in Brisbane's argument clearly and convincingly.

Writing: The essay writer's compositional skills remain strong to the very end, varying her or his writing with complex, compound, and compound-complex sentences.

PRACTICE ESSAY PROMPT

We've walked you through our sample high-level essay and explained all the reasons why it was so strong. Now it's your turn to strive for your own high score. Once again you will write an essay in response to the following prompt, and once again, you will use all of the knowledge you've accumulated over the course of this chapter to write the highest scoring essay you can write. When you finish your essay, try handing it and the scoring rubric to a willing teacher, parent, or (very smart) friend and asking that person to honestly evaluate and score your essay. Good luck!

As you read the passage below, consider how Bertrand Russell uses

- evidence, such as facts or examples, to support claims.

- reasoning to develop ideas and to connect claims and evidence.

- stylistic or persuasive elements, such as word choice or appeals to emotion, to add power to the ideas expressed.

Excerpt from *The Problems of Philosophy*, by Bertrand Russell

[W]e have to ask ourselves whether, in any sense at all, there is such a thing as matter. Is there a table which has a certain intrinsic nature, and continues to exist when I am not looking, or is the table merely a product of my imagination, a dream-table in a very prolonged dream? This question is of the greatest importance. For if we cannot be sure of the independent existence of objects, we cannot be sure of the independent existence of other people's bodies, and therefore still less of other people's minds, since we have no grounds for believing in their minds except such as are derived from observing their bodies. Thus if we cannot be sure of the independent existence of objects, we shall be left alone in a desert—it may be that the whole outer world is nothing but a dream, and that we alone exist. This is an uncomfortable possibility; but although it cannot be strictly proved to be false, there is not the slightest reason to suppose that it is true. In this chapter we have to see why this is the case.

Before we embark upon doubtful matters, let us try to find some more or less fixed point from which to start. Although we are doubting the physical existence of the table, we are not doubting the existence of the sense-data which made us think there was a table; we are not doubting that, while we look, a certain colour and shape appear to us, and while we press, a certain sensation of hardness is experienced by us. All this, which is psychological, we are not calling in question. In fact, whatever else may be doubtful, some at least of our immediate experiences seem absolutely certain.

Descartes (1596–1650), the founder of modern philosophy, invented a method which may still be used with profit—the method of systematic doubt. He determined that he would believe nothing which he did not see quite clearly and distinctly to be true. Whatever he could bring himself to doubt, he would doubt, until he saw reason for not doubting it. By applying this method he gradually became convinced that the only existence of which he could be *quite* certain was his own. He imagined a deceitful demon, who presented unreal things to his senses in a perpetual phantasmagoria; it might be very improbable that such a demon existed, but still it was possible, and therefore doubt concerning things perceived by the senses was possible.

But doubt concerning his own existence was not possible, for if he did not exist, no demon could deceive him. If he doubted, he must exist; if he had any experiences whatever, he must exist. Thus his own existence was an absolute certainty to him. 'I think, therefore I am,' he said (*Cogito, ergo sum*); and on the basis of this certainty he set to work to build up again the world of knowledge which his doubt had laid in ruins. By inventing the method of doubt, and by showing that subjective things are the most certain, Descartes performed a great service to philosophy, and one which makes him still useful to all students of the subject.

But some care is needed in using Descartes' argument. 'I think, therefore I am' says rather more than is strictly certain. It might seem as though we were quite sure of being the same person today as we were yesterday, and this is no doubt true in some sense. But the real Self is as hard to arrive at as the real table, and does not seem to have that absolute, convincing certainty that belongs to particular experiences. When I look at my table and see a certain brown colour, what is quite certain at once is not 'I am seeing a brown colour', but rather, 'a brown colour is being seen'. This of course involves something (or somebody) which (or who) sees the brown colour; but it does not of itself involve that more or less permanent person whom we call 'I'. So far as immediate certainty goes, it might be that the something which sees the brown colour is quite momentary, and not the same as the something which has some different experience the next moment.

Thus it is our particular thoughts and feelings that have primitive certainty. And this applies to dreams and hallucinations as well as to normal perceptions: when we dream or see a ghost, we certainly do have the sensations we think we have, but for various reasons it is held that no physical object corresponds to these sensations. Thus the certainty of our knowledge of our own experiences does not have to be limited in any way to allow for exceptional cases. Here, therefore, we have, for what it is worth, a solid basis from which to begin our pursuit of knowledge.

Write an essay in which you explain how Bertrand Russell builds an argument to persuade his audience that the idea that existence is just a dream cannot be proven. In your essay, analyze how Russell uses one or more of the features listed above (or features of your own choice) to strengthen the logic and persuasiveness of his argument. Be sure that your analysis focuses on the most relevant features of the passage.

Your essay should not explain whether you agree with Russell's claims, but rather explain how the author builds an argument to persuade his audience.

Sample Advanced Essay

Here is an example of a student response to this passage that would receive a top score from all graders.

The question of whether or not "matter" exists may seem like the kind of abstract question without any real grounding in reality philosophers tend to ask. Most people will agree that matter we can see and touch exists and that is enough proof. However, philosopher Bertrand Russell made such a seemingly unnecessary question seem necessary with the intriguing way he explores it in his *The Problems of Philosophy*, which illustrates the difficulty of distinguishing reality from dreams and hallucinations.

Russell begins his exploration of whether or not we can be sure that matter exists with a simple example anyone can grasp: a table. Russell notes how we can test the existence of this everyday object by seeing ("while we look, a certain colour and shape appear to us") and touching it ("while we press, a certain sensation of hardness is experienced by us"). Then he pulls the rug out from under these essential senses by reminding us that even touch and sight are psychological in nature. Russell does not explore this point in detail, and even states that he does not plan to question the idea that our senses of sight and touch can be affected by psychological influences. However, the mere introduction of it may make us readers begin to question these senses and get on board with an idea we might otherwise find difficult to grasp, the idea that it is actually isn't so simple to distinguish between reality and the unreal.

He continues to build on his study with support from a great philosophical authority. Russell introduces Descartes as no less than "the founder of modern philosophy," establishing Descartes as the authority to beat all other authorities on this subject. Russell goes on to quote Descartes with a philosophical statement so famous that you've probably heard it even if you've never studied philosophy: "I think, therefore I am." The authoritative nature of Descartes, the fame of his statement, and the fact that that statement is pretty easy for anyone to understand—he's basically saying that your ability to think is all the proof necessary to prove that you exist—not only forms the foundation of a strong argument but also makes it easy for anyone to understand and believe it.

Then Russell pulls the rug out from under "I think, therefore I am" and us trusting readers by questioning the very existence of who "I" is. Russell asks if the person you are today is the same person you were yesterday, which I assume takes into account the way one's beliefs, ideas, and perceptions can change from day to day. Admittedly, this is the point at which Russell's discussion might start getting away from the casual philosophy student. However, he had established himself in *The Problems of Philosophy* authoritatively enough by this point for us to go along with such an abstract and difficult concept. He had used a clear example of how we know matter exists (the table), referred to an authority (Descartes), and an essential philosophical statement that is easy for all to understand ("I think, therefore I am"). By gaining our trust and drawing us into the exploration so effectively, Bertrand Russell has also gained our trust in accepting less easy to grasp concepts. Also, by challenging a great philosophical authority with complex and convincing ideas, Russell strengthens his own authority.

I did not completely understand Russell's questions regarding what the "real Self" is, but I was willing to accept that such a real Self may, indeed, be hard to define since Russell is so in command of his argument. And by ending his discussion with a return to perfect clarity as he explains that dreams and hallucinations have the same sensation of reality that waking experiences do, he solidifies his argument that the things we are sure exist after testing them with our basic senses might actually require more testing. Clearly, this is just the introduction to a philosophical exploration Bertrand Russell will continue to pursue beyond this mere excerpt, and this excerpt is so intriguing that I really am curious to discover where it goes next.

Now here is an example of a scorer's analysis of the sample student essay.

Reading: Student clearly read this rather challenging passage carefully. While he or she did not understand every one of its concepts, student made an obvious effort to interpret it and was generally very accurate in her or his understanding of the passage. Examples are accurate and quotations are precise.

Analysis: Student's careful reading and creative thought have resulted in a strong analysis of the passage. He or she notes how Russell uses an authority (Descartes) to support essential ideas in the passage and strengthens her or his own authority by challenging the ideas of Descartes. Student also recognizes how the author establishes the strength of that authority (Descartes is "the founder of modern philosophy") and uses a famous quote ("I think, therefore I am") to get readers to go along with concepts that might be difficult to understand. Student indicates when Russell's complex analysis begins to get away from casual readers and also when it returns to greater clarity. Student briefly mentions that he or she was intrigued by Russell's passage to illustrate how the author's analysis appeals to readers without going so deeply into personal opinions that her or his own essay strayed from the analytical purpose of the SAT® essay.

Writing: Writing is high quality throughout with impeccable grammar, punctuation, and spelling. Student uses a fine variety of sentence structures to make his or her own writing interesting. Each paragraph maintains its focus on a specific aspect of Russell's passage. There is a clear introduction, trio of body paragraphs, and conclusion. The introduction grabs the reader's attention by indicating that Russell will contradict common notions ("However, philosopher Bertrand Russell made such a seemingly unnecessary question seem necessary with the intriguing way he explores it in his *The Problems of Philosophy*…") and ends strongly by indicating that student recognizes that there is likely more to learn from *The Problems of Philosophy* beyond this particular excerpt.

SUMMING IT UP

- The SAT® Essay is an optional portion of the test. Unless your school requires you to take the essay, you may decide not to take it, without this decision affecting your overall score.

- The SAT® Essay requires you to analyze an author's argument, NOT to agree or disagree with it.

- The prompt on which you will base your essay is a reading passage of roughly 650 to 750 words in length.

- You will have 50 minutes to complete your essay.

- You will receive three individual scores for your essay, each covering its own topic: reading, analysis, and writing. Your final score for each topic will be the sum of the scores of two scorers using a 4-point scale. For example, a perfect SAT® Essay score will look like this: 8/8/8—that's 8 points each in reading, analysis, and writing.

- According to the SAT® Essay rubric, a score of 1 indicates "inadequate," a score of 2 indicates "partial" proficiency, a score of 3 indicates "proficient," and a score of 4 indicates "advanced."

- The prompt for every SAT® Essay will always have the same basic introduction and directions.

- You will analyze the prompt passage writer's evidence, reasoning, and/or stylistic or persuasive elements in your essay.

- Taking notes is a key element of comprehending the prompt passage, writing your essay, and making the most of the 50 minutes allotted to write your essay.

- Your essay should consist of the three basic organizational elements of any essay: an introduction, a body, and a conclusion.

- Following a basic time table may guarantee you do not run out of time while preparing, writing, and editing your essay. Allow yourself 10 minutes to read the prompt passage and take notes, 5 minutes to outline your essay, 25 to 30 minutes to write it, and 5 to 10 minutes to edit it.

- Avoid common mistakes while writing your essay. These common mistakes include leaving blank space, misusing words and phrases, stuffing too many ideas into your essay, forgetting to support your conclusions with evidence, being too wordy, making new errors when correcting old ones, and panicking.

- Keys to getting a perfect score on the SAT® Essay include writing practice essays, evaluating your writing techniques honestly and carefully, understanding how writers use persuasive techniques effectively, and recognizing when their arguments suffer from logical fallacies.